The Embedded Corporation

The Embedded Corporation

CORPORATE GOVERNANCE AND EMPLOYMENT RELATIONS IN JAPAN AND THE UNITED STATES

■ ■ ■

Sanford M. Jacoby

PRINCETON UNIVERSITY PRESS   PRINCETON AND OXFORD

Copyright ©2005 by Princeton University Press
Published by Princeton University Press,
41 William Street, Princeton, New Jersey 08540
In the United Kingdom: Princeton University Press,
3 Market Place, Woodstock, Oxfordshire OX20 1SY

Library of Congress Cataloging-in-Publication Data
Jacoby, Sanford M., 1953–
The embedded corporation : corporate governance and employment
relations in Japan and the United States / Sanford M. Jacoby.
p.   cm.
Includes bibliographical references and index.

ISBN: 0-691-11999-6 (cl : alk. paper)

1. Management—Employee participation—Japan. 2. Management—Employee participation—United States. 3. Corporate
governance—Japan. 4. Corporate governance—United States.
5. Personnel management—Japan. 6. Personnel management—
United States. 7. Capitalism—Japan. 8. Capitalism—United
States. 9. Comparative management. I. Title: Corporate
governance and employment relations in Japan and the
United States. II. Title.

HD5660.J3J33 2005
338.6'0952—dc22   2004044328

British Library Cataloging-in-Publication Data is available

This book has been composed in Electra

Printed on acid-free paper. ∞

pup.princeton.edu

Printed in the United States of America

10 9 8 7 6 5 4 3 2 1

To My Teachers

■ Contents

	Preface	ix
1	Management and the Varieties of Capitalism	1
2	Human Resources Departments in Large Japanese Firms: The Way It Was	21
3	Inside Japanese Companies Today	41
4	The Evolution of Human Resource Management in the United States	78
5	Inside U.S. Companies Today	101
6	Comparative Survey Data	131
7	Taking Stock and Looking Ahead	157
	Acknowledgments	175
	Notes	179
	Index	211

■ Preface

This book is about the relationship between corporate governance and employment in large Japanese and American corporations. It takes readers inside the headquarters of a dozen selected companies to see how employment and business-strategy decisions are made in different industries and national contexts. It also presents the results of a large-scale survey of top-level executives in Japan and the United States.

Our window on many of these issues is the human resources (HR) department at company headquarters. HR executives are the senior managers responsible for designing a company's personnel policies. Studying these individuals, though it may seem an esoteric topic, in fact is a good way of understanding how companies reach decisions that determine the working lives of millions of people—everything from wages to layoffs to labor relations. HR executives are also the people whose job it is to link employment issues to overall corporate strategy. Analyzing their role in the corporation—including relations to CEOs and to other units like finance—can show us how employees figure, if at all, in the strategic decisions that drive a company's future.

Major corporate decisions usually are vetted by the board of directors, which means that corporate governance mediates the link between HR policy and business strategy. Corporate governance comprises the rules, practices, and procedures by which managers are held accountable to those who have a legitimate stake in the enterprise as well as the definition of who are those stakeholders. Issues of corporate governance include the duties of directors, methods of corporate financing, executive compensation, acquisitions and divestments, and other strategic decisions. Again, the issues are of enormous importance, not only to corporations themselves, but to people—shareholders, employees, customers, suppliers, and communities—who are affected by management decisions. Whether employees should have a role in corporate governance is a vital issue, both in Japan—whose traditional system of corporate governance is under challenge—and in the United States, where corporate governance is being reconsidered after the scandals—and job and pension losses—that occurred at Enron, WorldCom, Global Crossing, and other companies.

Large Japanese and American companies have taken different approaches to corporate governance and to employment. Japan has a type of stakeholder system that gives weight to the concerns of employees and other groups, whereas U.S. governance cedes sovereignty to shareholders. Also, as is well known, large Japanese companies tend to hire employees for "life" and to shelter them from market risk, whereas U.S. firms offer shorter job durations and more market-oriented employment policies. Teasing out how national differences in corporate governance are related—via the executive HR role—to employment practices is a major concern of this study.

Japan traditionally had a powerful HR-executive presence at corporate headquarters—if not the topmost department, then very close to it—whereas in the United States, HR has been weak as compared to other units like finance and production. Accounting for these differences requires a historical perspective on how corporate organization developed in the two countries, a perspective that is often missing from management and economic studies but which is provided here. It also requires an understanding of the distinctive ways in which corporations mesh with a nation's nonmarket institutions, including its legal structure, social insurance system, business-government relations, labor organizations, and norms of appropriate behavior. The idea that history and society matter—that a rational, economic entity like the corporation is embedded in the particularities of time and place—informs the analyses presented in this book.[1]

Globalization of world markets, the dominance of the U.S. economy, and prolonged stagnation in Japan have all raised the prospect that traditional Japanese approaches to corporate organization—ranging from the HR role to employment to corporate governance—are converging on the American way of doing things. Recently there has been an outpouring of opinion on the probability of convergence. Here we subject these claims to empirical scrutiny. Without doubt, the force of globalization is enormous. Citizens in both the advanced and the developing countries are far more exposed than sixty years ago to products, services, and ideas produced in another country. Globalization is propelling convergence, as we will see. However, we also will consider countervailing forces against convergence, such as the implosion of the U.S. model due to corporate scandals and slower growth; a desire of nations to preserve social standards; and a dawning realization that being different—whether corporation or society—is an effective way to compete globally. We also examine the reverse flow of ideas moving east from Japan to the United States.

A book like this has multiple audiences. It is intended not only for academics but also for practitioners and general readers. Some will be drawn to its focus on HR executives and the workplace, others to the corporate governance dimension, and still others to issues of convergence. Those interested only in Japan or only in the United States can ignore the comparative analysis, although there is plenty here for those concerned about the relationship between the two countries and, more generally, about the prospects for the world's varieties of capitalism.

In short, studying what goes on at corporate headquarters—and where HR executives fit into the hierarchy of power—offers a vantage point for answering important questions facing advanced industrial societies: Are employees best thought of as short-term costs or as long-term assets? What should be the balance of power between shareholders and others who have a stake in corporate decisions? What impact is globalization having on distinctive national approaches to corporate organization and on the social responsibilities of employers?

The Embedded Corporation

1

Management and the Varieties of Capitalism

DURING THE 1990S, CAPITALISM WAS ASCENDANT. The Soviet Union had collapsed, China was pursuing free enterprise, and in the United States businessmen were lionized as never before. Yet some social scientists observed that no such thing as pure capitalism existed or ever had existed. Rather, capitalism came in different varieties, a point first made by the German historical economists in the nineteenth century.

Today, capitalist nations vary along multiple dimensions. Industry networks, systems for innovation, employment relations, and facets of the business-government relationship are structured differently by different nations. Of recent interest are variations in the internal organization of corporations and in modes of corporate governance. One finds shareholder-oriented governance in the United States and the United Kingdom, statutory stakeholder governance in Europe, and voluntarist stakeholder governance in Japan and other parts of East Asia.[1]

Interactions between these subsystems within a nation yield distinctive paths to prosperity, each with its advantages and disadvantages. There is no one way that is best—no optimal point on what economists call "the production frontier." However, the force of this claim has been undercut by the performance of the U.S. economy since the late 1990s: Compared to its main rivals, the German and Japanese economies, it has been stellar. As a result, the focus of research and debate has shifted from analyzing institutional variety to predicting how quickly U.S. patterns of regulation, risk-sharing, and governance will take hold around the world.

Nowhere is the shift more noticeable than in Japan, which in the 1980s was held up as a model for a struggling U.S. economy and later served as a model of how *not* to run a modern economy. In the past, Japan distinguished itself for having, in addition to its high levels of coordination between business and government, a mode of corporate governance whereby the interests of different stakeholders—shareholders, customers, banks, and employees—were balanced, whereas in the United States sovereignty was given to shareholders. The stakeholder philosophy derived from, and contributed to, such Japanese labor practices as intensive training and long-term employment, the willingness to shelter employees from downturns, and ubiquitous enterprise unions.

A key element in the Japanese system was the headquarters human resources (HR) department, which administered employment and labor relations. Among its myriad duties were the rotation of managers around the company and the identification of employees for senior positions. HR was linked to corporate governance indirectly, through its grooming of individuals for the board of directors comprised of management insiders, and directly through the board membership of the senior HR executive. On the company board, the HR executive voiced employee concerns to other executives and served as the advocate of the *seishain*, or core employees, in strategic decision making.

In the United States, by contrast, the senior HR executive traditionally stood at or near the bottom of the managerial hierarchy. Epitomizing the function's dubious status was the relatively low pay offered to HR executives and the relatively high proportion of women in HR positions. The powerhouse functions inside the U.S. corporation have been production, marketing, and, more recently, finance.

HR did have its day in the sun. During the First and Second World Wars, HR (then called "personnel management") was temporarily elevated in status as U.S. corporations adapted to the rise of unionization or sought ways to avoid it. In some companies, the HR executive functioned as an employee advocate, being the two-way transmission point between employees and management. Facing new government regulations in the 1960s and 1970s, HR developed systems for complying with the law on affirmative action, occupational safety, and other issues. With respect to corporate governance, many large companies acted on the assumption that the firm was a social institution with responsibilities not only to shareholders but also to employees, customers, and communities, an assumption that boosted HR's internal status.

In the 1980s and 1990s, however, large U.S. corporations grew increasingly financialized—financial criteria dominated decision making, CFOs rose in prominence, equity prices became an obsession—and also singularly oriented to shareholder concerns. With ties between employees and companies waning, HR executives adapted, or were forced to adapt, to the status quo. They focused on flexibility and on treating employees as costs to be minimized. Some U.S. corporations, however, bucked the trend and sought competitive advantage not only in low costs but in having inimitable resources such as unique organizational processes and intellectual capital. This resource-based approach gave rise to Japanese-style emphases on organizational culture and employee participation.

Today Japanese companies are experiencing pressure to conform to U.S.-style corporate governance and to adopt market-oriented employment practices that would weaken the corporate HR function. Studying the role of the senior HR executive provides a unique window on the process of institutional change in Japan. As for the United States, there has been a decline of career jobs and of mutual loyalty between employers and employees, accompanied by a single-minded focus on share price. At the same time there is awareness that human and intellectual capital are increasingly a company's most important assets. Again, the HR function provides a vantage point for analyzing these countervailing U.S. trends and for understanding larger issues of national divergence and convergence.

The flow of management ideas in the 1980s was from east to west, resulting in discussions about the "Japanization" of work organization, quality systems, and industrial relations. Today the flow has reversed, with a huge debate in Japan (and other countries) over the costs and benefits of American modes of employee relations and corporate governance. There is now a sizable literature on convergence—on whether, in the wake of globalization, countries and corporations are becoming more alike. Those who emphasize "varieties of capitalism" tend to be skeptical of claims that convergence is occurring, and those who think that it is occurring tend to believe it spells the end of national business systems. Yet both sides, with some notable exceptions,[2] write about these issues from an often rarified, theoretical perspective. Here I focus on the less glamorous but nevertheless important *empirical* question of whether one can observe convergence in the organizational roles of HR executives in Japanese and U.S. corporations. For example, is it the case that HR is losing its high standing inside Japanese companies and becoming more like its counterpart in the United States?

The HR executive's status in the corporation cannot be understood without appreciating that corporations are more than mechanisms for maximizing profits—that is the textbook economics view—but are also the terrain for conflicts over whether and how to pursue that objective. One type of conflict is distributional: struggles among managers, shareholders, and other stakeholders over how much emphasis to place on profit maximization versus other goals and on how to slice the revenue pie. Different employment arrangements—whether to invest in human capital, for example—are associated with different risk and return patterns for shareholders and for employees. Often the tension is below the surface, but it may occasionally erupt, as in the shareholder-value movement of the 1990s, the post-Enron angst over corporate responsibility, and the current Japanese debate over corporate governance.

Then there are the internecine battles over which business unit or functional area will dominate executive decisions. These disputes are partly the result of a Machiavellian jockeying for power inside the organization, power that brings with it perquisites and organizational status, but they also represent disagreements over how best to pursue competitive strategy—whether to emphasize financial goals, market share, product cost, or employee talent. They also are a proxy for disputes among those who lay claim to a company's resources. Finance typically aligns itself with shareholders, marketing with customers, and HR with employees. These alignments can be merely opportunistic. Sometimes, though, a principle may be at stake. For example, from the 1920s through the 1960s, General Motors was marked by heated debates over the design of its M-form type of organization. The debates were really about the distribution of power and resources between managers and shareholders. Functional groups like finance represented the interests of shareholders, while other units, such as operations, were aligned with management.[3]

The power dimension tends be neglected in studies of corporate organization, whether in economics, political science, or sociology.[4] Those conducting comparative and historical research, however, cannot ignore it. For scholars examining corporations over time, it is hard to miss the interplay between shifting societal coalitions and changes in management orientation. Management, in other words, is socially embedded. Similarly, one can understand what makes American companies "American" only by comparing them to companies elsewhere in the world that operate under different rules of the game. Although some analysts still think that corporations are the epitome of rational decision-making, in fact they are places where power contests and social norms shape what managers think and do.[5]

Recently a flow of excellent comparative and historical studies of management has been appearing. However, one problem with this literature is its tendency to treat management as a monolith: Executives are assumed to share common views on strategy and policy. For example, research focused on employment issues tends to lump a company's (or a country's) executives together as "employers." In fact, during normal times most executives do not care a great deal about employment issues, and during critical periods they tend to form little consensus on how to proceed. The path finally chosen may appear historically determined but is also influenced by an element of uncertainty—of contingency—that is introduced by factional and other disputes within and outside corporations.

Methods

This study combines two different levels of analysis. Through "in-country" analysis, it attempts to identify how recent changes in the workplace are related to changes in the role of the HR executive in each country. The aim of the "between-country" analysis is to determine whether globalization is producing convergence in corporate organization between Japan and the United States. The study uses historical methods to examine changes in the HR role over time, and analyzes contemporary Japan-U.S. differences through case studies of paired corporations and through a survey of HR executives.

All the organizations discussed in the book are large public companies, and the HR executives I study are the senior individuals in their firm. In Japan, they are general managers or directors; in the United States they typically are executive vice presidents reporting to the CEO. In both countries, the role of HR—what decisions HR executives make, how the function is organized, how much power HR has relative to that of other units—is affected both by factors unique to the company (diversification, organizational culture) as well as by industry factors (technology, labor shortages) and national institutions (modes of corporate governance, government regulation, social norms).

On an everyday basis, HR executives make policy decisions concerning the structure of the employment relationship. They decide, for example, the mix of market principles and internal factors that will guide pay, promotions, and employee relations. Most HR executives also participate in strategic decisions about the company's future. They *mediate* the impact that various factors have on decisions related to employees and to corporate strategy. The more pressing or uncertain the factors are—for example, labor shortages, union threats, or legal constraints—the greater will be the power of the HR executive and the greater will be the impact of employee relations on business decisions. This book looks both at the determinants of the role of the HR executive and at the consequences of that role for employment and other business outcomes.

Field studies are an established research technique in sociology and industrial relations but have been adopted slowly in economics. Gradually, however, economists are beginning to appreciate that this kind of research enables them to explore areas for which little data has yet to be collected. And talking directly to senior executives and other economic actors provides information on their objectives and constraints, and that can be the basis for future theorizing and research.[6] At the same time, supplementing qualitative case studies with quantitative survey data allows the researcher to triangulate the subject by combining methods whose strengths compensate for each other's weaknesses.[7]

WHAT'S HAPPENING IN JAPAN?

After more than a decade of slow growth, Japan is convulsed by debates over its economic future. Critics have taken aim at everything from child-rearing practices to the old-age pension system, although the main nodes of dispute center on corporate organization and on the appropriate design of government economic policy. I will have relatively little to say about the latter, which is discussed in a vast literature on deregulation, trade policy, banking reform, and related topics.[8]

Targets for a steady barrage of criticism are the employment and governance structures of large Japanese corporations. For much of the postwar era, employment in large firms was based on the so-called "three pillars"—lifetime employment, seniority-based pay, and enterprise unions—which supported a host of complementary practices, including flexibility of work organization, employee participation in management, and high levels of investment in worker training, Related to these practices was a system of corporate governance that, compared to the Anglo-American model, did not privilege shareholders, permitting management to balance the interests of employees, banks, suppliers, customers, and other stakeholders.[9]

Foreign observers praised these practices when the Japanese economy was riding high in the 1980s. But the mighty have fallen. Now observers say that what was appropriate or at least tolerable during the postwar decades of catch-up industrialization has become dysfunctional in the current economic climate.[10] Emerging economies like those of Brazil, Korea, and especially China are capturing Japanese export markets. Meanwhile the United States and Europe are moving rapidly into new industries, including biotechnology, the Internet, and telecommunications. The Japanese are being forced to compete in markets that place a premium on risk and speed, neither of which is encouraged by traditional practices such as consensus management and strong corporate cultures. Companies are criticized for being dominated by powerful HR departments that are beholden to enterprise unions and reluctant to make jobs more flexible and market-oriented.

Meanwhile, Japan's consumer and financial markets are opening to foreign competition. Japanese companies, especially those serving the home market, face stiff pressure to reduce costs. Foreign investors are buying up shares in Japanese companies and urging them to adopt shareholder sovereignty, accounting transparency, and a focus on quarterly results. Postwar Japanese governance values are being displaced by these Anglo-American norms, a process that is spilling over to the employment sphere. Companies find it difficult to sustain practices (e.g., carrying surplus employees during recessions) that favor employees over shareholders, that give employees a voice in governance, or that require long-term investment horizons, such as career employment and training.

The critics contend that Japan has much to learn from the American experience of the 1980s and 1990s, when large U.S. corporations faced the same pressures now confronting the Japanese: intensified global competition, sluggish domestic industries, and difficulties in sustaining competitive advantage. What revived the U.S. economy, say the critics, were deregulation and the advent of a more active market for corporate control, that is, for challenging and replacing incumbent managers. These developments led to mergers, divestitures, and restructurings. Newly streamlined companies shifted to a focus on shareholders and share prices. With the change in governance came an effort to reduce costs by cutting jobs—not only frontline workers but also middle managers and senior staff at corporate headquarters. Part-time and contingent employment increased, while companies made a point of disavowing—in word, if not always in deed—career-employment principles.

The strong medicine that is believed to have saved American industry is now being prescribed for Japan. Today, Japanese managers are being urged to use resources more efficiently—to stop hoarding labor, cease investment in unrelated and unprofitable ventures, and return excess cash to shareholders. The primary prescription for organizational change is to reform corporate governance. Alignment of managers with shareholders will require an overhaul of corporate boards, which customarily are appointed by the president and staffed with insiders. The boards are huge, comprising sometimes more than fifty individuals, and allegedly incapable of making decisions or of criticizing the strategy of the incumbent president.

Until recently, stakeholder, rather than shareholder, philosophies were the norm in Japan. Even in the mid-1990s, 97 percent of Japanese managers agreed that the company exists for the benefit of all stakeholders and disagreed that shareholders should have priority.[11] Critics contend that, while emphasis on the stakeholder model may have provided the solidarity necessary to rebuild Japan in the postwar years, it now inhibits the willingness of Japanese companies to make tough decisions—to eliminate surplus jobs, close down weak units, and cut ties with high-cost *keiretsu* partners.

Next in the crosshairs of the critics of Japanese corporations are HR departments, the corporate nerve centers of the organization-oriented employment system. Traditionally these departments are in charge of labor relations and employee-welfare services. They also hire employees into lifetime jobs and control their careers through a centralized system of training, performance evaluation, career planning, and job rotation. Through their role in the development of managers who will become the company's leaders and board members, HR departments are indirectly involved in corporate governance. Their more direct involvement is through the senior HR executive, who holds a seat on the company's board of directors and has a say in strategic corporate decisions.

Encapsulating the critique of HR departments is *Corporate HR Departments Are Not Needed*, a recent book by economist Naohiro Yashiro, president of the Japan Center for Economic Research. Yashiro asserts that powerful HR executives, whom he casts as both gods and dictators, are preventing internal reform of large Japanese companies.[12] He argues that Japanese firms should shift to systems of employment and corporate governance that are more decentralized and market- and shareholder-oriented. Others criticize Japanese HR managers for administering policies that generate excessive conformity and that compare unfavorably to practices prevailing in Silicon Valley or on Wall Street. The current system is said to undermine creativity, individualism, and competition.[13] As we will see, the depiction of HR departments as all-powerful bureaucracies is a dated stereotype. Nevertheless, it contains sufficient truth to make Yashiro's book a plausible brief for reform and a contribution to the debate over the Japanese corporation.

Still, defenders of the distinctive Japanese approach to employment and to corporate governance continue to be heard. Within Japan, those who urge preservation or incremental reform of current corporate practices include academics, labor leaders, and corporate executives—and not only from HR departments. All of them think that corporations are being blamed for problems that originate in other spheres—the macroeconomy, politics, or banking.[14]

Seen as excessively short-term and individualistic, U.S.-style corporate governance and employment practices are thought to be inappropriate for Japan because they clash with social norms regarding the corporation's responsibilities—norms embraced both by liberals and by more-conservative nationalists. Some defenders of the Japanese approach express concern that a shift to U.S. practices will erode Japan's comparative organizational advantage in customer and supplier relations, product quality, incremental innovation, firm-specific human-capital formation, and speed of execution. Even decentralization, a mantra in the United States, is criticized as being one-sided. Its critics say it represents a failure to recognize the many structural advantages that centralization offers to Japanese companies, who tend to have smaller divisions and therefore can rely on headquarters to achieve economies of scale and scope in pursuing strategy, research, and innovation.[15]

Those who favored a go-slow approach to organizational change faced an uphill battle in the late 1990s, but recent events have lent credibility to their skeptical perspective. The bust of the U.S. stock market and the spate of corporate scandals in the United States have called into question previous assumptions about the innate superiority of U.S. corporate governance. The fall to earth of dot-com companies and other high-tech start-ups has coincided with successes for some Japanese companies, and that has cast doubt on the assumption that organization-oriented employment practices are incapable of sustaining innovativeness.[16]

Just how far change has proceeded, and in what direction, will be examined in this book. It analyzes the impact that globalization, recession, and the declining strength of unions have had on Japanese HR departments and employment practices. Is shareholder sovereignty taking hold in Japan? Are HR departments losing their centrality and clout? Is employment becoming more market-oriented? Are companies listening to critics like Yashiro and U.S.-based investors or to those urging gradual reforms consistent with established Japanese practices?

THE AMERICAN SCENE

In the United States too in recent years, a debate about HR's role has occurred, but its point of departure is different. Unlike its counterpart in Japan, HR in U.S. companies has never been a prestigious executive function. Few American CEOs have a background in HR; the salaries of HR executives tend to be lower than those of other corporate specialists; and, until the late 1970s, most HR executives reported to the vice president of operations, or to an officer at similar rank, rather than to the CEO. During certain periods, however, the HR executive did have some clout, typically when confronting problems that created uncertainty for the corporation. These included the rise of mass unionism in the 1930s and 1940s and increased federal regulation of employment in the 1970s. Although jobs in the United States never were as stable as those in Japan, many companies treated their employees like "lifers" and, in most other respects (employee representation not being one of them), had a Japanese-style system of welfare capitalism.[17] Companies shared with government the provision of social benefits. And senior executives saw themselves as having responsibilities not only to shareholders but also to employees, customers, and communities. Around 1980, substantial overlap existed between the policies and corporate cultures typical of large U.S. companies and those typical of large Japanese companies.[18]

During the past twenty years, those corporate cultures have diverged. In the United States, jobs have become more market-oriented—a boon for some knowledge workers but for many others a source of greater instability and insecurity. The strength of unions continues to decline, and the impulse to regulate labor markets has tapered off. Viewed internally, big companies can be seen to have weathered a period of deconstruction. They are more decentralized, and as a result their headquarters are smaller, they rely more heavily on outsourcing, and they invest more power in the hands of line management. Corporate governance in U.S. companies has taken a sharp turn in the direction of shareholder sovereignty. The notion of employees as stakeholders has been widely repudiated.

For HR executives, these changes were, at least initially, traumatizing. Decentralization meant not only fewer standard procedures to ensure company-wide equity but also a transfer of operating authority from the central HR unit to line managers. Under the new approach, as management scholar Peter Cappelli explains, "managers in each office or shop, often at the level of the supervisor, make their own decisions about who should get hired—and fired. They also have the flexibility to set pay for their employees, reflecting local market conditions, and to structure compensation so that it is heavily contingent on performance."[19] Whereas the exemplar of the old approach was IBM—it had career jobs, extensive training, and a powerful headquarters HR function—the new exemplars were the intensely market-oriented companies of Silicon Valley, whose employees had no expectation of continuing employment and whose jobs were structured to meet ever shifting market requirements. Corporate loyalty, on both sides, was considered a sucker's game. The new employment contract was that people would work hard in return for learning opportunities, or even less, at firms like Wal-Mart.

HR executives in U.S. companies are struggling to redefine their responsibilities. With finance dominating corporate decision-making, HR executives stress their contribution to cost-cutting and their role as strategic business partner, that is, as advisor to other managers. Gone are notions of employee advocacy. Having assumed the business-partner role, HR has given up "pacifying disgruntled employees" in favor of "consulting with internal customers."[20] The management literature uses a lot of buzzwords to describe what HR executives should do, but exactly what HR executives *are* doing as "business partners" remains something of a mystery.

Against this tendency is a contrapuntal movement based on a different conception of what makes companies profitable: Instead of a focus on low wages or market power to boost shareholder value, a resource-based approach is proposed.[21] In the resource-based view of strategy, a company's competitive advantage derives from inimitable resources, such as intellectual property or unique physical assets, that it possesses and other companies do not. The resource-based view is more inward-looking than the market-oriented approach and, as such, is more concerned with strengthening organizational processes that make a company distinctive. It emphasizes that companies may do better to develop their own talent than to purchase it on the open market. Exemplars of this strategy include Southwest Airlines, knowledge-based companies like software-maker SAS Institute, and more downscale retailers like Men's Wearhouse and Costco.[22]

Companies taking the resource-based approach construe employees, and the HR function itself, not as cost burdens but as sources of competitive advantage.[23] Headquarters HR has the job of creating a company culture that encourages employee commitment and creativity, monitoring line management to ensure that employees are being trained and treated fairly, and developing HR policies to support good customer and supplier relations. All this means having personnel policies that are organization-oriented. There are similarities between this approach and the tenets of traditional Japanese HR. In fact, Japanese researchers developed an early version of resource-based strategy to explain how Japan's focused organizations used human capital to build core competencies. These ideas flowed west during the period when Japan served as a model for the United States.

On balance, then, the HR functions of U.S. companies show conflicting tendencies. Some HR executives emphasize shareholder sovereignty and the value of commodifying labor, while others endorse stakeholder governance and a resource-based approach. Which approach is dominant? What do they mean in practice? Note that in Japan the resource-based approach has traditionally been associated with HR power and influence. Does this observation apply to the United States? Finally, it's not clear what role U.S. human resource executives play in top-level decision-making in decentralized, market-oriented companies. Does HR have any role, in fact, to play there at all?

Convergence and National Models

Over the past twenty years, advanced nations have become more economically interdependent as a result of increased trade and rising capital flows. Some prefer to say that the world economy remains inter-national rather than global,[24] but no one disputes that the economic integration of nations is tighter now than in the past. The big debate is over the consequences of globalization. Does it mean convergence of previously distinctive national systems, of the varieties of capitalism? If so, will convergence be disproportionately influenced by the American model—shareholder sovereignty, arm's-length employment and business relationships—or will some new hybrids emerge?

The Japan-U.S. comparison offers a way of exploring these questions. Because of globalization, Japanese and U.S. companies increasingly must satisfy the same customers and investors, and that is a potential source of convergence. More generally, what favors convergence is that the two economies are enmeshed with each other. U.S. investors and consultants are active in Japan, trying to persuade local executives to adopt U.S.-style business practices, just as U.S. policymakers have been urging the Japanese government to emulate American laws regarding trade, commerce, and intellectual property. On the other side, Japanese companies have made massive investments in the United States and now have a sizable number of U.S.-based employees, some of whom return to Japan regularly. As companies on each side of the Pacific become more aware of each other, they compare themselves and are more likely to adopt each other's practices, especially at the level of the industry in which they compete.

Because the United States is a global hegemon, however, some practices and ideas flow in only one direction. American values are transmitted through advertising, mass media, and other channels. Japanese youth model themselves after their counterparts in the United States. Young college graduates are leery of jobs in big companies and more inclined than their parents to take risks and assert their individuality. Affluent Japanese of all ages are more individualistic than were affluent Japanese of earlier generations. Japan today is marked by considerably less social solidarity than in the decades immediately following the Second World War, and by less willingness to tolerate egalitarianism in social policy and at the workplace.[25]

The HR executive's role in large corporations is just one of many reference points for the study of convergence, but it has the advantage of providing material in which any tendencies toward convergence are likely to show up in sharp relief, as Japanese and U.S. companies entered the 1980s with rather different approaches to HR, employment, and corporate governance. On average, Japanese companies were relatively *organization-oriented*, meaning that employment was of extended duration and turnover low; training was extensive; and internal considerations—equity, seniority—dominated decision making on wages and allocation. Stakeholder corporate governance and enterprise unions supported the firm's organization orientation. All these features undergirded a high-status, centralized HR function in Japan.

In the United States, employment practices tended to be more *market-oriented* with shorter job durations and higher turnover, low training expenditures, and pay and allocation based on going rates and other external criteria.

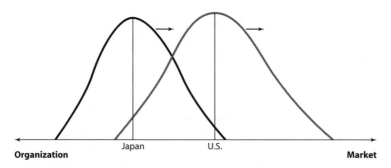

Organization   Japan   U.S.   Market

Figure 1.1 Corporate Employment Systems in the 1980s

Corporate governance privileged shareholders, and unions were either industrial in orientation or, more commonly, did not exist. Compared to Japanese
employees, dissatisfied workers in the United States were more inclined to
exit, and they had fewer opportunities for "voice." The HR function lacked
the centrality and influence of its Japanese counterpart.[26]

Figure 1.1 represents the distribution of corporate employment systems in
U.S. and Japanese firms in the early 1980s. What we see is that the United
States and Japan had disparate means (assuming normal distributions). That
is, on average they took different approaches to managing employees. One
interpretation of convergence is that the Japanese mean is moving gradually
closer to that of the United States. We will consider that hypothesis as we
analyze the respective developments in the two countries.

The story, though, is more involved than that. Although Japan and the
United States started from different positions, from the beginning there was
overlap between them, as is shown in figure 1.1. Some Japanese companies
and some U.S. companies resembled each other more than they adhered to
their national central tendencies. It is possible that, over time, the variance of
the national distributions will widen so that cross-national overlap increases
while the central tendencies change little, if at all. This too could be considered a type of convergence.

Complicating the situation is the dynamic nature of the distributions. Their
shape and location are changing over time. If both countries shift in a market-
oriented direction, as indicated by the arrows, it is possible that the distance
between the national means will not change. In my view, this would still be
an instance of convergence—what I call 'directional convergence.'

The existence of national models that other countries emulate is not unique
to the present period of globalization. In famous essays on "economic backwardness," Alexander Gerschenkron argued that late-developing countries
like Germany and Russia were able to accelerate their industrialization process by borrowing ideas and institutions from more advanced countries like

England.[27] In Japan, the Meiji modernizers of the nineteenth century looked to Europe, and to a lesser extent the United States, for lessons in designing the army, the police, the schools, the legal system, the postal service, and other political and social institutions.[28] The Meiji reformers picked and chose the national models that were considered "best practice" of the day, but they favored those that fit with preexisting Japanese characteristics—hence their preference for the French police system, which was centralized, over the English version, which was comparatively decentralized. Later, after the First World War, when large Japanese companies sought ways to spur efficiency without labor strife, they looked to the United States—it was industrializing rapidly without a strong labor movement—and borrowed practices such as scientific management and welfare capitalism.[29]

After the Second World War, Europe and Japan attributed America's role in the Allied victory to the superiority of its economic and political systems.[30] Within the United States, too, social scientists in the 1950s and 1960s were infatuated with the idea that American institutions were the most advanced in the world, and they predicted that eventually other countries would converge on the U.S. model. Modernization theorists expected convergence not only of business institutions but also of labor unions (with U.S. business unionism seen as the "mature" approach), of societal culture (individualism would supplant "collectivism"), and of political systems (pluralist democracy would become the norm and totalitarianism would disintegrate under the logic of industrialism). Just to be sure, America's foreign-aid and development programs, like those that defined its occupation and economic rehabilitation of Japan, prescribed the adoption of U.S. practices.[31]

In the 1950s and 1960s, Japanese businessmen and government officials made regular study trips to the United States to learn about the ostensibly superior American system. In economic-development jargon, this was a "demonstration effect." But, as in the Meiji era, the reformers selected only those elements that fit with Japanese practices. They grafted their borrowings onto existing Japanese institutions. The net effect was to preserve the underlying structure, as was the case with Japanese labor law.[32]

The postwar U.S. economic boom came to an end in the early 1970s. Productivity declined, inflation rose, and imports began to claim a larger share of the U.S. market. Against the debacle of Vietnam and the end of the Bretton Woods system, the economic giant that was the United States appeared wounded. No longer was it touted as a model for other countries. It was precisely at this moment that a new "varieties of capitalism" literature began to flourish. First it was the corporatist European economies, and then Japan, that were held forth as desirable alternatives. In the 1980s, political economists such as Lester Thurow and Michel Albert predicted that three types of capitalism—European (the "Rhine" model), Japanese, and Anglo-American—would contend for market share in an increasingly globalized world.[33]

Students of the Japanese model were impressed by its highly trained workers, high-quality products, and efficient manufacturing systems. Cooperation—between workers and managers, suppliers and users, business and government—was thought to be the key to Japanese success. Also, Japan played Gerschenkron's late-developer role with consummate skill.[34] By the 1980s, the tables had turned. Now it was U.S. businessmen who took regular trips to Japan to learn the secrets of its manufacturing prowess, while Japanese companies used their surplus profits to purchase real estate in downtown New York. Just as in earlier periods the Japanese had tried to adapt U.S. practices to their native economy, now U.S. companies struggled to assimilate quality circles, just-in-time methods, and union-management cooperation. Not only in manufacturing but also in the semiconductor and other high-technology industries, the Japanese appeared to be beating the United States and had long since outpaced the British, who in the 1980s tried to market themselves to Japanese investors as a low-wage assembly zone for export to Europe.[35] Economic fortunes fluctuate, however, and the 1990s saw another reversal. Now the United States recaptured the lead, as Japan and Europe experienced slow growth and record high levels of unemployment.

Our brief history of national models suggests the following principle: When a nation enjoys macroeconomic success, it will be regarded as a model by its slower-growing peers. Consistent with this prediction, U.S. ideas and institutions in the 1990s were once again prescribed as good for what ailed the stagnant economies of Europe and Japan. The performance of the U.S. economy in the 1990s, especially its ability to generate millions of new jobs, silenced earlier assertions that Rhenish capitalism—or Nordic, Northern Italian, or East Asian capitalism, for that matter—were superior to the U.S. version. The shoe was now on the other foot, and it was the American model—flexible employment arrangements, shareholder sovereignty, decentralized companies, and venture capital—that was held up as the exemplar.

The problem, however, is the difficulty of identifying which micro-level institutions are responsible for a country's superior macroeconomic performance. Hence, those who wanted to emulate American success had little idea of where to start. Some countries, or the companies within them, imitated U.S. accounting practices; others set up venture-capital funds; still others tried to build business-university linkages, in hopes of creating new Silicon Valleys.

Cynics said that *nothing* was worth imitating, because U.S. success was simply a matter of luck, of so-called first-mover advantages—it was first out of the chutes with information and Internet technologies. Others, more taken with the idea of national systems but less sanguine about convergence, noted that economic systems are composed of myriad small pieces that fit together as a result of having coevolved over long periods of time. That is, "institutional complementarities" exist that make it difficult, if not impossible, to chip off an institution from one setting, implant it in a different matrix, and have it achieve the same results.[36] For example, Silicon Valley requires not only venture capital and university talent but also high employee mobility and particular kinds of intellectual-property law. The parts fit together in fortuitous ways that are difficult to replicate piecemeal.[37]

In light of these developments, the varieties-of-capitalism literature became more cautious about advocating models. Now there was closer examination of the costs as well as the benefits of different national systems. On the upside, the U.S. economy in the 1990s generated millions of new jobs, thousands of new businesses, and a booming equities market. Shareholder sovereignty meant that companies were willing to take risks on behalf of their investors. On the downside, wage growth was slow and unevenly distributed; output per hour was about the same as in Western Europe; and per capita growth rates were not higher than in other advanced countries, including Japan. The downside of shareholder sovereignty became clearer after the U.S. boom ended in 2001, as news about managerial self-dealing and ineffectual boards came to light. Even so, productivity recently has improved greatly in the United States and, if that turns out to be a lasting development, proponents of the U.S. model will have something to crow about, assuming, however, it does not sink under the weight of its current-account and budgetary deficits.[38]

At this moment, though, much remains unclear, including the extent to which America's "new economy" is driven by first-mover technological advantages that may not be sustainable for very long. Since the 1950s, in fact, the United States has at different periods seemed to enjoy an advantage that was soon dissipated by overseas entrants with different economic institutions. It happened in transistors, consumer applications of integrated circuits, and, for a while, in semiconductors. It may happen yet again, or it may not.[39] Economic success at any point in time is often a matter of having all the right pieces at the right moment. (Perhaps that is what's meant by luck.) If economic actors don't know what contributes to a country's success and the success of the companies within it, it may elicit less imitation—and less convergence—than proponents of convergence believe should occur.

Consider corporate governance, for example. In the late 1990s, it was popular to blame the collapse and slow recovery of the Asian "tigers" on their corporate-governance systems, which were said to be opaque and prone to insider cronyism. Japan was criticized on the same grounds. In both cases, the exemplar for corporate governance was the United States, where ownership was dispersed and corporate boards were small and composed of outsiders. These features of the U.S. model were held responsible for the high growth rates and booming equity prices in the United States in the 1990s.

What many failed to realize is that the U.S. governance model is substantially the same as that found in Britain and Canada, whose economies in the 1990s were far from stellar. Britain's per capita GDP levels were below Japan's, while its output growth lagged behind Germany's throughout the 1990s. In

per capita income, Britain's rank among the nations actually declined between 1980 and the late 1990s, at a time when it was imitating other features
of the U.S. model. Canada's performance was even worse: In per capita GDP,
it fell from third to seventh, despite what by U.S. standards was an enviable
corporate-governance system.[40]

Putting to one side the hubris of Wall Street and The City, note that any
attribution of America's recent economic performance to shareholder sovereignty (which also exists in Britain and Canada) is based more on faith than
on facts. The absence of certain knowledge of how, or even if, U.S.-style governance contributed to America's economic performance sharply curtails the
incentive that other countries might feel to emulate American practices.

There are other problems with convergence theory. The notion of a dominant model may have more to do with how social scientists think than with
the realities of economic growth. As economist Richard Freeman observes,
the assumption that there exists an optimal set of institutions for governing
firms and markets owes much to the idea, ingrained in economics, of single-
peak optimality. The historical evidence suggests that a wide variety of economic systems foster growth—that there are multiple equilibria—and that
what appears as the best model is shaped as much by fad and fashion as by
evidence. With respect to the same example, corporate governance, the data
show no relationship between different types of corporate governance and
variations in per capita GDP. Hence one should be wary, once again, of claims
that there is one best way of structuring modern economies.[41]

Another defect of the dominant-model form of convergence is that it tends
to minimize or ignore the diversity that exists within a nation. For small (and
relatively homogeneous) countries, this may not pose a significant problem.
For large countries, however, it does. What the convergence literature gives us
is—instead of a realistic portrayal of a large nation's economic institutions—
something resembling a Weberian ideal type. The dominant-model school
focuses on national means and ignores within-country dispersion (see figure
1.1). Japan has long been characterized as a country with substantial economic
dualism—its small and middling firms are significantly different from its large
ones. Today that characteristic is magnified by the split between Japan's export-
oriented companies and companies, such as those in the retailing and construction industries, that are based on the home market In the United States
too, companies divide along various lines, such as that between unionized and
nonunionized, between family-owned and public, and between diversified and
focused. Hence, in some sectors in Japan and in the United States, companies
resemble their counterparts across the Pacific more than their national models,
and that causes the distributional overlap shown in figure 1.1.

This, however, raises a question: Does globalization lead to convergence at
the industrial level, resulting in greater within-country dispersion and fewer
companies clustered near the national mean? Referring to the idea that it

does, the economists Harry C. Katz and Owen Darbishire write of "converging divergences." They find evidence of this phenomenon in the employment systems of telecommunications and automotive firms in Europe and the United States. In the past, distinctive national institutions, such as collective bargaining—the laws and customs of which vary from country to country—molded corporate employment practices. Today, according to Katz and Darbishire, those institutions exert less influence than do the common technological and competitive forces operating at the industry level. Industry-level convergence is, however, rather different from what is seen in the dominant-model view: It is limited to particular sectors and implies the declining significance of macro-level national institutions. Another implication of the industry-level view is that national economies, instead of converging on the U.S. approach, borrow and imitate in multiple directions, as, for example, European and U.S. automotive firms copy Japanese work practices, while Japanese financial companies move to the more decentralized wage systems characteristic of the United States.[42]

One difficulty for the converging-divergences argument is that economic actors adapt to common environmental pressures in different ways. At the end of the adaptation process, the institutions have changed—they are now hybrids of some sort—but national differences persist. The logic underpinning this outcome is rooted in the theory of path dependence. Countries begin the development process at different starting points and move along separate trajectories. Over time, a nation's economic institutions interact and form complementarities. Think of diesel versus rotary engines: The parts are different but the function, generating torque or horsepower, is the same.[43]

Some countries are what economist David Soskice calls "coordinated market economies," in which, over time, complementarities among their systems of employment relations, labor relations, corporate governance, and external relations (relations with government and others businesses) develop. In Sweden's economy, for example, the parts that yield coordination may be different from those in Germany, the Netherlands, or Japan, but in each case the purpose of those different sets of parts is similar.[44]

The same observation holds true of the U.S.-Japan comparison. Japan has been repeatedly criticized for lacking a well-developed venture-capital industry like that found in the United States. That's one reason why Softbank, the Internet incubator of Masayoshi Son, created such a stir in the late 1990s. What was not well understood at the time is that Japan has an alternative mechanism for funding new ventures: growing them inside large companies and then spinning them off as independent entities. Another example of countries arriving at similar results through different approaches is that companies in Germany, Japan, and the United States, while differing from each other vastly in their systems of corporate governance, share the same response to sagging corporate performance: They are equally likely to replace top executives. It is precisely the response one would expect from a well-functioning corporate-governance system.[45]

When a common environmental change is felt, each national system tends to adapt incrementally and to do so in ways that fit existing structures. Because of complementarities, an adaptation that works in one system would fail in a different national context. (The reduction of emissions from a diesel engine and from a rotary engine requires two different methods.) While nations in theory could implement an entirely new set of institutions, sunk costs and uncertainty keep them from straying off a given path; incrementalism trumps synoptic change.[46]

An example: Technological innovation in the 1980s called into question existing systems for regulating telecommunications, but nations (including the United States) did not respond with across-the-board deregulation. Instead they made incremental adaptations that constituted what political scientist Steven Vogel calls "re-regulation," whereby national differences were preserved, even while the different adaptations tried by various countries moved each of them in the same direction. An example from the corporate level is the steel industry of the advanced nations, which since the 1970s has been plagued by excess capacity and competition from low-cost producers. All the advanced countries have shrunk their capacity, but their means of achieving that result varied: rapid downsizing via layoffs and bankruptcies, pay cuts, gradual job cuts combined with government subsidies. Choice of adjustment strategy was dictated by existing labor-management and business-government relations. A third example comes from the automotive industry. When confronted with quality problems in the 1980s, U.S. manufacturers at first tried imitating Japanese quality practices but quickly found that in the U.S. context they failed to perform as intended, and eventually fashioned their own alternative methods.[47]

Path dependence also provides an explanation for a conundrum relevant to the U.S.-Japan relationship: the high level of exchange between the developed countries of the North. What could be the basis for comparative advantage between countries with similarly efficient industries and endowments? Path dependence suggests that different national starting points and subsequent trajectories can give rise to institutional diversity, and that some constellations of national institutions may be better than others at facilitating certain types of innovation or business strategy.[48] Companies, and the countries in which they are embedded, can then secure international markets by specializing in particular product types, because competitors with different institutional structures will have difficulty imitating them. The emphasis, therefore, on human capital—high training levels—in Germany (craft skills) and Japan (firm-specific skills) supports production-based technological learning, incremental innovation, and high-quality products. By contrast, U.S. institutions encourage resource mobility, general skills, and high short-term rewards. That has the effect of directing resources to big-bang technological breakthroughs but not to implementation prowess. Path dependence, then, offers not only an explanation for North-North trade but also a larger lesson: Sustaining institutional diversity permits nations to reap continuing benefits from trade with each other.[49]

The implications for convergence theory are straightforward. At the gross level, diverse national infrastructures may appear to be designed to yield the same results, just as different engines all generate horsepower or torque. At a fine-grained level, however, those institutions are in fact defining slightly different production possibilities, which permit companies to occupy disparate competitive niches, just as some engines are better for powering a truck and others work best in marine applications. At that level of analysis, countries can be seen as not only structurally but also functionally dissimilar, and successful adaptations are those that prevent the dissipation of national advantages. Convergence pressure from common environmental changes may be resisted or may lead to a form of hybridization that preserves national diversity.

These observations lead to four different predictions about the role of HR executives and the nature of employment practices in Japan and the United States. First, the national-model argument: At the present time, the United States is an exemplar for other countries, including Japan, so one can expect to see Japan move in a more market-oriented direction, toward shareholder-oriented corporate governance and weaker ties to employees, other businesses, and government. The pressure for convergence could follow myriad paths. It might arise in product markets or in financial markets, or it might come as a result of legislation. Whatever the source, the result will be movement of the Japanese mean towards the U.S. mean shown in figure 1.1, leading to a weaker HR function in Japan.

Second, according to the converging-divergences argument, national patterns in all countries, including the United States and Japan, will fade as companies grow more sensitive to industry-level competition and model themselves on each other. Borrowing will be bidirectional, as it is not in the national-model case, so the net effect will be a two-way reduction in the distance between national means. At the same time, national dispersion—the variance around the mean—will increase. With respect to HR executives, one would expect to see greater industry-specific commonalities, with ideas and practices flowing between Japan and the United States.

Third, according to the weak-path-dependence prediction, national economies will adapt to common environmental changes in a similar way but will fashion those adaptations to fit preexisting institutions. The result is hybridization in each country. In terms of figure 1.1, national models will move in the same direction—both Japan and the United States will become more market-oriented—but the distance between their national means may not change. For

HR, this might mean greater decentralization in both Japan and the United States but within the confines of differently organized corporate structures.

Finally, according to the strong-path-dependence prediction, countries will preserve their dissimilarity—to sustain comparative advantage, because they find it too costly to change in the face of complex interdependencies, or because vested interests block reform and promote inertia. Figure 1.1 remains fixed, a case of *plus ça change, plus c'est la même chose.*[50]

A Look Ahead

To understand developments in Japan and the United States, and to determine whether convergence is occurring, requires a close look inside large corporations that dominate each nation's economy. Admittedly, the present situation of HR executives is only a piece in a much larger puzzle about the future directions of corporations and capitalism in different parts of the world. But a clear advantage of studying these executives and what they do is that it offers a unique vantage point from which the larger process of change can be seen. Because the HR function mediates between the economic environment and corporate practices, its organizational role affects a broad range of decisions—about business strategy, employment policy, and corporate governance. These decisions lie at the heart of what constitutes the varieties of capitalism.

Figure 1.1 offers a guide to the structure of this book. In chapter 2, I analyze the traditional Japanese system—the central tendency that existed in the early 1980s—and then examine the pressures for change that have developed over the past twenty years. Chapter 3 presents findings from field research inside large Japanese corporations, focusing on the diversity that exists in Japan today. Chapter 4 is devoted to the evolution of the HR function in the United States. There I look at the traditional U.S. system and at changes that have occurred since the 1980s. Chapter 5—which presents field research on a set of U.S. companies matched with the Japanese firms—examines U.S. diversity as well as industry-specific overlap with Japan. Chapter 6 presents survey data on the central tendency in each country today, allowing us to gauge how near to— or distant from—each other the countries are. Chapter 7 rounds out the book with a summary and conclusions.

Human Resources Departments
in Large Japanese Firms: The Way It Was

MOST OF THE RESEARCH on Japanese HR departments was conducted prior to the 1990s, that is, before calls for reform of traditional practices had grown loud and insistent. In the 1980s, when confidence in the Japanese model was at its peak, Japanese corporations had headquarters HR departments that, based on the number of personnel staff per hundred employees, were twice the size of their U.S. counterparts,[1] and they were regarded as powerful and influential as well as large. The reasons for that reputation are diverse, ranging from factors internal to the corporation (employment and labor relations, corporate strategy and governance) to societal forces such as postwar Japan's egalitarian ethos. We will examine these issues in detail and then consider recent changes in Japan's economy and society that are challenging the centrality of corporate HR departments.

Organization Orientation

One reason for the size and power of HR departments is the broad range of organization-oriented activities that large Japanese companies pursued on behalf of their employees: managing the training, development, and promotion sequences of an employee's "lifetime" career; negotiating and consulting with ubiquitous enterprise unions; weighting employee pay toward internal factors such as age, seniority, and merit rather than the external or market rate that a person might command; and maintaining centralized programs for employee training, recreation, and welfare (dormitories, lunchrooms, vacation facilities, etc.).

The origins of these practices are diverse and unplanned, ranging from a dearth of social insurance programs to shortages of skilled labor to successive waves of worker militancy. Some of them date from the 1940s and 1950s and others from earlier in the century. Over time, they intertwined and came to reinforce each other. Long-term employment and the rarity of interfirm mobility had the effect of increasing training expenditures borne by employers.[2] Enterprise unions, while helping to convince employees that the returns on firm-specific investments were being fairly divided, also provided some voice to employees for whom the possibility of exit was blocked. The "white collarization" of blue-collar jobs and the membership of middle managers in the union helped to align the interests of unions and management. Tying pay to seniority created a sense of equity among the organization's "lifers," although promotion to the organization's upper echelons remained dependent on ability. Long-term employment generated a steady stream of information that managers found useful for judging the abilities of employees and for assigning them to appropriate postings. Thus lifetime employment, the seniority system, and enterprise unionism, the three pillars of employment in Japanese corporations, were mutually reinforcing.[3]

The job of the headquarters HR department was to administer the internal labor market through standardized rules and procedures. It also had the responsibility of recruiting recent graduates to join the organization as new employees. Over time, the department became the repository for a steady stream of information on an employee's work history and abilities, enabling it to identify those employees who were most qualified to fill key positions in the corporate hierarchy. Finally, the headquarters HR department oversaw training and the administration of employee-welfare activities, two labor-intensive duties.[4]

Generally, the power of a firm's HR department was related to the homogeneity of its labor force. In companies where a single occupational group was dominant, be it blue-collar auto-assembly workers or white-collar banking employees, huge economies of scale could be realized from the centralization of HR activities for recruitment, training, and compensation. Of course, homogeneity of the workforce was related to the structure of the corporation itself— that is, to strategic decisions that corporate directors had made about specialization versus diversification.

Strategy and Structure

Compared to their U.S. counterparts, Japanese firms were and remain centralized and focused. By the mid-1980s, more than three-fourths of U.S. companies had adopted the decentralized, M-form structure that became popular after the Second World War. In this organizational model, corporate divisions are given autonomy in return for their meeting strategic and financial criteria set by headquarters. In Japan, however, the majority of companies (55 to 60 percent) at that time had a functional, or U-form, structure: Sales, finance, planning, and HR were centralized at headquarters; no divisional or other structures intervened between headquarters and local units; and product diversification was relatively low.[5]

Some researchers interpret the prevalence of U-form organizations in Japan as a sign of economic immaturity. What is not well understood is that, because of the ease with which they could create subsidiaries (*kogaisha*), Japanese companies had less need of, and interest in, an M-form structure. When new technologies or market segments did not fit with the core technological and strategic competence of the parent company, it would spin off units. This allowed the parent to "stick to its knitting" and reduce diseconomies of scale and scope. At the same time, as an independent subsidiary a unit enjoyed more independence than it would have as a division of the parent company. Some *kogaisha* eventually shed their subsidiary status and became fully independent entities, albeit the parent company held an equity stake. Toshiba in 1988 had thirty-three subsidiaries in which its stake exceeded 50 percent and another couple of hundred in which its holdings were less than that.[6] The parent company typically placed a substantial amount of business with the affiliate and, during hard times, might ask it to absorb some of its surplus employees. Partly because of these *kogaisha*, the comparison of U.S. and Japanese firms shows the latter to be less diversified, although it's a bit like apples and oranges.[7]

Opinion is divided on the question of why spin-offs were (and are) more prevalent in Japan. To some observers, they are a sign of capital-market imperfections. Others claim that the popularity of spin-offs in Japan reflects a management philosophy that favors specialization and competition on the basis of core competencies. In this view, the Japanese method of handling unrelated diversification is more effective than the U.S. method, which is based on the M-form model. The latter is said to result in greater bureaucracy and less internal competence and focus than are yielded by the *kogaisha* approach combined with the U-form model.[8] Also, in Japan there are lower legal and administrative costs associated with managing spin-offs than in the United States. Those lower costs can be attributed in part to accounting rules that, in the past, permitted a parent company to report earnings on an unconsolidated basis, so that labor and other costs transferred to *kogaisha* did not appear on the parent's books. The effort by troubled companies to use this method to shift costs is one reason the number of spin-offs has risen in recent years.[9]

Another reason that the cost of managing spin-offs is lower for parent companies in Japan is that social controls and the concern for reputation—which tend to be stronger in Japan—are more effective at inhibiting opportunism on the part of a spin-off's managers than U.S.-style contracts and litigation.[10] Whatever the explanation, the prevalence of *kogaisha* has had the effect of reducing corporate heterogeneity and thereby making it feasible for companies to remain relatively centralized.

Even the 40 to 45 percent of Japanese firms that by the 1980s had adopted the divisionalized, M-form structure had fewer divisions and less unrelated diversification than did comparable American companies. When Japanese companies diversified, they tended to spread narrowly into related industries. Also, their functions in marketing, accounting, purchasing, and HR were more centralized at headquarters.[11] For example, Matsushita Electric, a giant electrical company that, like General Electric, had numerous operating divisions, nevertheless centralized at headquarters its sales, marketing, R&D, and

HR functions. Such an arrangement is typical of Japanese M-form companies. It explains why Japanese headquarters staff was (and remains) substantially larger—by a factor of five, according to one expert—than that of the typical European or U.S. multinational firm.[12]

A key advantage, then, of a large headquarters staff is that it helps to coordinate and integrate the activities of divisions that operate in closely related markets. While divisions within the Japanese corporation would in many ways operate independently, they were expected to cooperate in sharing technology and personnel and in managing strategic alliances with customers and suppliers. Permanent interdivisional teams were much more common in Japan, while bonuses based on divisional performance—which in the United States tended to be considerable—were small or nonexistent.[13]

In a system of that nature, headquarters had the role of identifying and developing the company's core competencies by helping line departments build expertise in marketing, production, and technology. Human resources accumulated and distributed knowledge throughout the company, as did other functions. Eventually, a company would compete on the basis of these inimitable assets and tacit knowledge. This would become known in the West as the resource-based approach to business strategy.[14]

While a strong headquarters might seem like costly duplication of functions at the divisional level, in Japan the constrained role for divisions meant that headquarters coexisted with a flat organizational structure. Given the close relationship of divisions in matters of technology and markets, it was feasible to centralize functions at headquarters and thereby achieve economies of scale.[15]

Constraining divisions from below were powerful factory units that were crucial sites for the codevelopment of technological and manufacturing expertise. At Toshiba, another *sōgō denki* (diversified electrical company) that resembled General Electric, divisions were first introduced in 1949, and by the 1970s their importance was firmly established. However, caught as they were between headquarters (which usurped strategic planning and interdivisional coordination,) and semiautonomous "focal factories" (which combined production and applied research), Toshiba's divisions enjoyed less autonomy than G.E.'s did.[16]

It would be wrong to conclude that Japanese divisions were entirely toothless. At Toshiba, certain key divisions—examples include industrial electronics in the 1970s and semiconductors in the 1990s—carried considerable clout at headquarters. Divisions at Matsushita Electric sometimes engaged in bitter competition, as when the TV and video divisions both began producing VCRs.[17] All the same, when measured in comparative as opposed to absolute terms, Japanese corporate divisions had less vertical and horizontal autonomy than did their U.S. counterparts.

Another difference between Japanese and U.S. corporations is that the Japanese were less diversified, even after they began to invest surplus cash in new and often unrelated businesses in the 1980s, as they sought not only new markets (in an environment where acquisitions were difficult) but also new opportunities for incumbent employees. Some of the new businesses were successes; others were not, and the employee-oriented Japanese approach was often blamed, especially by those who thought that the surplus cash should have been returned to shareholders. In the end, diversification levels remained lower than in the United States, partly because of the practice of hiving off unrelated operations and turning them into independent subsidiaries.[18]

Centralization of HR in Japanese companies not only resulted from but also contributed to a focused business strategy and constraints on divisionalization. Headquarters HR departments were expected to help maintain a unified company through "soft" controls such as a strong corporate culture, intensive employee training, standardized working conditions, and the circulation of management personnel across different parts of the company. Because of the power of the central HR office, divisional HR units, where they existed at all, usually played second fiddle. M-form companies in Japan were less than half as likely as those in the United States to have personnel functions at the divisional level.[19]

The same factors that boosted the status of central HR departments also weakened that of finance departments. Because corporate divisions were tied by commonalities of technology and markets, and because long-term employment and intrafirm mobility fostered firm-specific knowledge, headquarters executives had a good grasp of the business fundamentals of various units and so in their decision making did not have to rely so heavily on financial criteria. The set of criteria on which business units were evaluated was broad; it included their synergies with other units and their technological prowess.

Many of these senior executives had been trained as engineers and so were steeped in the culture of "making things rather than making money."[20] Like their German counterparts, who also tended to have engineering backgrounds, they put a premium on product quality, even if it sometimes meant raising costs. Their productivist orientation made Japanese engineer-managers wary of finance departments, and it led them into alliance with HR departments, who provided the systems necessary to train workers to produce high-quality products. The net effect was that finance departments were left to serve more as borrowing strategists than as auctioners of internal capital. Critics of this approach would argue that it drove headquarters to engage too closely with functional goals when it should have been disinterestedly monitoring divisions and allocating capital to benefit shareholders—the pure M-form approach.[21]

Thus it comes as no surprise that, in a cross-national survey, Japanese executives gave lower influence ratings to their finance departments than U.S. executives gave to theirs. Conversely, HR departments in Japan received higher influence ratings than did those in the United States. Compared to the United

States, then, Japanese firms assigned a smaller role to the finance function and its "hard" controls and showed greater appreciation for HR and its soft (or, as the Japanese say, "wet") controls.[22]

Kingmakers

Contributing to the influence of Japanese HR departments was their reputation as corporate kingmakers. The vast majority of Japanese managers spent their careers with a single company and were selected rather late in their careers for executive positions. It is unclear precisely why Japanese companies developed the system of managerial rotation, intensive training, and late selection. Viewed superficially, it can be seen to mirror practices developed for blue-collar workers, who also are intensively trained to be versatile. More to the point, however, is that in the context of long-term employment, late selection allows the organization to conduct a series of tournaments that managers must win to rise to the top, a method by which it can identify the most competent insiders.[23]

The particular form that systematic rotation would take in a manager's early years was determined by central HR, which would assess how best to expose young managers to different parts of the company while insuring that each of those parts received adequate contact with the best and brightest young managers. In the majority (65 percent) of Japanese companies surveyed in the late 1980s, job rotations of three to five years were decided jointly by the HR department and department heads; in only a relatively small percentage of companies did the HR department (15 percent) or the individual divisions (13 percent) make these decisions unilaterally. Even in firms in which divisions ran their own rotations, it was usually understood that the central HR department had the right to overrule a division that refused to circulate talented managers whom other units of the firm needed.[24]

Japanese managers were subject to detailed performance assessments, at least twice a year in most cases. Employees were evaluated by their superiors, but central HR departments intervened to review the assessments and ensure that they were fair and conducted consistently across the company. In U.S. companies, that kind of top-down involvement would be resented by line managers prone to see it as "meddling" in staff issues. That attitude was less common in Japanese firms, because the corporate ethos there dictated that training and development be taken seriously (line managers were themselves evaluated on how they developed their subordinates) and because the central HR department had the power to command respect.[25] Adding to the perception of central HR's legitimacy was that, in the politicized world of Japanese companies, it had a reputation for being a neutral arbiter.

An oft-cited symbol of the HR department's power were the dossiers it kept on every employee in the company, from the president down to the lowest-ranking employee.[26] These contained all of an employee's performance assessments as well as other accumulated information. As if to affirm the saying that knowledge is power, the HR department could determine the fate of those moving up the management ranks. For those who had reached the uppermost management strata, however, its power was attenuated, as decisions about who would be promoted to the rank of department head (*buchō*) or senior executive were in the hands of the company president and the managing board, not the central HR department. Nevertheless, because the HR department was keeper of the organizational memory, the president would consult it to vet candidates for the corporate board or to design an executive succession plan, whose outcome in any given instance would, of course, be subject to the president's approval.[27]

Unions

Another institution bolstering HR's status and influence was the enterprise union. Enterprise unions represent "core" employees from entry level to mid-management and in large firms enroll 80 to 90 percent of all regular employees.

During the 1950s and 1960s, Japanese companies put a priority on developing a *modus vivendi* whereby their enterprise unions would be integrated into the corporate structure and culture. Many of the unions were founded as militant class-conscious organizations after the Second World War, and they still contained left-wing activists who were deeply suspicious of management. The task of isolating the militants and encouraging a more moderate union leadership was considerable, and it fell to central HR departments. The carrots it dangled included seniority-based wages, no-layoff guarantees (layoffs were the cause of bitter disputes in the 1950s), and other concessions; the sticks ran the gamut from the formation of second unions to the provision of special benefits to loyal workers.[28]

This left HR departments open to criticism from other managers, who blamed them both for strikes when they took a hard line and, when they took a softer line, for being too cozy with and accommodating to union leaders. In fact, union leaders and headquarters HR managers had a symbiotic relationship. Union leaders preferred to deal with the headquarters HR department instead of the line managers because companywide policies emanated from headquarters, and its understanding of the union's needs was more nuanced than that of most line managers. Headquarters HR often shared business information with union leaders, who reciprocated by sharing with HR information on issues of concern to employees.

Managers at headquarters HR understood that their influence with other managers derived in part from HR's relationship to the union. At times this put HR in the position of defending the union to fellow managers. Yet even when other managers criticized HR for being too sympathetic to the unions, it was respected, because the tensions inherent in the evolving union-management relationship demanded careful treatment and getting that relationship right was deemed crucial to the company's health. The issues that turned on that relationship—labor costs, labor peace, and managerial legitimacy—were seen as too important or too difficult to be relegated to line managers.[29]

The advent in the late 1950s of labor's spring wage offensive (shuntō) had the effect of centralizing wage negotiations at the company's highest levels and of sending, again, a particularly vital issue—in this case, compensation costs—into central HR's court. Although initially opposed to shuntō, firms adapted to it by consulting and cooperating with other employers, which thrust HR departments into the middle of complicated boundary-spanning interactions with suppliers, customers, competitors, and business-group (keiretsu) firms. HR executives were regular participants in activities organized by Nikkeiren, the national employer's organization, whose prestige—as reflected by its distinguished leadership, regular mention in the press, and close ties to key government agencies—enhanced their own. Like employers' organizations in other countries, Nikkeiren was a response to its national-level counterparts on the union side. In later years its ambit expanded to include social-welfare policy, such as pension reform, and dissemination of "best HR practice" in training and work organization, for example, although labor relations remained a key focus.[30]

These facts contrast sharply to those obtaining in the United States, where determination of union wages was more decentralized and unions were less prevalent outside the manufacturing sector. Even in unionized companies, most senior U.S. executives had little direct experience with unions, whereas in Japan the practice of including low- to mid-level managers in the union meant that, by the early 1980s, many department heads and board members and some presidents had once not only belonged to the union but even been active in it. Some individuals made a direct move from the union to a position on the board or audit committee.[31] A Nikkeiren study in 1982 found that three-fourths of Japanese firms had at least one managing director who had been a union leader; one-sixth of all directors were former union leaders.[32] These figures are unsurprising, as the same interpersonal skills that are necessary for effective union leadership also help to advance one's career in management. Hence a panoply of the corporation's most important officials—chairmen, presidents, board members, and department heads—understood the labor relations role of the HR department, respected the effort to maintain cooperative relations with the union, and were unlikely to harbor the kind of antiunion assumptions typical of American executives.[33]

While U.S. firms that were unionized responded to the oil-shock inflation of the 1970s with aggressive antiunion policies intended to reduce labor costs, Japanese HR departments were able to extract wage concessions in return for job preservation—a quid pro quo that steered Japanese companies through the most difficult economic crisis they had faced since the end of the Second World War.[34] At the same time, many Japanese companies adopted labor-management committees that formalized consultation and information sharing between the company (as represented by HR) and the union.[35]

Careers in HR

Japanese managers hoping to become board members traditionally viewed a posting to the headquarters HR department as favorable. Data from 1981 show that the top unit for promotion to a directorship was marketing, which contributed 18 percent of all directors, and that HR, which contributed 12 percent, followed. The figures for finance and accounting were 5 percent.[36] A study done in the early 1990s found HR about halfway down the list of functions to which a posting was the precursor to a top executive position. It ranked behind marketing and production but ahead of R&D, engineering, and overseas jobs.[37] A tour of duty in HR, particularly at an intermediate stage in one's career, was helpful, as the department was a good place to meet and network with managers throughout the company and to view the lay of the land. One-fifth of the directors in manufacturing firms and one-third of those from firms in other sectors reported having had previous experience in the HR function.[38]

Experience in HR was thought to give candidates being considered for top executive positions the advantage of a background that tended to make them well rounded. The typical career pattern for senior HR managers was that of a generalist with exposure to multiple functions. In the early 1990s, a third to a half of the typical career of a senior HR manager was spent in HR, and the rest of it in other corporate functions.[39] The generalist pattern was not unique to HR but more prevalent there. For buchō in HR in 1990s, the comparison of years spent there to years spent in the function to which the longest rotations of their career had been devoted showed a ratio of .41. In marketing, that figure was .53, and in finance it was .70. In other words, buchō in HR were more likely than those in marketing to have been exposed to accounting, finance, and strategic planning, and more likely than those in finance to have worked in production and sales.[40] This stands in sharp contrast to the Anglo-American model, wherein HR managers are professionalized and specialized but have scant exposure to other specialties and rarely become CEOs or board members.

Corporate Governance

To understand both the prominent position of HR and the distinctive nature of employment practices inside the Japanese firm, it is necessary to analyze the corporate-governance system. Japanese corporate governance is a form of stakeholder capitalism, in which, at least until recently, "nobody gives a great deal of thought to owners. Firms are not seen as anybody's 'property.' They are organizations—bureaucracies much like public bureaucracies that people join for careers, become members of. They are more like communities."[41] The community is run by its board of directors; these boards were larger than those of U.S. firms, some of them having thirty to forty (or more) members, although usually a subgroup, the management committee, headed by the president, made key strategic decisions. The directing board is composed entirely of incumbent managers who serve staggered terms of two to six years.[42]

There are two ways of interpreting this enterprise community. One is that, broadly, its members include not only employees but others who have a stake in the enterprise as a going concern: customers, suppliers, banks, and shareholders. In this view, the job of the managing directors is to mediate between the interests of the various stakeholders and to make decisions that are in the best long-term interest of the enterprise as a whole rather than in the immediate interest of any one group, including shareholders.[43] Those who have a stake in the company do so by virtue of having made investments in it, including investments in tangible and intangible assets. Shares are held by banks— in the past they played a key role in governance—and on a reciprocal basis by suppliers and business-group members. (In 2001, financial institutions owned 39 percent of shares; corporations held 22 percent.)[44] In recent years, employee stock-ownership funds also have played a role. Despite these stable ownership blocs, there are active equity markets in Japan, and ownership is less concentrated than in many parts of Europe. On the other hand, control of the Japanese corporation is in the hands of managers who mediate between the various stakeholders. This conception of the corporation extends back to the years before the Second World War and was reinforced by the wartime administration.[45]

The other, narrower interpretation is that the Japanese company is a species of labor-managed firm. The primary members of the enterprise community are the regular employees, the *seishain*, who include everyone from the lowest ranks to the company president. Internal egalitarianism—small pay differentials between top and bottom, single-status policies (the same programs and perquisites are offered to managers and nonmanagerial employees), and the willingness of managers to take pay cuts before employees do—helps to create a strong sense of common interest among the firm's *seishain* and insure that board members take employee interests into account.[46] Financial devices also help to align employee interests with those of senior management. Research shows that, when employee bonuses increase, so does the director's pay, which also rises in response to job-preservation efforts.[47] Job preservation in turn is enhanced by the existence of "patient capital": long-term shareholding by main banks, affiliated companies, and other entities. In the past, stable stockholding slowed the speed of employment adjustment, because dedicated owners were willing to let the firm absorb the cost of carrying redundant employees in the short term so that it could expand more rapidly during recovery.[48]

According to the labor-managed interpretation, the Japanese system of corporate governance is conducive to long-term employment, a sense of corporate loyalty and community, and efforts to promote the formation of firm-specific human capital.[49] There is a history of employee interests winning out when they conflict with short-term share performance. During the oil shocks of the 1970s, companies made heroic efforts to protect jobs, and when they resorted to layoffs it was with the intention not of benefiting shareholders but of preserving *seishain* jobs.[50] In some instances, the proliferation of spin-offs and the rise of unrelated diversification in the late 1980s were the result of efforts to generate employment opportunities for core employees. Also supporting the labor-managed interpretation is the predilection of companies to make dividend cuts prior to staff reductions.

Still, employees—managers included—were not entirely shielded from risk. They were expected to accept any job assignment offered to them, even if it involved their transfer to a lower-paying position at a company subsidiary or a supplier far from home.[51] Because a substantial portion of their compensation came in the form of a bonus that fluctuated with firm performance, employees accepted pay cuts as the price of job protection.[52] Thus there is also support for the first, broader interpretation of the enterprise community: Employees were treated like other stakeholders. Their investments, in the form of firm-specific human capital, were substantial, and they shared in risks and returns. What distinguished them from most other classes of stakeholders was that it was more difficult for them to liquidate their investments and exit.

The question naturally arises: Under this system of corporate governance, who watched management? Because of stable cross-shareholding, managers had little reason to fear hostile takeovers, and share prices were seldom penalized for mediocre short-term results. On the other hand, directors could not and did not ignore the banks that held equity as well as debt, nor could they ignore other shareholders with large blocs. Through monitoring devices like bank auditors (who sat on corporate boards) and the presidents' council (composed of heads of firms in a *keiretsu* grouping), both classes of stakeholder kept an eye on the directors. If a company was performing poorly, the bank could and occasionally did appoint its own directors. The downside of monitoring by the banks, however, was that they often intervened only to protect their debt streams and ignored corporate performance when it was poor but not accompanied by other red flags.[53]

Another party engaged in the monitoring of company directors were the employees themselves. The retailer Mitsukoshi in 1983 and the scandal-ridden Snow Brand Dairy Company (Yukijirushi) in 2000 are among the several recent examples of companies at which enterprise unions and informal employee sentiment played a role in the dismissal of the company president.[54] Middle-level managers also have been to known to engage in monitoring of senior executives, realizing that their future advancement, salaries, and pensions depended on those executives acting in the company's best interests. Senior executives in turn monitored the president and chairman to ensure that they made correct decisions.

Finally, there are a variety of soft controls to insure that managers do not put their narrow self-interests above those of other stakeholders. A senior manager in a Japanese corporation spends a lifetime being socialized to do what is in the best interest of the enterprise as a whole. As compared to the United States, social status—being promoted to the executive ranks—is a more important motivator than financial rewards. In Japan, stock options and high salaries remain rare. The occasional instances of malfeasance by corporate managers, as in the recent Snow Brand scandal, usually involve the gouging of consumers or the government in an effort to benefit employees and shareholders. No Japanese version exists of the Enron, Tyco, and WorldCom cases, which exemplified systematic self-enrichment at shareholders' expense and may well be more common under the U.S. system than had been appreciated.[55]

It might seem that in this kind of monitoring—by banks, *keiretsu* partners, unions, and middle ranks of management—the relationship between the watcher and the watched is too cozy, especially as compared to American practices intended to achieve accountability on the part of upper management. As mentioned previously, however, Japanese (and German) executives are as likely as U.S. managers to lose their jobs when the firm suffers poor stock performance or earnings losses.[56]

How does HR figure in these corporate-governance issues? The tasks most crucial to effective corporate governance—socializing managers so that they share the company perspective and then selecting the best of them to govern the community—are the responsibility of the HR function. Through its management of employee rotation and its impartial record-keeping, HR helps to winnow out weak contenders and to identify the middle managers who are most able and least self-interested (and potentially venal). Personal character matters a great deal: Ideally the president is someone who is unselfish, honest, committed to the common good, and unlikely to abuse power for personal ends. Many corporate leaders, though of course not all, have channeled their ambition into the company, not their more narrowly defined self-interest. Late selection enables HR to identify officers who will be dedicated and competent. To discourage entrenchment, the tenure of any board member is defined by a maximum limit, and mediocre directors serve shorter terms. Typically, corporate leaders want their own successors to be successful, a trait sometimes lacking in U.S. CEOs, especially those brought in from the outside, who seek quick financial gains for themselves and then leave without grooming a replacement.[57]

The other responsibility of HR in corporate governance is to communicate employee concerns to senior managers and to the board. In the past, the boards of most Japanese companies had at least one member who either headed or had recently headed the corporate HR function. Usually, the union would bring its concerns to the headquarters HR department, which through the HR managing director relayed the information to the board. The HR managing director also kept the union informed about strategic business issues, including restructuring, capital spending, and new technologies.[58] The HR director, then, served both as the voice of the *seishain* on the company's board and as the intermediary between the board and the union. Managers of other functions served on the board, but HR often was first among equals, and was seldom eclipsed by the finance director because the finance department, and financial measures of performance, did not dominate corporate decision-making.

PRESSURES FOR CHANGE

As we have seen, the status and power of Japanese HR departments can be traced to four main causes: organization-oriented employment policies, focused and centralized corporations, encompassing enterprise unions, and stakeholder corporate governance. Together, these form a system of reciprocal structures. In the past, career jobs, enterprise unions, and other organization-oriented practices supported a resource-based business strategy that leveraged employee skills; stable ownership and stakeholder corporate governance promoted the use of those organization-oriented practices; and business strategies and corporate governance were supported by headquarters centralization.

Beyond the large company were a host of complementary institutions, ranging from government subsidies for layoff-avoidance and educational testing of student skills (which reduced the risk of lifetime hiring) to cross-shareholding practices (which stabilized incumbent managements). The interlocks among these institutions ensured both the centrality of employees to the Japanese firm and the pivotal role of the HR department. They also contributed to the view of the Japanese business system as a structured totality—Japan, Inc. The experience of Japanese firms as they absorbed the oil shocks of the 1970s reinforced the impression that they could withstand any major economic crisis without undergoing fundamental change.[59]

What distinguishes the recession that began in the 1990s from earlier economic crises faced by Japanese companies is its duration and scope. It has affected many different parts of the business system and so has raised the possibility that the cumulative changes for which it is responsible might lead to systemic change, as the interlocks that define the system begin to snap. Factors that in the past had the effect of strengthening HR are now working in reverse. Corporate organization and corporate governance are changing as companies seek greater efficiency and profitability, sometimes by moving operations to mainland Asia. Deflationary tendencies add pressure to cut costs. Meanwhile, social norms are in flux, so that today the values of individualism and privacy receive greater emphasis than in the past.

The prolonged economic stagnation has made government receptive to foreign investors, economists, and others who argue that the system needs to be reformed—specifically, that shareholders be privileged and that the stakeholder compromises of the postwar era be superseded. Alongside the search for efficiency is an effort to change the distribution of risks and rewards so as to benefit financial capital over human capital, principals over agents, and managers over workers. Not a few Japanese executives look longingly at the high salaries and perquisites earned by their U.S. counterparts and ask, Why not us?

The Search for Efficiency

The Japanese approach to corporate organization involves costs as well as benefits. The benefits were touted in the 1980s and early 1990s: high trust, high human-capital formation, high quality of products and services, and rapid execution of decisions. More was heard about the downside, though, as the decade progressed: the cost of carrying excess employees, torpid decision making, excessive centralization, overinvestment in existing businesses, and low rates of new venture formation.[60]

Japanese managers have their eyes on Western multinational corporations whose restructuring has the effect of expediting decision making. They hope that by restructuring their firms through spin-offs, consolidations, and the like they can become equally nimble. Investment outside the country is resulting in the kind of hollowing out that took place in the United States in the 1980s, as companies decide that the benefits of a skilled Japanese workforce are outweighed by the low cost of third-world, often Chinese, labor.

Other forms of corporate restructuring intended to spur efficiency are being undertaken. Spending on information technology is on the rise, and so companies need fewer clerks and managers. Where Japan might diverge from the United States is that focused companies, which are more prevalent in Japan, have less incentive to restructure or to shrink headquarters, because the logic holding these companies together is more than purely financial. In the United States, by contrast, conglomerates and other unrelated diversifiers are more common and have been responsible for the greatest amount of restructuring.[61]

Meanwhile, the slow growth of the 1990s and the failure to clean up the financial overhang from the bubble economy have caused a severe banking crisis in Japan. One response of banks has been to unwind their long-term holdings in the companies with which they do business. Supervision by a company's main bank was previously a key feature of Japanese corporate governance, and it remains to be seen what institution will take the place of the main bank. A long-term shift from debt to equity financing is underway, however, so the unwinding of bank holdings may not be as consequential as it would have been twenty years ago. All the same, the bank crisis provides support to the various groups seeking to sensitize Japanese companies to shareholder interests.[62]

Those who wish to change Japanese corporate governance are guided by mixed motives. For some, the primary objective is distributional: to redivide the allocation of corporate resources so that more flows to shareholders and less to retained earnings and to employees. This is the position of the investing community, both foreign and domestic, about whom more in a minute. On the other hand, some managers and business reformers genuinely believe that, by changing the Japanese system of corporate governance, they will help to make companies more efficient and the Japanese economy more prosperous. The reformers include corporate liberal groups like the Keizai Doyukai and prominent businessmen like Nobuo Tateisi, chairman of Omron, who has established an organization to encourage stock options, more transparent accounting, changes in the composition of the board of directors, and other governance reforms in keeping with the Anglo-American model. Still, Tateisi and others like him, such as the Corporate Governance Forum, insist that they want to preserve many of the stakeholder features of the Japanese governance model even while increasing the power of shareholders. They are what I would term "incrementalists" interested in adapting, not junking, the Japanese model.[63]

As we will see in the next chapter, one reform that has proven popular—it has been adopted by about a third of Tokyo Stock Exchange companies—is the so-called corporate-officer system (*shikkō yakuin*), pioneered by Sony. It reduces the size of the company board from as many as fifty members to a dozen, or even less, and includes independent outside directors, such as a prominent university professor or business leader (Carlos Ghosn of Nissan now sits on Sony's board). The other twenty or thirty former board members— heads of functional areas and divisions—form another body that is more akin to an operating or management committee, leaving the board to concentrate on strategy, or so it is hoped.[64]

Social Values

As they strive to become more efficient, Japanese companies also feel pressure to accommodate their employment policies to a younger generation that is more individualistic and less enchanted by the prestige of working for a big company than their parents were. Signs abound that social values are changing: Some young people (so-called freeters)[65] are postponing their careers to take a series of short-term jobs; divorce rates are up, slightly; and the social solidarity that characterized the postwar generation is waning.[66] Caution is in order, however. For example, a recent survey trumpeted that Japanese workers today are less loyal and satisfied than workers in the United States and concluded that this finding represented a "Westernization" of Japanese attitudes toward the workplace, but survey data from twenty years ago showed the same disparity between Japan and the United States.[67]

Whether the social changes are subtle or stark, companies perceive that employees are seeking greater individual recognition, and that is one reason for the proliferation of pay systems in which weight has been redistributed from seniority and age to individual performance.[68] Further, Yashiro and other critics of the Japanese HR system argue that career planning by HR departments is paternalistic and out of step with an increasingly individualistic and assertive workforce who want to have more say in their work assignments and other decisions affecting their employment.

Unions

Both absolutely and as a proportion of the labor force, membership in Japanese unions has been declining steadily.[69] Union density has slipped from about 35 percent of the labor force in 1970 to about 20 percent currently. Unions have a hard time attracting new members, in part because enterprise unions—which make up the bulk of the Japanese labor movement—have little incentive to organize. Also, in some cases employers have found it preferable to deal with nonunion consultation groups. However, observers agree that the causes of union decline have more to do with changing employee attitudes and the peculiarities of enterprise unionism than with employer resistance—a crucial factor in the United States.[70]

Back in the 1980s, the Japanese labor movement could be divided into four categories of union. A union was oriented toward asserting employee views on distributive issues, toward participating and cooperating with management to improve productivity, toward both of these modes, or toward neither (the passivity often found in smaller companies). About 70 percent of unions were split between the last two categories. The consensus among labor experts is that enterprise unions that are concerned both with pie expansion and pie distribution are becoming less militant on distributive issues, although there is some disagreement about how to interpret that development. One argument is that unions are showing restraint in return for access to sensitive company information that management is providing them. Others point to falling strike rates as evidence that management is punishing unions who defend their members and that this is the source of restraint.[71]

Another indicator of declining union strength is the disappearance of Nikkeiren, the Japanese employer's federation, as an independent entity. In 2002, Nikkeiren merged with Keidanren, a business group focused on government economic policy, to form the Japan Business Federation, along the lines of Britain's Confederation of British Industry (CBI). Nikkeiren's absorption was a sign of the declining significance of labor relations as an issue capable of uniting large numbers of employers. In recent years, Nikkeiren had staked out a centrist position on corporate governance, stressing that respect for the interests of shareholders and employees alike could coexist. It was relatively moderate on employment issues, expressing tolerance for labor unions and affirming the importance of employment security (it supported a Rengo—the national labor federation—plan for job subsidies to prevent layoffs). But it also recommended that personnel policies reflect greater sensitivity to market conditions, and it called for greater use of temporary workers. Nikkeiren's absorption into Keidanren will likely result in a more conservative employment policy issuing from the new federation.[72]

Distributive Issues and Social Norms

Labor's weakness creates openings for those whose efforts to change the Japanese system are informed less by the project of increasing efficiency than by distributional or ideological concerns. Many of the efforts to reform corporate governance and labor practices in Japan have as their motive the desire to replicate what happened in the United States since the 1980s, when the purpose of corporate restructuring was not only to improve efficiency but also to change the distribution of corporate resources going to retained earnings, shareholders, senior managers, and other employees. Ordinary employees and lower-to-middle-level managers lost out; implicit contracts based on career-type employment were shredded. The subsequent ballooning of CEO salaries shows clearly the distributional consequences of corporate restructuring.[73] There is evidence that a similar process now is underway in Japan. For example, one study finds that, as foreign ownership of a company increases, so does the company's inclination to downsize and engage in asset divestment.[74]

Reslicing the corporate pie in Japan, however, is trickier than in the United States, because the Japanese institutions that determine who gets what are based on norms embedded in Japanese society—for example, the obligation of employers to employees, of suppliers to customers, and, what discourages hostile takeovers, of companies to each other. More generally, norms include the conception of the corporation as a community whose interests transcend in importance and longevity those of ordinary shareholders. Anyone endeavoring to change social norms will soon bump up against the collective-action problem: Actors will not switch norms unless they see that everyone else is doing the same. That creates an opening for norm entrepreneurs, people who seek to create the impression that norms are changing, so that a bandwagon effect is created and social criticism becomes self-fulfilling prophecy.[75]

Who are these norm entrepreneurs? One group consists of foreign share-holders, who have no stake in the relational business system and now hold about 18 percent of shares listed on the Tokyo Stock Exchange, up from 4 percent in 1990. Prominent in this group are U.S. mutual funds and pension plans like TIAA-CREF and the California Public Employee Retirement System (CalPERS), who have strongly advocated shareholder-oriented corporate governance in the United States and are now proposing a shift toward that governance style in Japan. There are other groups that stand to benefit not only from higher equity prices but also from greater merger and acquisition (M&A) activity, associated fees, and a more active market for corporate control generally. They include investment banking houses, brokerages, and other financial service companies and consultants. Sometimes these groups work together, as in the creation of the Investor Responsibility Research Center, a joint venture among CalPERS, Mizuho Securities, and the Rockefeller Foundation. The center's aim is to persuade Japanese companies to adopt U.S.-style governance practices.[76]

The business press in Japan, the most prominent example of which is the *Nikkei Shimbun*, Japan's equivalent of the *Wall Street Journal*, regularly beats its drum for a new corporate-governance system. The justification typically is the contrast between Japanese and U.S. economic performance, the assumption being that Japan's economic performance would improve if it adopted American practices.[77] The editorials are sure to please the *Nikkei*'s main advertisers, which are primarily financial-service companies, and the large portion of its readers who work for them.

While many Japanese managers still identify with fellow employees as much or more than with shareholders, a significant minority of them seek to reform corporate governance out of a belief that they would personally benefit were executive pay linked to share price via stock options and the like. This opinion is usually couched in other terms; greed may be considered something of a virtue in the United States but is still socially unacceptable in Japan. A recent study identified a group of Japanese executives who would like to reform the corporate-governance system and contrasted their views with those of the majority who remain supporters of it. One of the questions over which the two groups held divergent opinions was whether in the future the presidents of Japanese companies would earn more than fifty times as much as rank-and-file employees. Reformers are more inclined to see that as a possibility, in what one suspects may be an expression of wishful thinking.[78]

Statutory Reform

The Liberal Democratic Party (LDP), which has ruled Japan for most of the postwar period, in recent years has catered to the interests of financiers and investors seeking a change in corporate governance.[79] In Japan, the government is the first mover on legislation, not the Diet, and the government tends to be more ideological and less pragmatic than the business community. It also tends to be more sensitive to foreign investors who demand reform of the corporate-governance system. While the government would like to use governance reform as a costless (at least to the Treasury) way of spurring recovery, it is also acting at the behest of financial interests. The result has been a raft of business law legislation since the mid-1990s.[80]

In addition to a major financial deregulation law that took effect in 2001, statutory reforms include a 1997 law permitting companies to purchase their own stock, thus creating a channel for returning excess cash to shareholders. Since then, the law has been revised three times to simplify corporate M&A activity. Corporate restructuring is also facilitated through regulatory changes whereby the number of board meetings needed to approve mergers is reduced and companies are permitted to merge operations through equity swaps. In addition, the postwar ban on holding companies has been lifted, in an effort to move big companies further in the direction of M-form, finance-driven structures. To align manager and shareholder interests, laws regarding stock options have been liberalized, first in 1997 and then subsequently. In yet another legal reform designed to make Japanese corporate boards more like those in the United States, a firm is now permitted to eliminate its board auditors if it creates a CEO position and adds outside directors to the board. The net effect of these changes is to push Japanese corporate governance in a direction that privileges shareholders at the expense of other stakeholders.[81]

The government is also chipping away at the legal underpinning of the Japanese employment system. Its achievements in that sphere have not been as thoroughgoing as those related to corporate governance, in part because the labor movement represents an organized constituency opposed to change; the opposition to reforms in business law is weaker and more diffuse. Under the Japanese system, labor groups have the opportunity to comment on legislation before it goes to the Diet, and tripartite roundtables (business, government, labor) exist for the purpose of discussing employment and social policy.[82]

Nevertheless, under the guise of "flexibilization" the government has sought to push employment policy in a more market-oriented direction. The first of recent reforms that relax restrictions on the ability of a firm to hire temporary workers was the Worker Dispatch Law, which, enacted in 1999, increased the number of occupations in which they could be employed. In a concession to preserving the norm of employment stability, the law requires an employer to offer permanent jobs to temporary workers after they have worked a year (and possibly more). On the other hand, the Koizumi government recently proposed legislation that would codify judicial standards for dismissal and make it easier for employers to lay off permanent employees, a controversial step opposed by Rengo and employers alike. Interestingly, the reason some employers oppose the legislation is that they fear codification will actually hinder them in their ability to resort to layoffs—a position that should remind outside observers that job cuts can and do occur in Japan.[83]

Confronted by all these pressures on the traditional systems of corporate governance and employment, to which has been added the burden imposed by years of slow growth, how is the executive HR function inside Japanese corporations faring? Is it still a powerful kingmaker? By focusing on the HR function, we can gain a better sense of how corporations in Japan are adapting to the changing legal, social, and economic environment.

Inside Japanese Companies Today

ONE WAY TO UNDERSTAND what is happening in Japan is to analyze the organizational traits of individual companies. We studied seven of them. At each, we interviewed the general manager of the corporate HR department and members of his staff. At some companies we also interviewed the managing director of HR (a board member) and senior executives from the corporate-finance department.[1]

The companies represent a variety of industries: securities, package delivery, auto parts, electrical manufacturing, construction, and electronics. In one industry, construction, we studied a pair of companies, which provided a broader base for our examination of sectoral effects. We coded interviews, making it possible to compare evidence from the cases, identify patterns, and advance some generalizations about causality.[2]

What is immediately apparent from the case studies is the diversity in how Japanese corporations organize their headquarters HR department. The power, responsibility, and influence of the headquarters HR unit differ from one company to the next, and these differences are linked to subtler variations in employment practices. The more closely one looks at an individual company, the harder it is to see in it the kind of national and central tendencies discussed in the previous chapter.

It is useful is to distinguish companies that are diversified from those that are specialized and derive most of their revenues from the same business. Previous research has shown that in specialized Japanese companies the divisions tend to be weaker and the headquarters staff larger than in diversified companies.[3] This was evident in our sample.

- The two most diversified companies, which I will call J. Electronics and J. Electrical, both have a long history of strong divisions and plants that wield internal clout. Highly diversified manufacturing companies characterize the sector they are in. Headquarters HR units have modest strength. (Note that J. Electronics largely produces electronic consumer products while J. Electrical offers a mixture of heavy electrical products, motor-driven appliances, and consumer electronics.)
- Conversely, three of the more focused companies—J. Parts, J. Delivery, and J. Securities—have relatively weak divisions and powerful headquarters units, including the central HR unit, and two of them are service-sector companies.

- Finally, the construction companies are harder to classify. Although they are specialized firms, they have powerful geographical divisions that challenge directives from headquarters.

In short, what we will see is that there is no single way of structuring central HR but rather that there are different patterns related to business strategy and to sector. This point sometimes gets lost in facile (or central-tendency-focused) descriptions of the "Japanese model."

AN OVERVIEW OF THE COMPANIES

The literature on organizational power identifies several features that make an organizational subunit relatively powerful: (a) *operating authority*; (b) *centrality*, or ties to many parts of the organization; (c) *possession of information that other units depend on*; and (d) *influence over the company's decisions about resource allocation*.[4] These features correspond to the following observations we make about a "powerful" or "strong" headquarters HR department:

- It is in an authority position vis-à-vis corporate divisions and line managers. (a)
- It sets companywide policies for evaluation, rewards, and various procedures. (a, c)
- It controls unit headcount and employee allocation—i.e., recruitment, promotions, and intracorporate transfers and rotations. (a, b)
- It collects data on the performance of employees. (c)
- It plays the lead role in selecting senior managers. (b, d)
- It influences strategic decisions (e.g., on spinoffs or overseas investments) through its positions on the board and the management committee and through other channels. (d)

In what follows, we describe each of the companies and examine the structure of its headquarters HR department. We look first at the companies with the most powerful central departments and then turn to those with departments that are somewhat weaker with respect to other functional units and/or the operating divisions and plants. After discussing all of the companies, we return to examine changes that are underway in each.

J. Securities

J. Securities is one of the largest and oldest investment houses in Japan. Its main business is brokerage services, which it provides through a network of 125 retail offices in Japan and 40 offices overseas. The company also offers a complete range of fee-based corporate services, including asset management and investment banking (origination and underwriting of debt and equity, M&A services, etc.), and this has generated a growing portion of revenues in recent years. Still, most of the company's nine thousand domestic employees (the company employs an additional three thousand employees overseas) are in the retail branches. J. Securities has ten wholly owned subsidiaries related to its core business. These include a bank and an asset-management company. It also has some partially owned subsidiaries. Total revenues have declined sharply in recent years, partly as a result of trading losses. Commissions, which provide three-fourths of net revenue, have kept the company afloat.

Banks and brokerages have a reputation for being among the most traditional companies in Japan, and J. Securities is no exception. Among the companies we visited, J. Securities most resembles the stereotype of the corporation with a powerful headquarters HR function. Of its multiple divisions—for example, investment banking, corporate finance, and asset management—none has its own HR unit. The divisions are located at headquarters and are under close supervision of headquarters management. The core of the business consists of the domestic retail branches. Each is a business center that reports directly to the senior executive director of retailing—an arrangement that gives the branch managers some operating autonomy. On the other hand, there are no local HR units, and the headquarters HR department closely scrutinizes retail employment decisions.

Headquarters HR is divided into two units: Employee Relations and Personnel. The split goes back more than thirty years. Employee Relations handles the administration of companywide programs such as employee welfare facilities, health programs, and cafeterias. It's also responsible for negotiations with the union and for ensuring compliance with Japan's web of employment laws. All domestic employees below the level of branch manager belong to the enterprise union, which, in addition to negotiating contracts, serves as a two-way conduit for information and communication between management and employees. The union cooperates with, and is accepted by, management. Its main office is at J. Securities headquarters in Tokyo. Union leaders typically serve terms of two to three years and then return to the ranks. One of the company's current board members was formerly president of the enterprise union.[5]

Personnel, with thirty-five employees, is the more powerful of the two HR units because it oversees person-specific decisions on recruitment, assignment, performance evaluations, rotations, training, and compensation. In fact, the power of this department to make or break careers is enormous. Like many other large Japanese firms, J. Securities still guarantees employment to its managerial and professional employees through age sixty. Hiring decisions, which are therefore considered to be of consequence, are handled by the headquarters HR unit. Although the company's business is flat, it has been in the labor market each year to replace younger employees who are being poached by foreign financial and consulting companies seeking to expand their Japanese operations.[6] Headquarters recruits, hires, trains, and assigns young graduates to their initial posting. From the very start, then, employees have a close connection to the headquarters Personnel unit.

J. Securities is famed for providing extensive on-the-job training through formal methods and systematic rotation during an employee's initial ten to fifteen years on the job. The first cut of the rotation plan is developed by headquarters, which examines employees' performance records and weighs them against the needs of the company's various businesses. Rotations include postings to the company's wholly owned subsidiaries, so that careers span the parent and its *kogaisha*. The Personnel department initially presents its rotation plan to the Personnel Development Committee (PDC), which is composed of Personnel's general manager, board members representing the three main retail regions, and five senior managers from other parts of the business. The PDC attempts to resolve conflicts that divisions have over which one will get (or get to keep) the best and brightest young managers. In PDC meetings, the head of Personnel tries to defuse sectional interests by emphasizing what is good for the company as a whole, pointing out that less glamorous, slow-growing divisions need an infusion of talented people; that talented managers headed for the top need exposure to multiple facets of the business; and that fast-growing, "hot" divisions must take on a share of the company's mediocre employees, not just the stars. Thus the HR department is greatly concerned to ensure internal parity, both across divisions and among the company's lifetime employees. While J. Securities is known for fast-tracking its rising stars, it also takes seriously the development of those managers and professionals who, though talented, are less stellar.

This concern is demonstrated by the extraordinary practice whereby a manager from headquarters Personnel annually interviews every nonclerical employee. In the course of a year, each manager visits approximately seven to eight hundred employees. The interviews are conducted on-site, whether in Beppu or Bahrain. This enables headquarters to assess and compare the evaluations and bonus recommendations it receives from the company's far-flung units. Headquarters then performs its own evaluation and ranking of all line managers, and it checks to insure equity in the award of bonus payments. Units usually agree to any adjustment ordered by Personnel, although about half a dozen disputed cases go to the PDC each year. Interviews are also a way for Personnel to learn of any local problems and to take note of the employee's own career plans and preferences. However, when an employee's preference (say, to live in Tokyo) and the company's need (as assessed by Personnel) conflict, the company's need is usually decisive—the employee is sent to Hokkaido.

The HR function is well connected not only to the managerial rank and file but also to the corporation's top leaders. The general managers of the HR units report to HR's managing director, who sits on the company's board of directors. At board meetings, the managing director raises the concerns of the two units and transmits strategic information back to his general managers. The general managers are part of the companywide general managers' group, which meets with the president and the directors twice a year to discuss strategic issues. To strengthen his influence, the general manager of Personnel meets individually with every board member at least once a year. These arrangements do not give HR a unique ability to influence strategy but merely put it on an equal footing with other departments. Because of HR's international savvy and its attention to the interests of the *seishain*, however, its managing director is sometimes more influential than other board members.

Despite the importance of the Personnel function at J. Securities, none of the senior managers whom the company assigned to Personnel had previously worked in HR-related positions. The company's policy is to rotate managers in and out of the department every two to four years. Rather than indicating any weakness in the HR function, the generalist orientation and short terms of the managers are consistent with a career-development pattern throughout the company: Its rising stars are rotated around key positions—in marketing, sales, personnel, and planning. Because Personnel comes into contact with many people in the company, its role and function are widely understood. If asked, an employee can be sent to Personnel and brought up to speed rather quickly. The division's general manager, who was in the job for less than a year, had previously handled investments for the fixed-income division. His younger assistants confided that their boss was an outstanding person, well regarded in the company and destined for greatness. From their perspective, Personnel was a good place to learn about the company's diverse parts, strategic direction, and organizational politics.

J. Delivery

J. Delivery is one of Japan's leading overnight-package-delivery companies, in an industry that barely existed twenty years ago but has grown rapidly. The company's founder is well known in Japan for having tackled government regulations that hampered private package delivery. Until recently, he was active in managing the company. Older employees remember him well and fondly; their loyalty to him is part of the company's legacy, as is his loyalty to them.

J. Delivery has eighty-six thousand employees, of whom a large number— forty thousand—are part-time workers. The bulk of J. Delivery's sales are in Japan, and its organizational structure is geographic. There is a geographic division for each of Japan's major regions. The divisions in turn are divided into bases, to each of which a number of neighborhood centers report. J. Delivery has more than 2,500 of these local centers, one in every neighborhood in Japan. Given such an infrastructure, it can reach nearly every business and household in the country. Its sales and net income have increased steadily in recent years, despite the recession. It is capturing sales from other transporters, including the postal service, and is creating new markets with, for example, its business-to-business parcel deliveries, rapid delivery of fresh produce, and, for vacationers, express delivery of golf clubs and ski equipment.

In recent years the company has undergone some limited diversification. Its expertise in information technology and in logistics enables J. Delivery to provide solutions to other businesses needing help with their distribution systems. Because the logistics consulting business requires skills and strategies that are very different from those of the package-delivery business, it was recently spun off into a separate subsidiary. For overseas delivery, the company has a joint venture with a U.S. company. However, given the compact size of the Japanese market, its reliance on air freight within the domestic market is slight.

The heroes of this focused company are its drivers, who not only deliver packages to homes and offices but also solicit new business and sell products—consumer nondurables such as tissues and bottled water—from their trucks. As the main point of contact with the consumer, the driver is expected to be not only efficient but courteous and friendly. To attract the best and brightest of Japan's shrinking number of high school graduates, the company pays the drivers high wages—the highest in the industry. To boost productivity, J. Delivery has invested heavily in information technology and communications equipment. The technology allows customers to choose the precise hour for receiving their delivery and, from their cell phone, to learn of a shipment's progress. J. Delivery is hoping to cash in on the rising volume of Internet sales by making deliveries to convenience stores that sell products online and by offering to collect payments from consumers who are wary of posting credit-card numbers on the Internet. The HR department is heavily involved in formulating these new business strategies, whose success hinges on the skill and motivation of the company's drivers.

The company offsets the high cost of drivers' wages also through the use of part-time employees in its sorting, warehouse, and back-office facilities. Nonpermanent employees make up more than half of J. Delivery's workforce—the figure has increased moderately over the past ten years—and the bulk of these are part-timers who work a few hours a day. Many are housewives who come in at 5:00 A.M. and work for three hours sorting packages for the morning delivery. Others are seasonal workers hired for a period of two months or less.[7]

As the company's success depends on providing high-quality personal service to its customers, it is unsurprising that the central HR department occupies an important place in J. Delivery's operations. The HR department designs all personnel systems—for hiring, wages, promotions, and training. The large regional divisions, even in Osaka and Tokyo, do not have their own HR departments and rely on headquarters. At headquarters, the senior HR managers are specialists who have been assigned to that department and have spent the better part of their careers there. During their early years they are rotated around the centers and branches before returning to headquarters. The HR department has sixty employees; its chief reports to the HR managing director, who sits on the company's board and is highly influential and respected.

One responsibility of the central HR department is maintaining the company's good relations with the enterprise union. Because driver morale is crucial to good customer relations, the union carries considerable weight in its dealings with management. The union's structure mirrors that of the company: It has leaders at the bases (which include several delivery centers), branches, and headquarters, where, on the top floor of the building, the union has its head office. One of the union's main concerns is the company's growing reliance on part-time employees. The company, by agreeing not to use part-timers as drivers, demonstrates that it takes the issue seriously. Many company managers formerly belonged to the union, and some lower-to-mid-level managers—about half of the heads of local centers—currently do. This mitigates any sense that management and union are separate entities. The central HR department reinforces "unitarianism" through employee-involvement programs and single-status personnel policies.[8] Neither the company's benefit packages nor its welfare facilities discriminate between managers and drivers or between white- and blue-collar employees. Company headquarters are spartan and the company's senior managers are notably homespun. Senior executives and uniformed drivers dine together in the headquarters cafeteria.

Base managers are free to hire their own drivers and other employees, train them, and evaluate them, but only within guidelines set by the headquarters HR department. There are guidelines for hiring new drivers, standardized exams for drivers seeking to become center managers, and a unique evaluation system that emphasizes the driver's personality and incorporates comments from customers and peers. The extensive local training staff themselves are trained at headquarters. Like many other Japanese firms, J. Delivery invests heavily in employee training: The ratio of trainers to drivers is an astounding 1:7.[9] Base managers are trained by headquarters HR, which meets with every base manager at least twice a year. Union leaders at the local level bring complaints about managers to headquarters; this provides headquarters HR another channel for monitoring local affairs.

Headquarters HR plays a major role in selecting branch managers, who are the senior line managers in the company. It also runs the annual recruitment of college graduates for headquarters positions, and it oversees rotations and promotions for headquarters managers up to the level of department head. As befits the egalitarian ethos of this company, many who have risen through the ranks to become managers at the branch and headquarters levels have not attended college.

J. Parts

J. Parts is a diversified multinational company that began as a subsidiary of a major automobile manufacturer. It has fourteen divisions, twelve of which are organized into product groups focused on the automotive industry: power-train, electric systems, electronic systems, and thermal systems. The other two divisions manufacture innovative industrial products, such as robots and bar-code readers. All divisions share a centralized HR department, a centralized research laboratory, a centralized sales-and-marketing group, and facilities at the company's large Japanese plants as well as at several plants overseas. The company has about forty thousand core domestic employees. When these are added to the employees of its seventy affiliates and subsidiaries, its total domestic headcount rises to more than seventy thousand. Of the forty thousand core employees, 60 percent are blue-collar workers and 40 percent white-collar: clericals, managers, and engineers. The company's products are renowned for their high quality and technical sophistication. Total sales have recently risen after declining for several years in the late 1990s. Profits, while positive, have been shrinking.

Like the large automotive assemblers it supplies, J. Parts prides itself on the quality and reliability of its products. A producerist company par excellence, it places a premium on clever engineering, skilled workers, and hard work. Almost everyone at the company is a "lifer," whether blue- or white-collar. It has a strong corporate culture that stresses equity, both horizontal (across plants and divisions) and vertical (between managers, engineers, and manual workers).

At the hub of this hard-working, homogeneous organization is the central HR department, which employs more than two hundred people in three subunits: recruitment and planning, training, and welfare services. Centralization of HR reflects the company's geographic organization. The headquarters office is also the site of the main manufacturing plant. Together the office and the plant account for nearly a quarter of the company's domestic employees. Most of the other eleven domestic plants are located nearby in the same prefecture. Geographic concentration is a conscious strategy intended to keep the company's plants in close proximity to each other and to major customers. This allows coordination, the sharing of innovation across plants, the tailoring of products to specification, and coordination of R&D with manufacturing processes.

HR centralization is also related to the company's enterprise union, which fifty years ago led a major strike, of which today's managers, some of whom weren't even born yet, are still mindful. Although the union now is a far cry from its militant past, it retains a strong presence at headquarters and in the plants. It cares as much about consistency across plants as does the company, albeit for different reasons: The union is concerned to prevent plants from undercutting each others' wage and effort standards, while management seeks ease in transferring employees and processes. Similarly, the company and the union have coalesced around the issue of vertical equity. For the union, minimization of pay and status differences is a matter of fairness; for management, it helps to boost employee loyalty and build trust across the ranks.

HR centralization has resulted in a uniform system for recruitment, training, promotion, and reward. Recruitment is highly centralized and, despite weak sales, continues—the search for "fresh blood," it is called. The engineering department, not HR, handles the training of engineers, on which the company places a high priority. The primary functions of the central HR department are to train and rotate managerial employees, but it also administers the company's industrial junior college and an annual companywide training conference, and it designs systems for compensation, performance evaluation, and job rotation. Decision making under these systems is based on a delicate and presently changing balance among the HR department, the product groups, and line managers.

Divisions and plants have their own HR departments, which can make unilateral decisions on career planning, evaluations, and promotions for engineers and skilled workers, within guidelines formulated by central HR. Until recently, central HR had the final authority to evaluate managers and, even when the division or product group disagreed, assign them to postings where, in its judgment, they could best serve the interests of the company as a whole. Now the divisions share with central HR responsibility for these decisions on lower- and middle-level managers. Even under the present arrangement, however, the divisional HR staff are in close contact with central HR—partly out of self-interest, since headquarters controls their careers.

Because the enterprise union, which remains important to the activities of the central HR department, has two centers of influence—in the plants and at headquarters—it serves as a back channel for bringing plant-level concerns to the attention of headquarters. Central HR meets regularly with the union to discuss employee issues, this in addition to the annual wage negotiations. Former union leaders are sprinkled throughout upper management: Two former union leaders are employed in central HR (one is the department's labor-relations specialist); others hold senior management posts; and one of the company's managing directors is a former union leader. The union, especially now that it is moderate and cooperative, is spoken of with respect and is regarded as a vital part of the company's employee-relations system. As one senior HR manager put it, the company and the union are joined like the wheels on an axle, but the relationship goes forward only when the wheels are balanced.

Sometimes, however, HR's connection to the union puts it in a difficult position. A senior manager explained, again speaking metaphorically, that the department is the bridge over the river that flows between management and the union. HR represents management's views to the union and the union's views to senior management and, via the HR managing director, to the board. To serve this function, HR must have the trust of both sides. We were told that top management trusts HR and understands why it must sometimes take a neutral or even pro-union stance, but we also gathered that some younger managers are skeptical of this approach.

The top HR executives at J. Parts are a mixture of generalists and specialists. The managing director has a generalist background in corporate planning, materials procurement, and product planning—all of them "dry" areas. Having a dry manager represent HR on the company board bolsters the function's credibility in the eyes of board members who are skeptical of "wets." Traditionally, the position of HR managing director is regarded as a powerful one, because of the union's power and because the *seishain* are considered stakeholders. Of the four other senior HR managers, three are specialists—the head of education and development; the head of welfare operations (dormitories, resorts, hotels, meals, and recreation), and the labor-relations manager.

J. Electrical

J. Electrical is a multinational company that sells products (cellular phones, laptop computers, and home appliances) to consumers but also makes a vast array of industrial products (information systems, electrical power equipment, elevators, medical devices, and semiconductors). Reflecting its diversity, the parent company has ten product groups comprising thirty-six divisions—a classic example of the comprehensive Japanese electrical company (*sōgō denki*). J. Electrical was among the first companies in Japan to adopt an M-form structure, and its divisions are relatively independent. Of its 60,000 employees, 70 percent are white-collar workers, half of them engineers. More than three hundred affiliates and subsidiaries employ an additional 140,000 workers in Japan and overseas. Parent-company sales in recent years have been flat, reflecting the company's continued dependence on the Japanese market (around 60 percent of sales). Net income has been negative or very small.

J. Electrical's headquarters HR department is divided between a planning group of thirty-five people and a group of fifty people who administer employee-welfare facilities and services. This division resembles the arrangement at J. Securities but is of more recent vintage. It reflects an attempt to put some distance between the union and HR decision making and to align HR decision making more closely with strategic planning. The HR planning group takes the lead in introducing companywide systems. Recent initiatives have included a new pension plan, a performance-oriented pay scheme, and modifications to overtime-pay practices. Divisions, which are required to adopt these systems, have few distinctive HR policies of their own, the only example cited being a flextime plan that the R&D unit recently established on an experimental basis.

Career rotations of managers occur within the divisions, each of which has its own HR unit. While there is a companywide committee that reviews the divisional rotation plans, it typically rubberstamps them. Employees can change divisions by bidding through the company's open posting system, with central HR acting as the switchboard. In the past year some three hundred engineers and a number of managers used the system, but this is far from being an open internal labor market, because employees have to receive transfer permission from their divisional HR unit. If the unit does not approve, corporate HR will try to mediate the situation, although it almost always defers to the originating division. On the other hand, when headquarters itself has its eye on promising managers, divisions are afforded less deference. They might be able to keep their managers for a year or two but, as one executive said with a wry smile, "Eventually headquarters gets what it wants."

Strong as the company's divisions may be, the best and brightest managers at J. Electrical are still destined for headquarters positions. This is a source of central HR's power. One of the department's main responsibilities is to identify and rank candidates for executive positions. Its recommendations are discussed by a standing executive HR committee made up of the company's chairman, other top officers, and the head of central HR. Each divisional president meets with this committee to discuss his stars as well as the divisional succession and rotation plans. Central HR helps the company president develop a succession plan for headquarters' executives, and it identifies suitable appointees to the board of directors.

In a more subtle fashion, central HR influences divisional HR departments. Following the diversified-manufacturing pattern, the plant and divisional HR staff—more than four hundred people—in effect have dual reporting relationships, as central HR controls their career rotations. Staff of the central HR department themselves are mostly specialists who have spent their careers inside HR, doing their rotations in plant and divisional HR units. The divisional HR managers meet monthly with the general manager of HR planning to discuss issues such as recruitment and union relations. Occasionally this group will form a task force to develop a new companywide program, as it did several years ago when it designed an online system allowing employees to change their address, family status, and other personal information. Divisional HR managers and their staff try to stay on good terms with central HR, in the hope that eventually they will be moved to headquarters. The physical move is actually only to a different floor, as most of the divisional HR units are located in the same building that houses central HR. This propinquity reinforces the influence that central HR exerts throughout the company.

Construction Alpha and Beta

These companies belong to the Big Five group of general contractors. They design and build major projects—everything from bridges and tunnels to hotels and office buildings—for the public and private sectors. The firms do not directly employ manual laborers but instead hire subcontractors to do the construction. Each company has a central HR department of approximately seventy employees, headed by a general manager who reports to the managing director for human resources; at both firms, the managing director is a board member.

Roughly 70 percent of Alpha's eleven thousand employees are engineers, designers, and architects, many of whom work at headquarters. The company has three divisions: civil engineering (which is mostly public works), Eastern Japan construction (including Tokyo), and Western Japan construction (including Osaka). These divisions, which oversee a slew of geographic branch units, are responsible for generating business in their territories. The company also has several overseas subsidiaries, a real-estate-development division (a big money loser), and eighty-one affiliates (*kogaisha*) in the engineering and construction industries. Despite record government spending on public works, orders have steadily declined over the past four years.

Beta's organizational structure resembles Alpha's. Beta has three main units: a construction division with eleven geographic branches, which are financially independent entities; an architectural and engineering division; and a real-estate-development division. Like Alpha, Beta employs only white-collar workers. Of its thirteen thousand employees, two-thirds are architects and engineers. Orders have fallen over the past two years and the company is operating in the red. Beta has overseas subsidiaries as well as a collection of affiliated companies whose businesses range from engineering to architectural publishing to resorts.

Intense rivalry exists between the engineers and the architects and designers. Both companies have evolved similar strategies for keeping the central HR department above the occupational fray. HR staff do not have technical backgrounds, and that helps them maintain neutrality in factional disputes. Despite their lack of credentials, they can act with some authority because, before their assignment to HR, they rotated around different functions at headquarters and in the field, holding both staff and line positions. The general manager of Alpha's HR department had been there for six years, prior to which he worked in on-site construction and before that did corporate planning at an affiliate company; Beta's general manager was previously employed in on-site nuclear-power construction.

Rivalries exist also between the geographic divisions of the two companies. Each division has its own set of customers but competes with other divisions for capital and technical assistance from headquarters. The power of the divisions is reflected in their control over recruitment and rotations, which are not centralized. Here too, by acting as neutral mediators, the central HR units exert some influence. For example, Alpha has a companywide committee for planning career rotations and promotions. On it sit representatives from central HR, from the HR departments of the major divisions, and from the separate HR departments for engineers and architects employed at headquarters. The central HR representatives try to balance any competing interests by emphasizing the companywide perspective. However, in contrast to the arrangement at J. Securities, this committee is not under the control of Alpha's central HR department, so divisions can and sometimes do retain the employees they want.

The independence and clout that each Alpha division enjoys is enhanced by its being represented on the company board. The same is true at Beta, where the eleven main geographic branches have seats on the company board. In planning rotations, Beta's central HR department defers to the branch HR departments, although it reviews their decisions and occasionally may question them. Disputes are handled by a companywide HR committee chaired by the HR general manager, but the committee meets infrequently.

At each company, further power accrues to central HR by virtue of its responsibility to maintain dossiers on all employees. At Alpha, the department head and managing director of central HR regularly report to the president their informal opinions regarding his intended appointments to the board and to senior management positions. Nonetheless, the power that derives from controlling this knowledge is less than that wielded by central HR at a company like J. Securities.

Another way that central HR asserts its views is through dotted-line relationships to the divisional and branch HR departments. Meetings between those departments and central HR are common; staff rotation occurs in both directions; and relations are friendly. In 1998, Alpha, moving to a new salary scheme that put greater weight on individual performance, adopted a plan that central HR designed and then fine-tuned by working with the heads of the various HR departments and the union. The same procedure was followed later that year when Alpha adopted a restructuring plan to cut jobs via attrition, early retirement, and reduced hiring.

Nearly all of the companies' technical staff—engineers and architects—belong to the enterprise union. (At Beta, 80 percent of employees are in the union; they are employed in all ranks up to the level of section head.) Central HR conducts annual wage negotiations with the union and also holds special meetings throughout the year. Despite, or perhaps because of, their lack of militancy, the unions are treated respectfully by central HR and the rest of senior management, many of whom are former union members themselves. Several former union leaders are employed in central HR at Beta, and the current president of Alpha was once the head of the enterprise union. One senses—especially at Alpha, the more egalitarian and less paternalistic of the two companies—that senior management feels a sense of responsibility to incumbent employees, views the union as the *shain*'s legitimate voice, and gives credit to the HR department for trying to shape the views that the union and top management have of each other. Still, neither Alpha's nor Beta's central HR department is as pivotal as those of the companies discussed earlier.

J. Electronics

J. Electronics is a multinational electronics company well known in Japan as an organizational innovator. Of the companies we visited, this is the most decentralized and has the most market-oriented employment policies. The parent company has five major business groups: home products, information technology, core technology, communication systems, and semiconductors. Each operates as a semiautonomous company with authority over its constituent divisions. The groups employ nineteen thousand people, of whom 70 percent are engineers. J. Electronics has more than one hundred affiliated companies, both in Japan and overseas, most of them wholly owned by the parent and related to the parent's product lines. The affiliates employ approximately fifty thousand people in Japan and one hundred thousand overseas. The company's sales have been flat in recent years. While operating income is positive, it has been trending downwards.

J. Electronics had a conventional multidivisional structure until 1994, when it began to reorganize itself to put units in closer contact with product-market trends. In effect, it decentralized. Where there had been centralized sales departments at headquarters and thirteen product groups, there were later eight (then ten) product groups, each with its own sales department. These "companies within a company" had relative autonomy in areas such as marketing, R&D, and investments, functions that were relocated from headquarters to the new groups.

The reorganization occurred at this time for several reasons. First, the company, which has more foreign shareholders than most other Japanese firms, was under fire from Wall Street for a disastrous acquisition that caused red ink to flow. Radical decentralization was a good story to pitch to investors, and, indeed, the association between foreign ownership and restructuring is not unique to J. Electronics. Second, after years of being managed by a founder and his successor, the company had been taken over by a youthful new manager who included in his personal network Jack Welch of General Electric, Lou Gerstner of IBM, and Percy Barnevik of ABB—all of them Western apostles of the lean corporation. Finally, the new president wanted to redirect the strategy of J. Electronics away from its historic base in consumer electronics to more computer- and Internet-oriented digital products. The hope was that decentralization would unleash "a small-venture-capital spirit" and move the company into the digital age.

Two years ago J. Electronics swung back from extreme decentralization and went to the present arrangement of five product groups. The groups are more manageable when their number is fewer. It is easier for headquarters to interact with them and for them to interact with each other. Each of the five product groups is large. Home Products, for example, contains six divisions: audio, visual, mobile, broadband, procurement, and sales, the latter two being former headquarters units. The central HR department is being asked to identify and groom future company leaders and otherwise to help achieve "centripetal" synergy across the five business units.

In the mid-1990s central HR split into two units: a strategic department of ten employees and a service center of ninety. The strategy group develops systems, such as a stock-option plan for the new Internet group. Although it has no role in the formulation of business strategy, it is responsible for developing HR strategy that fits with the company's business strategy. As at J. Electrical, the existence of two departments is part of an effort to align HR decision making with corporate strategy and to put a wedge between strategy formulation (which might require downsizing) and the union. The service center is in charge of routine operations such as recruitment, labor relations, welfare services, and international HR. Executives of central HR include both generalists and specialists who have rotated around the company in various HR positions.

Each of the five business groups has its own HR department, which has considerable autonomy with respect to divisional personnel decisions. The group HR departments are more powerful than in most Japanese companies, but, even so, their autonomy has its limits. Meetings are held twice a month with central HR to coordinate recruitment, compensation, and other policies, and additional meetings are held to discuss specific projects or topics. Recruitment is a shared responsibility between headquarters and business groups. Each group sends its recruiting plan to central HR, which then balances divisional needs and develops a master plan. The plan is sent to a companywide "organization committee" composed of managing directors from each business group and chaired by the HR managing director. Here the groups can air their differences and revise the master plan, as the HR director plays the role of mediator. The final plan is referred to central HR, which is responsible for hiring fresh graduates. The whole process is a good example of the persistence of a traditional, Japanese practice—consensus decision making (*nemawashi*)—in a company that considers itself (and is regarded by others) as a corporate bellwether for the adoption of Western-style management practices.

In contrast to recruitment, rotation decisions fall largely to the groups. There is no systematic interdivisional rotation. In earlier years, central HR oversaw rotations. Under the present system, however, rotation occurs within the product groups and is planned by them. Headquarters intervenes only when employees seek to move to another group (in which case they contact headquarters HR through the new "free voice" system) or when one group targets an employee in another group. Generally, the internal labor market is more fluid and decentralized than in the other companies we visited.

An important exception are the five hundred employees who have been identified as future company leaders. These rising stars—they include some non-Japanese—are picked by the president, or so it is said, although central HR is the power behind the throne in deciding the group's composition. Those who make the cut are groomed by central HR, which manages their careers, including overseas assignments. Central HR also has the responsibility of vetting individuals who are being considered for promotion from general manager to vice president, although it is the business groups that initiate the process and the organization committee that makes the final decision.

The sharper line of independence is between the parent company and its subsidiaries, who have their own personnel policies, rotation schemes, and compensation practices. One reason for so many subsidiaries is that they operate in industries whose pay structures are disparate with the parent company's pay norms. When they are spun off, they are taken out of the parent company's orbit of comparison, and this helps to contain costs. The parent company and each of the subsidiaries have separate unions and conduct separate negotiations with them.

Against this background story of continuity amidst change, corporate governance stands out as one area in which the company has transcended its past to a degree that affects central HR profoundly. Until recently, J. Electronics was governed like most Japanese companies. It had a large board of directors, whose forty members included representatives from the divisions and from headquarters departments such as HR. Although J. Electronics has been traded on the New York Stock Exchange since the early 1960s, share-price movements had never been a strong determinant of the company's business decisions.

In the mid-1990s, however, that began to change. Foreign investors had long been calling for greater attention to shareholders, greater accountability of directors, and speedier implementation of new business strategies. Smaller boards were viewed as a means of achieving those objectives. With its heavy foreign ownership, J. Electronics was particularly sensitive to criticisms of traditional Japanese governance. In 1997, it, like Sony, implemented a corporate-officer system (*shikkō yakuin*) whereby the number of members who sat on the board was slashed from forty to twelve, and three outside individuals were brought in to serve on it. Tellingly, the company's chief financial officer remained on the board, while the HR managing director (a former union leader) was cut. He and the other former board members are now part of a management committee that, although lacking power to make strategic decisions, has beefed-up authority for handling operational issues. Shareholders showed their approval by boosting J. Electronics' stock price; the financial press lauded the change.

Some have argued that the move to the new board system is mostly cosmetic, since power remains in the hands of insiders. In fact, the new system can be viewed as a formalization of the past practice by which a small management committee, headed by the president, made key strategic decisions and presented them to the larger board for approval.[10] From HR's perspective, however, the new system constitutes a real change and a direct cut in its own power. The strategic influence wielded by employee-stakeholders has been reduced. Whereas previously the board had included the HR managing director and other individuals with direct HR experience, now it has none. Senior HR managers told us they were disturbed that finance, but not HR, was represented on the new board. They felt that this signaled that the corporate culture was shifting toward greater emphases on financial criteria and favoring shareholders over employees.

Consistent with this shift, J. Electronics is moving faster than most Japanese companies in adopting stock options that are supposed to align management's actions with the interests of shareholders. Options are paid all the way down to the level of general manager, and sometimes lower. Senior executives, whose annual options in some cases are worth more than their annual salary, receive the juiciest payouts. At lower levels, options are less than 20 percent of salary. As a result of recent drops in the company's share price, management is rethinking the heavy use of options and converting to cash those options that are "under water." This response suggests that, despite the lip service paid to owners, managers are still at the helm.

CHALLENGES AND CHANGES

In all the companies, efforts are under way to make headquarters smaller, more focused, and more efficient. While less affected by early rounds of cost-cutting than were local units, headquarters were still reduced, in response to the prolonged recession and in an effort to make the organizational structure of these large companies more responsive to the quickened pace of global markets and technologies. Shrinkage of headquarters is also intended to curry favor with foreign shareholders, whose response to news of staff cuts has become increasingly positive.[11] In the companies we visited, HR is not being singled out. That is, the economy measures that the companies have made are across the board and do not have a disproportionately negative impact on central HR departments.

Another set of changes, however, *is* weakening the standing of central HR in the corporate hierarchy. These are associated with the distribution of power between shareholders, managers, employees, and unions. Corporate-governance reforms are undercutting the stakeholder approach by giving more weight to shareholders and to finance-driven decisions. Union weakness, as at J. Electrical, is reducing the perceived relevance of corporate HR departments. Employment practices—and the social norms underpinning them—are gradually becoming more market-oriented. As a result, a sense of anxiety is building in some corporate HR units, where staff worry that their influence in the corporation is eroding.

Headquarters Reorganizations

Headquarters jobs are being reduced in the companies we visited, but not all the cuts are permanent. Both Construction Alpha and Beta are moving headquarters staff into sales jobs—a shift that presumably will reverse itself when the construction sector recovers from its present malaise. Nor is HR necessarily being singled out. The approximately 20 percent by which J. Parts cut its central HR staff is in line with cuts in other headquarters units. The reduction in HR was achieved through hiring freezes and the transfer of employees to divisional units.

One effect of job transferal to divisional units is to make HR decision making less top-heavy. During the past two years, J. Parts has been moving HR and other responsibilities to its product groups (divisions). Rotations up through the rank of middle manager are now handled almost entirely by the product groups, who communicate with each other rather than through central HR. The latter intervenes only to vet plans and oversee the careers of high-ability individuals who are in demand throughout the company. Also, while central HR reviews promotions and can advise the product groups about them, it can no longer overrule promotion decisions made by the operating units. Considerably more power accrues to the product groups and divisions as a result of these two changes. To a large degree, most management careers are still characterized by "central planning," but now it takes place one level lower, in the divisions. Central HR increasingly focuses on the high-flyers destined for the upper ranks.

As economic problems continue and pressure mounts for additional budgetary savings, some HR departments are being forced to make changes more radical than those imposed on other headquarters units, because HR is so much larger to begin with. In 2001, the president of J. Parts announced plans for a second round of headquarters cuts, this time by 50 percent, a huge amount. HR could meet a cut that size only by spinning off its welfare and training divisions into independent companies. That change became effective in 2002. The welfare division, which administers recreational facilities, restaurants, and medical services (the latter are legally mandated), is now J. Parts Well, a stand-alone company with a budget of $76 million. The new training company, which has 150 employees and a budget of $24 million, will sell its services back to J. Parts and, it hopes, to other companies.

Other companies have already gone down this road. In 1999, J. Electronics spun off its training unit and turned it into an independent company that is trying to sell training programs to J. Electronics as well as to other companies. This move, like the spin-off at J. Parts, was part of an attempt to reduce the number of headquarters jobs. The training-unit employees were given the choice of staying with the parent (but being transferred to another position), following the spin-off, or striking out on their own. Some employees in the third category resigned and became independent trainers who now are hired on a contract basis by the spin-off to provide services to the parent company. The same people are doing the same work as before but are now two steps removed from the parent's payroll. So far, the spin-off has not generated sales from third parties. That is hardly surprising, as the companies (in heavy manufacturing and financial services) that pioneered this approach earlier in the 1990s never had great success at finding new clients. In fact, J. Electrical was among those companies. In the mid-1990s it spun off its 130-person training department, but since then it has failed to garner a single client outside the J. Electrical family. However, and this is critical to bear in mind, the training spin-off continues to receive substantial funding from the parent company and to maintain an extensive panoply of employee training programs.

Despite its experience with its training subsidiary, J. Electrical is currently planning to spin off its welfare units (including both headquarters and divisional employees) in response to the president's recent call for additional staff cuts. The new welfare spin-off will be an independent company, as at J. Parts. Although we heard claims that this would generate outside business, it is clear that the real purpose of forming these subsidiaries is not to gain external clients.

Why, then, do Japanese companies spin off welfare and training services? The reasons are both budgetary and strategic. From a budgetary perspective, a spin-off provides the cover for actions that would otherwise be difficult to effect. At J. Electrical, for example, the welfare spin-off will result in a cut of about one hundred employees over three years. About half of them will be farmed out to affiliated subsidiaries (and so might receive pay cuts); the other half are near retirement age and will not be replaced. The employer saves money, then—through head cuts and through pay cuts that would have been difficult to instate directly—and employees save face.

Strategic reasons for these spin-offs include, as mentioned, the advantages of decentralization. Another is that, as many believe, administration of hostels and cafeterias does not mesh neatly with the "core" function of HR and does not give the parent company any competitive advantage. Not only welfare services but also security, accounting, maintenance, and other "service" functions are being spun off or outsourced in Japanese companies. That may sound like "stick to your knitting," the rationale for outsourcing so often heard in the

United States, but the use of spin-offs for strategic purposes has a long history in Japan. In fact, experience with welfare and training spin-offs dates back to the early 1980s, before the current recession.

Finally, spin-offs are useful for shrinking the absolute size of the central HR department without having to cut jobs in core activities like HR policy and planning. At J. Electrical, the welfare and training spin-offs have reduced the size of the central HR department from more than 100 employees to 35, and of the divisional HR staff from more than 500 to about 250. These numbers, which are more in line with other staff departments that are less labor-intensive than HR, leave the HR core better positioned to deflect any future cuts.

Corporate Governance

A growing number of Japanese companies are following in Sony's footsteps and shrinking their boards and/or adopting the corporate-officer system. J. Electrical is a case in point: It implemented the corporate-officer system in 1999 and no longer has a designated board position for the HR managing director. Although HR still has a place on the executive committee, it feels the loss of a board seat keenly. HR at J. Electrical recently received the good news that its new managing director has been selected to become a board member—not, however, because of his HR responsibilities, but because he is widely regarded as one of the company's most capable executives. This will keep HR on the inside loop, at least as long as he remains the managing director, and allow it to bask in the glory of his prestige, but it is hardly a decisive victory for HR. This executive spent most of his previous career in finance and moved to HR only two years ago, when he was appointed managing director, the first in recent history to have no previous HR experience. The department's spin on the appointment is that it signals to the rest of the corporation that HR still matters enough to attract as its head one of the company's top stars: "The HR function was seen as old-fashioned and appointing someone from finance made us look more modern." But this interpretation should not obscure the reality that HR has an image problem and that it looked to finance, a function acknowledged to be on the ascendant, to improve its reputation.

If J. Electronics is a harbinger, the new corporate-officer system might change the internal balance of power. At J. Electronics, the CFO retains a seat on the board, which gives the finance function greater leverage in budget negotiations and which may prove to have a disproportionately negative impact on HR. Why? A department's budget initially is determined by the finance department and then negotiated by the department's general manager and by the general manager of finance. In the past, a department could always ask its managing director to seek forbearance from his counterpart in finance; both were board members with equal status. Loss of a board seat puts these departments at a disadvantage in budget negotiations. The same problem affects a variety of headquarters departments, but HR may be in a particular jeopardy because its contributions to the corporation are harder to quantify in ways that finance managers can appreciate.

Generally, the new arrangement calls into question the assumption that the central HR function represents not only its narrow sectional interests but also the collective interests of the *seishain*, the lifetime employees. HR's loss of a board seat signals that those interests, however important, no longer merit a seat on the board. Conversely, shareholder and investor interests are gaining weight through CFO-directors and the move toward the appointment of outside directors, typically academic economists or leading business figures. As a result, when boards make strategic decisions, they are likely to give less consideration to the interests of employees and more to the interests of shareholders. J. Electrical has a temporary reprieve because its managing director sits on the main board. When asked what will happen when the director retires, the general manager sighed and said, "Che sarà, sarà."

Even at companies that have not adopted the corporate-officer system, closer attention is being paid to financial markets, investor relations, and share prices. Here are some bits and shreds to support that claim. First, J. Securities is planning to pay stock options to board members and to list itself on the New York Stock Exchange. Second, managers at Construction Alpha openly admit that the company's restructuring plan, which trims headcount by 10 percent over the next three years (through early retirement and natural attrition) has been formulated with an eye to the financial press and the financial markets. Finally, at J. Delivery (13 percent of which is now owned by foreign investors), the effect that wage negotiations have on share prices is jointly monitored by the HR and investor-relations departments. HR is trying to sensitize the union to this issue.

Unions

Japanese unions find themselves in a weaker position today than at any time in the past thirty years, and, as noted, this is affecting the perceived importance of the central HR function, especially in manufacturing companies where unions once were powerful and occasionally militant. At these companies— like J. Parts and J. Electrical—HR's close relationship to the union makes it appear a little old-fashioned, like the union, and hurts its image Memories of the postwar labor accord are fading and some younger directors are skeptical about the need for unions. As we have seen, HR executives at J. Parts constantly have to explain to non-HR managers the department's role as the third party—a bridge or axle—between the union and the company. Workers, too, are losing interest in unions, particularly at companies whose core consists mostly of managerial and professional employees.

In the 1960s and 1970s, J. Electrical had a powerful enterprise union made up largely of blue-collar workers, who were about two-thirds of the company's employees. HR played an important role. It negotiated with the union, securing its cooperation with the company's plans and making concessions in areas such as employment security. But continuing mechanization and "hollowing out" (the shifting of production to subsidiaries and subcontractors outside Japan) has hit hard the ranks of the company's blue-collar workers, who are now less than 30 percent of its employees, and it is hiring few new ones. Given the shift in J. Electrical's occupational composition, the union has become less militant, less of a threat, and less important in the eyes of top management—and, as the union goes, so goes the central HR. Having once derived influence from its relationship with the union, HR now finds itself subject to charges that that relationship renders it out of step with efforts to make the company more streamlined and market-oriented. Even within HR itself, those who were once the department's elite—the labor-relations experts well-versed in the intricacies of union politics and labor law—are less important than thirty years ago.

Changes in corporate governance have affected management's relationship with the union. In the past, the company's board of directors would approve results of the annual wage negotiations. Now, in companies where HR lacks a board seat, executives think that it will become more difficult for negotiators to obtain the board's endorsement. Union leaders may try to make end runs around HR if they sense that the department lacks clout to settle deals. Another possibility is that the trend toward decentralization will make it difficult to maintain common conditions across different parts of the company, thereby undermining the union's solidarity.

Another significant development is the bifurcation of the HR function into a planning unit and a service unit that includes labor relations. On one side of the coin, the ability of the union to influence strategic HR decisions is limited. On the other side, HR's image is improved in the eyes of managers who in the past suspected it of being unable to advance a perspective that was not unduly affected by the union's. This development helps HR reorient itself to the senior-management team, a group whose interests may not coincide with those of the rank and file, the *seishain*. When the welfare and training functions are not just cleaved from HR but spun off into independent entities, as at J. Parts and J. Electrical, the result is fewer managers at headquarters who have close ties with, and often a background in, the enterprise union.

Keep in mind that in the past, the willingness of senior managers to tolerate the union was supported by egalitarian norms and by an array of single-status policies, including union membership for junior managers. Today, however, a growing number of managers are recruited at mid-career and have no particular loyalty to, or sympathy for, the enterprise union, as is corroborated by attitude survey data.[12]

Employment Practices

Most of the companies we visited had changed or were changing their pay systems, especially for white-collar employees, so as to give less weight to seniority and more to individual performance. Accompanying these changes has been a shift to accelerated promotions up the managerial ranks, although the speed with which fast-trackers can move varies from company to company. J. Electronics and J. Securities have some general managers in their mid-thirties, whereas J. Electrical has chosen to remain sensitive to traditional age norms with respect to assignments and promotions until a manager is in his forties.

The rewarding of performance is nothing new in Japan. What has changed is that the weight of performance—relative to that of seniority, age, grade, and other factors—tends to be greater now. The new pay systems have the effect of widening pay differentials for employees with similar seniority and grades. We found the largest differentials at J. Securities, where the bonus ratio between top and bottom has widened from 2:1 five years ago to more than 10:1 currently. J. Securities regularly has to fend off raids by foreign financial firms, who offer high salaries regardless of age, so its new pay system can fairly be called a market-oriented approach, and it includes market comparisons (from survey data) in designing its bonus payments. Another effect of the revised pay system is that it moves J. Securities further in the direction of creating specialist tracks alongside the traditional general-management grooming process.[13]

Other companies, however, face little or no risk of managers jumping ship for higher pay. They've introduced the new pay plans partly to accommodate younger managers, who are marked by an increasing sense of individualism and are less tolerant of age norms than are their elders. A company with a reputation for fast-tracking and for performance-based pay has an advantage in recruiting ambitious young graduates, so in this sense too the new plans are more market-oriented. Still, the portion of total compensation based on performance remains comparatively small. At J. Electrical, an engineer five years out can expect to have only about 10 percent of his pay based on individual performance. Another reason companies introduce these plans is what sociologists call "mimetic isomorphism" (what feeds all fads): They simply wish to appear progressive and on the cutting edge.[14]

One of the less-publicized but important reasons for performance-based pay is that, by curbing salaries of relatively low performers, it helps offset the cost of no-layoff policies. Part of the savings is reallocated to "star" employees; the rest enables the company to carry incumbent employees without resorting to layoffs. Greater pay differentiation, therefore, is the price of preserving lifetime jobs.[15] We saw evidence of this at J. Securities, where the current restructuring is intended to occur without any job cuts (though some positions in retailing may disappear if the company decides not to fill vacancies there). J. Securities insists that its headcount is not excessive. Rather, it says, the problem is the high floor for basic compensation, the guaranteed minimum paid to an employee. Under the new performance-based pay plan, the guaranteed minimum, which is built on seniority and age, will fall.

For central HR departments, the new pay systems are a mixed blessing. They are a high-visibility activity that central HR designs and rolls out, but at the same time the emphasis on performance is accompanied by operating decisions that are more decentralized. Organizational turf wars have ensued. At J. Parts, the central HR unit previously required line managers to follow a preset distribution whereby a given percentage of managers and engineers were slotted into each appraisal level. Now, divisions are free to reward performance as they see fit, so long as its total payroll falls within budgetary limits, which are still set by headquarters. J. Securities is moving in the same direction, but its central HR department, faced with the prospect of ceding to line managers its authority to make decisions about bonuses, is reluctant to do so until it has trained them to evaluate employees "properly." Even as it becomes more market-oriented, J. Securities remains concerned to maintain or encourage equity across company units, and that plays into the hands of the headquarters HR unit. The tension between centralization and decentralization—between companywide concerns and the more market-oriented interests of particular units—remains unresolved.[16]

Firms are accommodating employee individualism also by relaxing central control of job moves, as in the case of the "free voice" system at J. Electronics. J. Parts recently adopted a similar innovation that it calls the "free agent" and "open access" system, which give individuals greater control over their careers. *Open access* simply means that company units must publicize job openings; *free agent* means that employees can apply directly to the unit posting the vacancy. These reforms represent a move away from a "command and control" career system to one in which the employee has greater choice. HR introduced them as part of Vision 2005, a planned makeover of the J. Parts culture intended to make it more attractive to the younger workers it is trying to recruit. Designed by the HR department, Vision 2005 sententiously touts the company's "open corporate culture," which "treasures every single associate and assists each one in full self-realization." At J. Parts, "personal growth leads to company growth."

A company that frees up its internal labor market makes itself more attractive to mid-career movers (*chūto saiyō*) recruited from other companies. J. Electronics, J. Electrical, and J. Parts rely on advertisements and occasionally on headhunters to help them find people with scarce technical skills—for example, audio engineers who can design automotive navigation systems. The typical mid-career employee is an engineer in his early thirties who, for whatever reason, is unhappy with his current employer. While big companies could get the same talent by acquiring a company, M&A activity remains a relatively rare event in Japan, despite all the noise about it in the financial press.

More so than in the past, Japanese companies today rely on temporary and part-time employees, who can easily be dismissed if business takes a turn for the worse. In fact, temps were being laid off at J. Electrical during our visit. J. Delivery, which was heavily dependent on temporary and part-time employees to begin with, has become even more so, with the percentage of noncore employees rising from 43 in 1990 to 49 in 2002. J. Electronics recently spun off part of its HR department to serve as a temp agency for the company's various units as well as for other companies, although, like the training spin-off, this subsidiary presently gets almost all its customers from the parent company. The temps tend to be superannuated blue-collar workers, but some are white-collar employees seeking new jobs inside the company or at its subsidiaries. Neither group has ever actually been terminated. The function of the temp agency, then, is a variant of the traditional practice (*shukkō*) whereby surplus employees are transferred to subsidiaries and suppliers. This, along with natural attrition, is helping the company meet its goal of slashing its global workforce by 10 percent over the next three years. Investors boosted the company's share price after the job cuts were announced but probably don't understand how gingerly the company is moving in this regard.

The same circuitous approach could be seen at J. Electrical, which is in the midst of a three-year plan to cut its workforce by about 15 percent. The company expects about one-half of the reduction to come from attrition and the rest from spin-offs and voluntary early retirement. No one will actually be fired or laid off.

■ ■ ■

What do these changes—in centralization, corporate governance, labor relations, and employment policy—mean for central HR departments? The evidence shows that the further a company moves along any one dimension, the more it changes along other dimensions, in line with the institutional-complementarity hypothesis. J. Electronics, the company showing the biggest shifts toward shareholder governance and market-oriented policies, is also the company whose headquarters HR unit has suffered the greatest loss of power and prestige. At the other end of the spectrum are J. Delivery and J. Securities, where market- and shareholder-oriented reforms have been modest, and neither their basic policies nor the centrality of the headquarters HR units has changed.

In the middle are companies in flux. Here we heard mutterings that, while nothing has changed much yet, there is no telling what the future will bring. The gloomiest mood was at J. Parts, which, as mentioned, was about to institute a major across-the-board cut in headquarters jobs. Executives at central HR think that the union's weakness and the search for operating flexibility will continue to drive the transfer of the department's authority to line managers. Some of them fear that, if this process continues over time, eventually it will hurt the company's ability to manage its human resources optimally. Central HR's view of line managers is that they are incapable of adopting a company-wide perspective when handling promotions, and of understanding the long-term benefits of training. We were told that the same thing may occur with the union relationship as HR decentralizes. "Line managers don't understand the subtleties here, [so] the gap between the company and the union may widen." The executives were all familiar with Yashiro's book on HR departments and sounded defensive when speaking about it. Yashiro, they said, just didn't understand the economic logic of central procurement (as applied to recruiting and career rotation) or the risks of leaving employee relations in the hands of line managers.

These comments raise two interesting points. First, those urging change in the Japanese employment system have clearly hit a nerve. HR departments are uneasy about what the future may hold and are frustrated that their point of view is not being heard. Norm entrepreneurs like Yashiro have, at least for the time being, done an effective job of making the case for a change in employment practices. One hears few voices promoting an alternative perspective. Because HR is not professionalized, there is no organized response from HR executives themselves. HR departments do have allies, but they are a ragtag group: quality and production managers who believe in the virtues of training, union leaders who want to preserve jobs, and business figures like the head of Toyota, who recently struck a patriotic chord by publicly defending the Japanese business system against foreign critics.[17]

Second, most HR executives are not worried about their own jobs; they stand little likelihood of losing them. Rather, their concerns are for the company's long-term health. One senses genuine concern that competitive advantage will suffer if companies keep chipping away at the three pillars—lifetime employment, enterprise unions, and seniority—and all they support. Their unselfish focus on what is best for the company may yet countervail "outside" voices that promote other, more self-serving, agendas.

THE GLASS HALF FULL

Despite myriad changes throughout the corporate structure of these companies and even in the central HR departments themselves, there remains considerable stability—call it inertia, or call it continuity—in the role of the central HR function. Unlike his gloomy counterpart at J. Parts, the general manager of HR at Construction Beta dismissed Yashiro derisively, saying that the book was overly academic and made no business sense. His company, he said, had no intention of shifting power to line managers or of recasting fundamental HR structures. He characterized current changes as "add-ons": dry features like performance-based pay are being placed on top of existing "wet" institutions like seniority, lifetime employment, "familyism," enterprise unions, and strong corporate culture. Central HR, he said, would continue to occupy a privileged place because it is essential for ensuring equity, good relations with the union, and an efficient internal labor market. He also said that central HR is crucial to the company's business strategy, which is based on quality and customer satisfaction. We heard similarly assertive opinions at J. Delivery and J. Securities. It is, perhaps, not coincidental that these are companies whose business depends on employee-provided customer service.

Reorganizations

Several companies are undergoing reorganizations, which include spin-offs of diverse units and decentralization of management systems. For example, under a new matrix-inspired restructuring at J. Securities, divisions are being given shared responsibility not only for staff functions previously handled by headquarters but also for corresponding parts of overseas subsidiaries and affiliated companies. Under this approach, the divisions, not headquarters, will be the glue holding together the company's domestic, international, and *kogaisha* parts. A key responsibility being transferred to the divisions is decision making on employee bonuses. But while divisional line managers will perform evaluations and determine rankings, they will have to send their data to central HR, which retains power over final rankings and promotions. Under the reorganization, there still will be no divisional HR units. J. Securities, then, is preserving the power of the central HR unit even as it decentralizes.

J. Electrical, a company with a long history of semi-autonomous divisions, has recently made moves to advance its product groups on their own separate paths. Two years ago the groups were renamed "in-house companies," a term that is supposed to connote greater independence. Also, according to a plan not yet effected, a portion of an employee's semiannual bonus will be based on divisional performance—something that is still unusual in Japan. Other than that, however, the company has no intention to further differentiate HR practices at the divisional level. There persists a strong belief in using central HR to realize cross-unit synergies and to sustain a strong companywide culture that can hold the company's diverse pieces together.

Consultants

Central-HR executives are confident that they know what's best for their company and that outsiders—consultants, academics, foreign observers—really "don't get it." A sure way to get a laugh out of these managers is to ask what they think of the growing number of management consultants plying their services in Japan. At each company we heard the same story: They once hired a consultancy to see what advice it could offer on HR issues and problems, and that was that—they never rehired it. Why?

We were given various explanations—companies can think faster on their own, for example, or consultants don't understand the peculiarities of Japanese business. Also, many of the packages offered by consultancies are, like the assumptions underlying much of the psychological research on which they are based, highly individualistic, and so ill-suited to the collectivist incentive systems of Japanese companies. Age norms and egalitarianism remain important, so high-achievers know to temper their style; "cowboys" are pariahs. U.S.-style performance-appraisal systems are criticized for being too direct and unsubtle. Of course, cultural differences change over time and evidence suggests that Japan is gradually becoming more individualistic. Someday, foreign consultancies may find themselves doing a thriving business in Japan, but they haven't yet.[18]

This does not mean that HR departments are insulated from outside perspectives. When necessary, companies still secure information from the institutions that are legacies of "Japan, Inc."—peak organizations like the Japan Productivity Council and Keidanren; local business associations; and private networks like *keiretsu* affiliates, suppliers, and *kogaisha*. The ethos persists that competitors should share information that can advance the collective interests of Japanese business. Hence companies still trade data on pay rates, labor relations, quality systems, and a host of other HR issues. These are proprietary matters but typically do not involve the sort of information that can make or break a company's competitive advantage and its stream of rents.[19]

Through corporate networks, HR departments learn about new developments but also experience pressures to conform to what other companies are doing, even if it's inefficient or inappropriate. One sees innovations—quality circles in the 1960s and 1970s and performance-based pay in the 1990s are examples—mushrooming across firms and industries. This is different from HR fads in the United States, where the HR flavor-of-the-month idea is usually promoted by private consultants, each of which has its idiosyncratic plans and proposals, whereas the HR innovations in Japan have been sanctioned by government and by corporate pattern-setters, blue-ribbon firms like Sony, Toyota, and Toshiba. In Japan, the spread of HR innovations from one company to another follows a pattern that resembles the convoys seen in product markets, whereby bigger firms help smaller or less profitable ones.[20]

It is conceivable that this system might someday generate more radical change. For example, if major pattern-setters instituted a drastic reform—if they phased out lifetime employment, say, or gutted central HR units—they would lend it the legitimacy other companies would need to follow suit. That hasn't happened, at least not yet. When Nissan announced major layoffs and plant closures in 1999, some journalists predicted a domino effect, but executives we interviewed said that Japanese companies no longer consider Nissan a pattern-setter because its ownership (Renault) and CEO (Carlos Ghosn) are foreign. In the end, Nissan did conform to Japanese norms. It shuttered plants in Japan but offered laid-off workers jobs elsewhere in the Nissan system. "We didn't throw anybody out in the cold," an HR manager at one of the closed plants said. Some workers took early retirement; others opted for transfers.[21]

Employment Practices

An upsurge in *shukkō* transfers and mid-career hiring is making organizational boundaries more permeable and more exposed to market influences. One might think these developments would be shrinking the portfolios of organization-oriented HR departments, but the opposite is occurring: central HR departments are taking greater responsibility for managing movement across boundaries so companies can maintain internal pay and promotion norms.

Shukkō, the transfer of employees to another organization, is used for least three purposes: to facilitate technology transfer to suppliers, customers, or overseas partners; to codevelop products with customers or joint-venture partners; and to farm out surplus employees to subsidiaries and suppliers, forcing them to share the burden of the primary firm's no-layoff policy. In this last category—the secondments—the sending firm usually guarantees 60 percent or more of the transferee's salary. Secondments are the dominant form of *shukkō* in Japan today, although *shukkō* for all three purposes is on the rise.[22] Of J. Parts's core employees, two to three thousand are on *shukkō* to other entities. The factories with surplus employees choose personnel for *shukkō*, but otherwise the process rests in the hands of central HR. In addition to negotiating with the receiving firm over salary terms, housing allowances, and numerous other details, HR decides where seconded employees will be sent. At J. Electronics, J. Electrical, and Construction Beta, most of the *shukkō* is between the parent firm and its *kogaisha* subsidiaries. The pay scale at these subsidiaries is different from that of the parent firm—sometimes they were spun off for that very reason—so the issue of pay rates for *shukkō* employees is sensitive, and central HR handles that. These temporary reassignments often turn out to be quasi-permanent; in large companies, more than a third of *shukkōs* last for five years or more.[23]

Mid-career hiring (*chūto saiyō*) also is centralized, in part because traditionally recruiting falls to central HR, and in part because questions about pay equity are, in *chūto saiyō* as in *shukkō*, touchy. Many mid-career people are hired from subsidiaries and from suppliers, who tend to pay less. The source companies resent having their employees poached, and central HR is in a position to smooth over any hard feelings—another reason for its involvement. At both J. Parts and J. Electrical, central HR said they usually checked with their sales departments before recruiting *chūto saiyō* from customers or suppliers. Contrary to claims that the increase in mid-career hiring is a sign that labor markets are more open, most *chūto saiyō* are moving only within the corporate network of a core firm. A senior HR manager at J. Electrical put it bluntly: "There is still no open labor market in Japan."

One major function that has undergone change—decision making about managerial promotion and rotation—presents a complicated picture. In four of the seven companies we studied, central HR retains its mandate to oversee companywide rotations. In two others, J. Electrical and J. Electronics, divisions make decisions about managerial rotations, while J. Parts is moving in that direction. Yet in all the companies, even those that are decentralizing, central HR shows a countervailing tendency to take tighter control over career planning for the company's stars, identifying the best and brightest and grooming them for senior management positions. One reason companies need to exercise greater central control over the process is that it is sensitive, as stars are being promoted a little earlier and a little faster than their peers. Here, as in the matter of *chūto saiyō* and *shukkō*, companies are wary of riding roughshod over existing social norms; they are managing the change process carefully. The other reason a company puts stars in the hands of central HR is straightforward: Many of them are likely to end up at headquarters.

Again, sometimes market pressures have centralizing effects that are paradoxical. At J. Securities, the early identification of stars is intended to give them a sense they are destined for greatness and thereby stem the loss of outstanding employees to foreign competitors. In the initial phase of this plan, the company has targeted about fifty managers in their early thirties, who will receive special bonuses and career counseling from central HR.

Other functions over which central HR remains firmly in command are corporate recruiting, which continues to be aimed largely at recent college or high school graduates, and the design, although not always the implementation, of companywide compensation plans. Underlying both of these functions is what underlies many of HR's premises: the lifetime employment system.

Case studies admittedly are an imperfect means of gauging developments in the lifetime-employment system, but the evidence we did gather consistently and strongly suggests that companies are trying to minimize layoffs and preserve the jobs of highly trained career employees. Even the two construction firms, the most financially troubled companies we studied, have not resorted to layoffs. Alpha has a variety of methods for dealing with employee redundancies: reduced hiring, early retirement incentives, the shedding of temporary workers, and the transfers of technical and managerial employees to sales positions and, via *shukkō*, to subsidiaries. Still prevailing among senior managers is the belief that the honoring of long-term employment commitments benefits both the Japanese economy and the company. It improves morale, labor relations, skill retention, and social image. That is what we heard even at J. Electronics, the most market-oriented of the companies. "Today there are many people who cannot work productively, because the production facilities have moved to Asian countries, technologies have changed from analog to digital, and for many other reasons. But the company cannot terminate these people because of the long-standing heritage of the employment system." J. Electronics is trying to create a new set of expectations by no longer using the phrase "lifetime employment" in its publications, but its actions are hemmed in by social norms as well as by court decisions restricting mass layoffs.

These findings fit with data from other studies that show employers trying to reduce labor costs with a panoply of practices that lead up to, but do not include, layoffs of permanent employees. One such practice is the use of contingent employees. In Japan, the percentage of employees who are part-time has risen from 17 in 1990 to 25 in 2001. Since 1982, the number of temporary employees and freelancers has tripled.[24] Some companies cut pay, either asking employees to take unpaid leave days (a form of work sharing) or instituting straightforward, across-the-board pay reductions, not only in bonuses but in base pay. For the first time since the end of the war, Rengo, the national labor federation, is allowing pay cuts when they are a quid pro quo for job preservation.[25] Other adjustment policies include employment subsidies from the government to reduce the cost of carrying excess employees as well as *shukkō* transfers to affiliated companies and to suppliers. Indeed, because large firms squeeze smaller ones, unemployment is more problematic in the secondary labor market.

Nevertheless, layoffs at large firms are surprisingly few and, when they do announce layoffs, they don't usually terminate employees outright. Some of the employees designated for layoff end up on the payroll of affiliated companies or other joint ventures. Most of the job cuts occur through voluntary retirement or attrition. One should not underestimate the extent of employment shrinkage that has occurred through these methods. But remaining employees have relatively stable jobs and, for this reason, the data show little evidence of a decline in employee tenure at large companies.[26] Consistent with this stability are findings from recent surveys indicating, first, that a majority of employers prefer to cut pay and dividends before cutting jobs and, second, that a similar majority still expect employees to work for the company for a long time and to be loyal to it. Cracks in the dike, however, can be detected. In 2003, the proportion of companies giving awards to long-service employees was 82 percent, ten points below the 1992 figure of 92 percent.[27]

The most stable companies are the large, elite employers of the type examined in our case studies. Because of the sheer number of their employees, they are more alert to the social consequences of layoffs and to jawboning from government. They also are more likely to be unionized and to face lawsuits if they engage in mass layoffs. (Unions are empowered to handle employee complaints over unfair dismissal.) In these large public companies, employees continue to be viewed as stakeholders: The proportion of firms saying that they give weight to employees as stakeholders actually increased slightly from the 1990s to 2002. Further down the industrial ladder, however, norms of social responsibility are weaker, unions are less prevalent, and companies are inclined to ignore Nikkeiren's call for "globalization with a human face" (i.e., for hiring more contingents to subsidize the cost of carrying core employees).[28] Smaller companies are carrying the biggest burdens of adjustment, and, indeed, the data show that smaller and less prestigious firms are more likely to downsize.[29] Also bearing a burden are young people, for whom the unemployment rate is high. Japanese graduates find it difficult to obtain jobs in large, elite companies, where the low number of layoffs is counterbalanced by low hiring rates.[30]

Unions

Companies with strong unions or a history of troubled labor relations mention the union as a consideration in their no-layoff policies. In the 1980s, not so long ago, J. Electrical and its union fought. Since then HR has developed a more cooperative relationship with the union and, even though the union has lost power, the HR managers hesitate to propose drastic job cuts, which would open up old wounds. Not everyone at the company agrees with the approach HR has taken. A retired J. Electrical executive, who spent much of his career in overseas and finance positions, criticized HR for being too consensus-oriented and standing in the way of necessary headcount "adjustments." For now, however, the department is behaving like most of its counterparts, relying on reduced hiring, attrition, and layoffs of temporary workers to gradually shrink the payroll.

In interviews, officials of national union federations corroborated the situation exemplified by J. Electrical. We were told that executives without HR experience believe that cooperation with the union hinders a company's ability to move quickly on issues such as downsizing and divestitures. But enough former union leaders remain in senior management to keep it from calling into question the future existence of the union. On the whole, senior managers with a union background share the attitudes of other senior managers, but they are less likely to consider the company the property of its shareholders. Although managerial support for unions is eroding, executives still tend to regard them as more good than bad. In Japan, companies are seldom heard to articulate the U.S.-style proposal that they operate union-free.[31]

The symbiotic relationship between HR departments and enterprise unions endures. HR relies heavily on the union as a routine part of the employee-relations system. For example, Construction Alpha, preparing its new pay-for-performance plan, spent about a year discussing it with the union and revising it in response to union concerns. In those companies, however, that have recently split off the labor-relations function from HR, more distance has been created between the union and the core HR function, with the result that consultation between them in the future is likely to diminish.[32]

Perhaps the biggest problems enterprise unions encounter are not with management but with younger workers, who, according to one manager, do not remember the glory days of the union and are often unable to distinguish it from management. This puts the union in a dilemma. To stay in management's good graces, it must continue to cooperate, but over time that weakens the union's ability to command loyalty from its members. As loyalty diminishes, management finds the union less useful. The situation is more serious in small- and medium-sized companies, where unions in some cases are on the way out. In the large companies we visited, however, the glass remains half full: Enterprise unions, despite some decline, remain secure.

Corporate Governance

Although recent legal reforms have made permissible a variety of U.S.-style corporate-governance practices, Japanese companies have changed far less rapidly than the law itself. Perhaps the most dramatic change can be seen in the unwinding of bank shareholdings, especially by the big-city banks. By 2001, the percentage of Tokyo Stock Exchange (TSE) shares held by financial institutions had fallen from a peak of 46 in 1989 down to 39, but that is still more than the percentage that obtained in 1980. That is, much of the unwinding is of shares acquired during the bubble of the late 1980s. And while big-city banks have been selling shares, trust banks have been buying them. Even as banks sell their shares, they continue to play a role in corporate governance, as the recent management shuffles at Sogo and Daei demonstrate. Still, companies report that they give less priority to banks today than in the 1990s.[33]

Corporate cross-share owning has fallen more steadily: from a peak of 26 percent of shares owned in 1976 to 9 percent in 2001. Like bank shareholdings, cross-shareholding rose in the late 1980s as companies sought to take advantage of the stock market bubble, and so many of the shares being unwound today are from this tranche rather than from more relational holdings. If one looks at long-term holding relationships, a broader indicator of cross-shareholding, the decline has been more gradual: from 46 percent of shares in 1987 to 30 percent in 2001. And within the Big Six *keiretsu*, cross-shareholding actually was higher in 2001 than in the early 1980s, and other *keiretsu* companies likewise have been slow to unwind their holdings. Now as in the late 1980s, about 90 percent of companies engage in some cross-shareholding.[34] It continues to be used to solidify business relationships such as technology transfer, as in a recent deal between Toyota and Yamaha Motor. *Keiretsu* are regrouping, new suppliers and lenders are being sought, and companies are spinning off or merging superfluous divisions, so relational restructuring is obviously occurring, but it remains at the margin. Only 1 percent of large companies changed their main bank over the past three years, and 70 percent reported no change in the number of vendors from whom they procure products and services.[35] In short, majority ownership remains concentrated in relational blocs, thereby insulating companies, for better or for worse, from independent investors and hostile takeovers.[36]

Another ostensible change in corporate governance is the use of stock options to align managers more closely to shareholders. Despite a lot of press coverage about stock options, five of the seven companies we visited did not use and had no plans to introduce them. The companies that did use them offered less stock and to fewer employees than in the United States.

Likewise the corporate-officer system: Only two of the seven companies we studied had adopted it, which is roughly consistent with data showing that around 30 percent of firms utilize this system. With the introduction of the system has come a modest increase in the number of outside directors, who could be found at 24 percent of public companies in 2003. The five other companies we studied, where boards were still composed of insiders, including a managing director from HR, emphasized that they had no intention of changing their board structure, although a couple said they were interested in reducing their board size or putting an outsider on the board. Survey data show that the size of boards has been decreasing in about half of all Japanese companies, this after a run-up in the 1970s. Some argue that boards are reduced mainly to limit officer liability in shareholder suits and that shrinkage does not represent a functional change in corporate governance. Our impression is that, by limiting the influence of HR (and other corporate interest groups), the shrinkage of boards, through the corporate-officer system or otherwise, *does* have an effect on governance.[37]

Financialization of executive decision-making does not yet exist. In fact, what is striking at the corporate level is the extent to which finance managers espouse support for traditional governance arrangements. Finance executives at J. Delivery told us, with nary a hint of cynicism, that their company is a going concern in which it is important to "balance between the interests of employees and of shareholders." They noted that, because the company was a service provider, "people are everything. In this sense, human resource management is important to [our company]." At Construction Alpha, central HR does have to negotiate with the finance department over its annual budget allocation, but this was portrayed as a collegial meeting of equals. Indeed, the negotiators are the general managers of the finance and HR departments—each at the same rank and each reporting to his own board member.

While HR departments track quantitative data like wages and retention, we found no evidence that departmental budgets are tied to these criteria or that finance departments are questioning the value of soft expenditures like employee training, which are difficult to quantify. The one exception to these findings was J. Electronics, where the importance of financial criteria as guides for executive decisions is growing. Other companies may follow in its

steps as their foreign ownership increases. At this time, however, foreign owners still hold only about 18 percent of outstanding shares in Japanese industry,
and some foreign investors, including Merrill Lynch, have given up on the
Japanese market and closed shop. At the two hundred largest companies, foreign equity holdings constitute only 5 percent of outstanding stock. And for
every J. Electronics, there are several companies that continue to operate the
old way or even to move further away from the direction taken by J. Electronics. Toyota, a bellwether among the traditionalists, initially bucked the trend
by *adding* board members, giving it fifty-eight directors, this to the horror of
the *Nikkei Weekly*, which usually takes the view of foreign investors. However,
more recently Toyota adopted its own version of the corporate-officer system
and cut the number of board members. But the board remains quite large—
it has twenty-seven members—and all of them are company managers.[38]

Meanwhile, new institutions are emerging that reinforce management control and a stakeholder ethos. Employee-stock-ownership funds (*mochikabukai*)
are an example. They are composed of employee stock purchases and match-
ing employer contributions. These ESOPs, which are relatively new, have
grown steadily more popular since the 1970s. At Construction Alpha, the fund
holds 3 percent of the company, as it does at J. Delivery, where it is the sixth
largest shareholder. The amounts may seem trivial, but they provide companies with yet another source of patient capital and an extra margin of insulation from fickle investors.[39]

CONCLUSIONS

On close inspection, Japanese companies display considerable variety. On the key
indicator of centralization of operating authority, for example, headquarters
HR departments vary significantly, ranging from the highly centralized
(J. Securities, J. Delivery, and J. Parts) to the moderately centralized (J. Electri-
caland the J. Construction firms) to the moderately decentralized (J. Electronics).
Centralization—the traditional way—is associated with a set of interlocking
factors, which include a focused business strategy, organization-oriented and
egalitarian employment policies, and highly trained, fungible employees with
company-specific skills. Holding this nexus together are central HR and its
counterpart, the enterprise union.

Conversely, a company that is becoming more decentralized tends to have
employment policies that are more market-oriented, employees whose skills
are more general than firm-specific, and a corporate culture that is more differentiated. As the autonomy of divisions and product groups increases, companies have less need for a strong, central HR unit to orchestrate companywide
outcomes. In our study, decentralization is associated with a rise in the importance of shareholder concerns, as reflected in the use of the corporate-officer
system and stock options. Finally, where companies have revamped corporate

governance, the enterprise union is perceived as being much weaker than in the past. The result is that HR loses influence.

However, while it is tempting to see a chain of causation whereby exposure to global markets leads to changes in corporate governance and then specifically to decentralization of HR and shifts in HR policy, companies like J. Securities—which is quite globalized yet retains a powerful and centralized HR function—do not fit the mold. Like J. Delivery, J. Securities is a labor-intensive provider of services whose business strategy is affected by human resource considerations. Despite exposure to Anglo-American business models, these companies are reluctant to shed their traditional approach, with its heavy emphasis on firm-specific skills, because of its integration with their customer-oriented strategies. At both J. Delivery and J. Securities, central HR plays a role in setting strategy, both directly (through participating in decisions on new products, spin-offs, and the like) and indirectly (through its position on the board). HR's strategic role is limited, however. The initial stage of strategic formulation is handled by the planning department or by general administration (sōmu-bu). Even at J. Delivery, HR's strategic contribution tends to be more indirect and consultative than directly creative.

Corroborating the impression of variety are data on employee tenure. Average tenure rates in Japan range from eight years in real estate to thirteen years in manufacturing and as much as seventeen years in public utilities. We do not have tenure data on the case-study companies but suspect that they would show similar variations. We do know, however, about variation in the financial performance of the case-study companies, which include modestly profitable companies like J. Delivery and J. Electronics and struggling firms like J. Securities and J. Construction. It is also known that at the aggregate level some industries in Japan (automotive, machinery, pharmaceutical) have performed reasonably well in the 1990s, while others have performed abysmally.[40]

Take a step back, however, as we did in chapter 2, and a different picture emerges. Detailed differences fade and one sees greater uniformity. Even at J. Electronics, the most market-oriented and decentralized company we visited, the main tendency remains organization- rather than market-oriented. Turnover rates are low; core employees are still hired "for life" and distinguished from contingent employees; training expenditures, although outsourced to a subsidiary, are substantial and focused on firm-specific skills; the majority of employees are hired at entry level, despite rising numbers of chūto saiyō; and the company assumes financial and other responsibilities for the welfare of its employees. There have been layoffs, but the company has tried to minimize their effect through retraining and reassignment. While J. Electronics is hardly a classic gemeinschaft, it retains a strong sense of community and of ties that bind the seishain.[41]

All the same, changes have taken place at J. Electronics, and much of their impact on central HR has been negative. Compared, however, to a typical U.S. (as opposed to Japanese) company, the HR unit at J. Electronics looks more "Japanese" than "American." It has a substantial role in the organization-oriented employment system, tends to a stakeholder philosophy, and—despite loss of a board seat—still commands prestige in the executive hierarchy.

Moreover, even if J. Electronics represents Japan's likely future, it remains the case that most Japanese companies today do not yet resemble it. A recent survey attempting to present a composite picture distinguished between companies that were "J-firm types"—high internal promotion, pay cuts for managers instead of dismissals of nonmanagerial employees, stable shareholding, and an ethos that the company did not exist solely for its shareholders—and those that were not. Eighty-two percent of companies were found to be strong J-firm types; 18 percent were weak J-firm types or something else.[42]

To sum up: The reforms taking place inside large Japanese companies do not amount to a phase shift or what is fashionably called a "punctuated equilibrium." Corporate governance is changing slowly, sometimes more in form than in substance. The decline in union power has been a long, slow drift, taking place chiefly outside the large companies. And what the stronger market orientation evinced by many companies comes down to is greater choice in job assignments and some fudging with performance weights to accommodate high-flyers. The reforms are better characterized as incremental change—small movements along parallel continuums such as market-organization, shareholder-stakeholder, and individual-group. In some cases the reforms—whether of the pay system or of corporate governance—are being adopted for symbolic reasons without changing the "deep structure" of the organization.[43] The result is that the core features of the Japanese corporate system are adapted to a changing environment and thereby preserved.

How does all this affect headquarters HR? Generally, HR has lost power since its glory days in the 1960s and 1970s, but it still occupies a privileged position. Firms like J. Electronics that have moved farthest out on the organization-market continuum are not pacing the corporate convoy. Most companies are moving sluggishly to a hybrid system that takes a base of traditional features and adds on to it some market- and shareholder-oriented practices, such as performance-based pay and occasional stock options. Their borrowing from the United States has led not to convergence with U.S. practices but rather to the emergence of something new.

As yet, however, no consensus exists on what the hybrid ought to look like, no dominant alternative to the traditional model. For HR, this means that the role of the headquarters unit within the company is more variegated—coaching and monitoring line managers (J. Delivery), dispensing technical expertise and systems (J. Parts), or serving as conciliators between line managers (J. Construction). In short, a single new hybrid is not emerging, but rather companies are finding different ways to adapt the traditional practices to pressures from markets, investors, and employees.

4

The Evolution of Human Resource Management in the United States

UNLIKE THEIR JAPANESE COUNTERPARTS, U.S. personnel managers have formed themselves into a semi-profession with a distinctive history. Standard histories of U.S. personnel management present the field as a succession of techniques and philosophies divorced from the historical context that produced them. The standard histories also have little to say about the role that personnel managers exercised inside the corporation—that is, about their relationships with other managers and their influence (or lack thereof) on business decisions and strategies.[1]

Here we proceed differently, embedding personnel managers, and the firms employing them, in the matrix of American society. The role, status, and influence of personnel management *inside* the U.S. corporation have always depended critically on forces *outside* it. These include labor markets, government regulation, unions, and the social norms that contribute to prevailing notions of what constitutes "fair" employment. When there are labor shortages, new laws to comply with, or threats from unions—that is, when the external environment creates uncertainty—personnel managers have found themselves in relatively powerful positions, with substantial budgets and a role in strategic decisions. But these have been rare moments. When the external environment has been stable and predictable, personnel management has usually been low man—or woman—on the corporate totem pole.

Why have U.S. personnel managers as a group historically been so weak within corporate management, especially as compared to personnel managers in Japan? First, they deal with qualitative (or "soft") problems in a business culture dominated by those who think in quantitative terms. Second, managers in that field have never developed an intellectually consistent paradigm, despite the ready availability of models they might work from. They constitute a semi-profession, at best, in a world in which other business-oriented specialties—in engineering and accountancy, for example—have stronger professional identities, paradigms that are more coherent, and, consequently, greater claims to internal authority. In Japan, by contrast, everything is not done by the numbers. Also, Japanese business professionalism is relatively weak; managers usually do not spend a lifetime in any one specialty, so their expertise is well-rounded but firm-specific. Third, in their employment practices—job tenure is shorter, there is less training, and so forth—U.S. companies historically have been more market-oriented than Japanese companies and so have had less need for administrative rules and procedures to organize employment.

Finally, U.S. personnel managers derive their status in part from the status of employees inside the corporation. According to the prevailing interpretation of corporate governance, shareholders are the organization's principals, managers their agents, and employees a factor of production who are without the "stakeholder" claims enjoyed by Japanese *kaishain* (literally "company member," although usually translated as "full-time employee"). This has the effect of relegating employees to a low official position and of dragging personnel managers down with them. As we will see, though, the primacy of shareholders has itself sometimes been challenged, both by unions and by managers, and such episodes have been associated with an accretion of power for personnel managers.

THE EARLY YEARS

In the late nineteenth century, when the United States was emerging as an industrial society, companies, even large ones, rarely adopted a systematic program for managing their employees. Most were content to leave daily production and employment decisions in the hands of their first-line supervisors—their foremen—and sometimes even contracted out to them all managerial responsibilities for a given operation or department. But as technologies and organizations grew more complex, this decentralized approach created problems. The flow of production was hindered by a lack of coordination between various departments, and data on costs were not kept or were gathered irregularly. The result was that firms found it difficult to increase throughput speed—the key, as historian Alfred D. Chandler has argued, to corporate growth and to mass production and distribution.[2]

Between 1880 and 1920, the systematic-management movement (of which Frederick Taylor's scientific management was one strand) began to introduce new methods of coordination and control to industry, systems whereby foremen and skilled workers were told how to schedule production and the order in which to perform operations. The new systems included cost accounting and the creation of staff departments to handle technical and administrative duties, but by and large they left untouched the foreman's control over the hiring, firing, and payment of workers.[3]

The foreman did suffer, however, two incursions into his empire. First, industrial engineers introduced various incentive-wage schemes that, it was hoped, would boost productivity and thereby raise wages sufficiently to squelch any incipient labor unrest. Second, some companies took the hallmarks of the industrial engineers' approach to production—orderly proce-

dures, accurate records, and the departmentalization of routinized functions—and applied them to their hiring practices. They created so-called
employment departments, which interviewed prospective employees, kept
track of "problem" workers, and assigned new hires to departments where
they were needed. One of the earliest of these departments was established at
Goodyear in 1900.[4]

The late nineteenth and early twentieth centuries were an era of recurring
political and labor unrest, both in the United States and in Europe. In the
United States, socialist and anarchist ideas gained currency among not only
immigrants but also native workers and farmers. Craft unions periodically engaged in bitter disputes with employers; unorganized workers sometimes went
on strike or simply quit their jobs in search of better ones. Labor turnover
rates, already extremely high by modern standards, were exacerbated by the
foreman's readiness to hire and fire. In their search for ways to ameliorate
these problems, middle-class reformers were inspired by religious and secular
ideas of "uplift" and by the legislative experiments being tried out in Europe.[5]

Many companies began to practice what came to be known as "welfare
work," which ran the gamut from pecuniary incentives, such as profit sharing,
pension, and stock bonus plans, to programs aimed more directly at the worker's character, such as thrift clubs, citizenship instruction, company recreational activities, company housing, and company medical facilities. To run
these programs, employers hired specialized welfare workers who had backgrounds in social work, settlement work, journalism, and the ministry. As they
sought to exert greater influence in the companies that employed them, welfare workers at an early stage began to professionalize their activities through
the American Institute for Social Service, the National Civic Federation, and
similar organizations.[6]

Welfare workers were rarely involved in daily employment decisions about
the hiring, firing, and payment of employees. Their focus was on the employee's life outside work and particularly his life at home. At Ford Motor and
other companies, welfare workers practiced "home visiting." They went to the
employee's residence to check up on illnesses, offer advice on hygiene and
housekeeping, and extend a bit of familial warmth from an otherwise imper-
sonal corporation. While nearly all executives and managers during this
period were men, it was not uncommon for welfare workers to be women,
partly because they ministered to young workers or to other females and partly
because welfare work (like social work) was regarded as a low-status, "helping"
profession.[7]

Thus the various strands that would make up the personnel management
movement were woven together on the eve of America's entry into the First
World War. The emphasis on efficiency, administrative specialization, and
uplift caused the recognition among America's large and mid-sized companies
that they needed to pay more attention to how they managed their employees.

The movement operated on the belief that the hiring of specialized, educated employees to administer the workplace would humanize industry and usher in a more enlightened era. Prior to the war, though, only a minority of firms acted on that belief. The vast majority maintained traditional methods of workforce management. Labor was cheap and readily available, and foremen would complain about having to take orders from soft-handed college graduates. Consequently, most large companies lacked personnel departments. Ironically, though welfare workers saw themselves as employee advocates, employees resented them for their intrusiveness and for what they reflected of their employers' paternalism.

As labor markets tightened after 1915, employers were confronted with a host of problems that, while not entirely new, were of such magnitude as to cause them to reconsider their reliance on traditional methods of employment management. Unemployment rates fell to the lowest levels since the 1880s. Turnover rates skyrocketed. Meanwhile, strikes had become commonplace, along with government efforts to prevent them. Labor unrest was widespread, and productivity sank. Each of these factors—labor shortages, labor unrest, and government regulation—in itself was sufficient during later years to compel employers to establish new personnel departments or to boost the status and resources of those departments already in existence. What made the labor markets during the war period remarkable was the confluence and intensity of these factors.

The period from 1916 to 1920 witnessed a veritable "personnel boom" as companies rushed to create personnel departments that would help them recruit and retain workers, maintain labor peace, and comply with government regulations. Of firms with more than 250 employees, the proportion that had personnel departments increased between 1915 and 1920, from roughly 5 percent to about 25 percent. This rapid growth led to the creation of a new occupation almost overnight. Five hundred persons attended the first national conference of personnel managers, held in 1917; in 1920, at another conference, nearly three thousand were present. The previous work experience of these new managers was diverse. Some were former social workers or educators, but most already had backgrounds in industry—as welfare workers, safety experts, salespersons, and attorneys. Inevitably, personnel managers found themselves engaged in turf disputes with line managers, especially foremen, and with industrial engineers and production officials who, being reluctant to change traditional methods, were quick to blame personnel managers for driving up costs and for being too "soft" in dealings with employees. Personnel managers responded by forming professional organizations to bolster their status. These included the National Association of Employment Managers, which after several name changes became the American Management Association in 1923.[8]

Despite the resistance they encountered, the new personnel managers made substantial inroads into the foreman's domain. Their biggest advances included the adoption of central hiring offices, rules (which usually required the personnel manager's participation) for disciplining and dismissing workers, record-keeping of employment and wages, and more systematic approaches to training, performance evaluation, and promotion. Some companies introduced formal job analysis to aid in employee selection and to rationalize the hodgepodge of wage rates that was liable to have developed over time. A few hundred firms established their own employee-representation plans; others were compelled to do so by the War Labor Board and other government agencies. As a result of these reforms, companies found themselves better able to retain employees, control costs, and raise employee morale. Workers came to feel more attached to the companies that employed them; their jobs began to look more like careers. The potential for labor unrest diminished as the most egregious workplace problems were removed and many of the unions' own protective structures were replicated within the firm.

WELFARE CAPITALISM

During these tumultuous years, some large employers felt the need to shape the course of events more decisively and to set an appropriate direction for the personnel movement to follow. One result was the formation of the National Industrial Conference Board in 1916, an effort led by Magnus W. Alexander of General Electric (he was among the first to demonstrate the existence and costliness of labor turnover). Another was the creation in 1919 of the Special Conference Committee (SCC), made up of executives—CEOs and personnel managers—from ten of America's leading industrial corporations.[9]

The SCC had strong ties to the Rockefeller interests. (Clarence J. Hicks was the SCC's chairman from 1919 to 1933, during which time he also headed the personnel department at Standard Oil of New Jersey.) Early on it adopted a set of principles based on the belief of John D. Rockefeller Jr. that "the only solidarity natural in industry is the solidarity which unites all those in the same business establishment."[10] Each of the SCC companies had employee representation plans intended as a corporatist alternative to craft and industrial unions. The firms also were leaders in the introduction of pecuniary welfare benefits—pension plans, paid vacations, health insurance, profit sharing—that were seen as a less paternalistic alternative to traditional welfare work. Finally, the SCC companies all had personnel departments which ensured that employees not only had steady jobs but also received similar pay for similar work and reasonably fair treatment from their supervisors.

The SCC emphasized that the job of the personnel manager was to supply tools for line managers to use. It wanted the personnel movement to detach itself from the idea, which was popular among the movement's liberals, that the personnel manager was an independent professional who could overrule line managers in favor of employees. The SCC was in favor of power being returned to foremen but also of their being trained to use it. This reflected a desire to curtail what were considered excesses of the wartime period and to find a means of managing increasingly decentralized companies. Employee representation, welfare benefits, career jobs, foreman training, and pure staff-type personnel administration—the combination of these characteristics defined the standard that large progressive companies aspired to achieve.[11]

Most employers of the 1920s, however, failed to follow the example set by the SCC. After the war, the same forces that had fostered the formation of personnel departments went into reverse: Labor markets softened, labor unrest subsided, and government unwound its wartime regulations. Companies that had added personnel departments and adopted various reforms as a temporary expedient now cut their budgets and let their programs lapse. Others, which had resisted the trend toward personnel reforms, felt little pressure now, in the changed atmosphere of the 1920s, to reconsider them. By 1929, about 40 percent of industrial firms employing more than a thousand workers had personnel departments, many of which, however, were considerably less powerful than their wartime counterparts. While personnel managers tried to defend their budgets by citing hard data such as figures on labor turnover and its attendant costs, their arguments fell on deaf ears.

THE TURBULENT YEARS

Passage of the National Industrial Recovery Act (NIRA) set in motion a chain of events that brought government back to the labor market and rejuvenated the labor movement. Although unemployment remained high, the other two conditions (labor unrest and government regulation) for personnel formalization were in place, and the result was another boom for personnel management. The proportion of firms with personnel departments expanded dramatically between 1933 and 1936, as during the First World War. To bolster employee morale and forestall unionization, personnel departments moved aggressively to shrink the foreman's discretion, making labor allocation (hiring, promotion, layoffs, dismissals) subject to definite rules and procedures. Companies dusted off their foreman-training programs as a first line of defense against unions. Several hundred large firms also established company unions.[12]

None of these moves was sufficient to halt the tide of union organizing or a flurry of new labor-market regulations. Nearly 5 million workers joined unions between 1936 and 1939, notably in mass-production industries that previously had been nonunion strongholds. The Social Security Act brought government into competition with private welfare capitalism, although a place for private provision was carved out by insurance companies and well-placed managers such as Marion Folsom of Kodak. Still, the events of the 1930s called into question large parts of the welfare-capitalist agenda.[13]

The one part of the agenda to remain vital was the professional administration of corporate labor practices. Now a renewed importance was accorded to personnel managers, experts capable of designing employment policies that complied with new government regulations and also of negotiating with unions or of preempting union organizing. Under pressure from unions and from workers concerned about security, corporate personnel departments further formalized procedures for hiring, promotion, and layoff. Unions, or the threat of them, led personnel departments to develop conduct codes and publish handbooks in an effort to codify personnel procedures. It was also in response to unions that companies adopted definite procedures for discipline and dismissal, and personnel departments came to play a larger role in the disciplinary process.[14]

The Second World War saw government take an active role in coordinating the labor market, as in the previous war. One of the government's objectives was to prevent strikes from disrupting vital war industries. During the war, unions were more powerful than ever and added another 5 million members to their rolls. Now all three factors (labor shortages, labor unrest, and government regulation) favorable to the growth of the personnel function were in play, and the resulting growth was remarkable. Small and medium-sized firms that had never had personnel departments instituted them, while the status and size of the departments in larger companies reached an all-time high. Foremen were herded into training programs subsidized by the federal government, and what was left of the foreman's empire was brought under the control of centralized personnel departments. (Some foremen angrily protested by forming their own unions.) To gain control of pay structures for collective bargaining and to comply with federal wage controls, personnel departments embarked on a massive effort to establish job evaluation plans whereby they could rationalize pay structures. Because the War Labor Board allowed employers to circumvent wage controls through reasonable expenditures on fringe benefits, health and pension plans expanded by leaps and bounds during the war.[15]

The Golden Years

The end of the Second World War led to reductions in the budgets of personnel departments, but the cuts were small compared to those twenty-five years earlier. Why? Employment had become more organization-oriented during the previous years. Male employees now spent substantial amounts of time with their employer—job tenure was higher than at the turn of the century—and this required specialized staff to administer training, pay, and benefit systems. Also, unions were entrenched in manufacturing, transportation, regulated utilities, and other industrial sectors. Government, meanwhile, had become a permanent fixture in the labor market, through its activities to supervise union-management relations, restrain wage inflation, and regulate the provision of pensions and health insurance. To deal with unions and comply with regulations, a company now had to rely on a bevy of technical experts.[16]

Finally, American businessmen recognized the importance of being perceived as socially responsible in an era when unions and government were steadily chipping away at management's prerogatives. The public's infatuation with business was not what it had been in the 1920s. A "good" employer was now one who treated employees as members of the enterprise and provided them with economic security and fair treatment. The adoption of progressive employment practices was made easier by the separation of ownership from control, a phenomenon first explored by economists Berle and Means in the early 1930s. Professional managers had taken control of large companies and now had substantial discretion to run them as they saw fit.[17]

The American Business Creed, the classic study from the 1950s, gives striking expression to a managerial philosophy that would be considered heretical today. "Corporation managers," the authors observed,

> generally claim that they have four broad responsibilities: to consumers, to employees, to stockholders, and to the general public. . . . each group is on an equal footing; the function of management is to secure justice for all and unconditional maxima for none. Stockholders have no special priority; they are entitled to a fair return on their investment, but profits above a "fair" level are an economic sin.

While labor scholars usually think of "management rights" as prerogatives invoked by management as it tried to defend against union encroachments, for managers in the early years after the Second World War the term had another meaning: It also referred to managerial autonomy in the sense of immunity from shareholder pressure. Thus *'management rights'* was defined in *The American Business Creed* as "a sphere of unhampered discretion and authority which is not merely derivative from the property rights of owners." Management rights included the authority to plow profits back into the enterprise, a practice that the National Association of Manufacturers defended as "the way the American system works." Apportioning profits between dividends and retained earnings—and other claims on corporate resources—was seen in those days as "one aspect of the general function of balancing competing economic interests which devolve on corporate management."[18]

This philosophy continued to hold sway during the 1960s and 1970s. According to Gordon Donaldson, the typical mind-set of senior management in those years was an introverted corporate view . . . focused on growth, diversification and opportunity for the "corporate family." . . . It was a period when the social and legal climate encouraged management to adopt a pluralistic view of their responsibility to the various corporate constituencies. As career employees themselves, it was natural for management to identify with all constituents who were long-term investors in the enterprise and to view shareholders in the same light.[19]

As corporations took seriously their responsibilities as "good" employers, the personnel manager's status in the organization was boosted in the process. Companies aligned or combined their personnel departments and their public relations departments; both were aimed at what were now perceived as "stakeholders" in the corporation. The treating of employees as stakeholders did not put them on a par with shareholders, to be sure, but it invested them with a definite status in the corporate family. Employment was construed as a quasi-permanent relationship that endured through bad times and good. Benefits and other emoluments served to underscore management's common interests with employees. "'Loyalty,'" according to Donaldson, "was the key word — commitment to the success of the enterprise within which each constituent found economic and social fulfillment." Employment in the United States never became as organization-oriented as in Japan, but career-type jobs did become prevalent, and personnel managers were in charge of administering vast internal (corporate) labor markets.[20]

Another development of the postwar era was the growing importance of psychology to personnel management. Before the war, selection tests, attitude surveys, and other psychological techniques were used by only a handful of companies, chiefly as a guide in executive selection and for studying employee morale. Pioneering companies, notably AT&T and Western Electric, conducted large-scale studies of employee attitudes, as in the Hawthorne experiments run by Harvard anthropologist Elton Mayo. Mayo's ideas about "human relations," as his followers dubbed them, represented a break from the reliance on economic incentives and administrative processes that had characterized personnel management prior to the 1930s. The Mayoites argued that managers should pay greater attention to the worker's psyche and to his personal relationships at work — especially the relationship between employee and supervisor — and worry less about pay and perquisites. During the war, the government's Training Within Industry (TWI) program used Mayo's ideas to teach nearly half a million foremen how to motivate their employees. After the war, many behavioral scientists went to work in the private sector, either as management consultants or as corporate staff, a development that never took root in Japan.[21]

The impact of the behavioral sciences on personnel management continued to be felt into the 1960s and 1970s. Research on employee motivation was applied to compensation and work restructuring. Out of this came ideas like "vertical job leading," which showed how routine jobs could be made more interesting while at the same time eliminating supervisory positions. The most sophisticated techniques borrowed from the behavioral sciences were directed at managerial and professional employees. These included sensitivity training (for bolstering psychological acuity among managers) and the managerial grid (to help managers balance "people" and "production" problems). Personnel managers spearheaded corporate involvement with the behavioral sciences, whose academic stature they used to legitimate greater spending on training and organization-development (OD) programs.[22]

In the postwar decades, personnel management came to involve a distinction between "labor relations" and "employee relations," and the gap between them widened over time. Labor relations was the province of specialists concerned with collective bargaining and contract administration, while employee relations encompassed all other aspects of the employee-company relationship. Labor relations departments were found only in unionized firms, and already in the mid-1950s the percentage of the U.S. workforce they employed had stopped growing. As union organizing slowed and industrial relations matured, becoming more orderly and predictable, the importance of labor relations as an aspect of personnel management declined.

Employee relations departments were where the idea of applying psychology and the behavioral sciences took hold. At General Motors, for example, the first of the Big Three automobile manufacturers to develop a coherent industrial-relations strategy after the war, personnel management was Janus-faced: The unions faced a tough adversary in bargaining, while employees saw a kinder, gentler GM through the employee relations department. The department was in charge of, among other projects, conducting attitude surveys at GM plants around the country. In the late 1940s it also administered a contest in which workers wrote essays on "My Job and Why I Like It." GM invited Paul Lazarsfeld, an eminent survey researcher at Columbia University, to analyze the data. It also hired Opinion Research Corporation to find out what GM employees thought of the contest.[23]

For nonunion employees, the employee relations department often functioned as a third force between them and line management, mediating disputes and insisting that supervisors give workers the benefit of the doubt. A member of the personnel staff would serve as the employee's representative either informally or under a formal complaint system. That kind of employee advocacy was a throwback to the early days of personnel management. For unorganized blue-collar employees, a complaint system functioned somewhat like a grievance procedure in the union sector and reduced the appeal that a union might have. The systems also were a means of resolving disputes without the costs associated with quits or dismissals.[24]

Even in heavily unionized companies, labor relations by the 1960s no longer was the primary element in personnel management. A study of large companies found that union-management relations was the dominant person-nel activity in only 7 percent of surveyed companies; 55 percent did not even consider it important. Personnel units reported that they were focusing much more on management development, employee benefits, training, and com-munications. It is interesting that companies attributed this shift in activities not only to the stabilization of labor relations but also to the growth of internal markets for white-collar employees. Companies had "overwhelmingly decided that going outside the company to fill vacant managerial positions is unsatis-factory. Instead they staff from within wherever possible . . . [and this requires] monetary and other incentives for good men to come into and remain with the company, developing men for the future needs of the company, and setting up more efficient systems of inter-unit promotion and transfer."[25]

The 1950s and 1960s were the era of the "organization man," when U.S. companies were vastly expanding their middle-management ranks. Mean-while, they were also building up their overseas operations and becoming increasingly multinational as they moved decisively toward a decentralized, multidivisional corporate structure (the M-form), in which a headquarters unit oversaw the allocation of capital to semiautonomous divisions.[26] With these changes came the creation of new headquarters personnel units alongside divisional and plant units; more than half the headquarters units in existence in the mid-1960s were less than twenty years old. Headquarters personnel concerned itself primarily with companywide policy and with managing exec-utive careers. During the 1960s, despite corporate decentralization, headquar-ters personnel staff grew more rapidly than the company as a whole. Most corporate personnel departments were adding activities, and the vast majority felt that the importance of their unit inside the organization was rising.[27]

Yet even at the highest levels of the organization, where, as personnel execu-tives reported, their influence had increased, events were occurring that did not bode well for headquarters personnel.[28] The spread of the M-form struc-ture brought with it the elevation of the corporate finance function. To mod-ern financial managers, the firm is a collection of assets. Financial tools are used to judge the performance of divisions and units, which are bought and sold to diversify risk and/or improve overall share returns. During the 1960s, mergers and acquisitions rose sharply as more firms adopted the finance ap-proach, some of them taking it to its logical conclusion: the conglomerate model of unrelated diversification. Increasingly, CEOs and presidents came not from the operating side but from finance. For financial managers, quanti-tative indicators were paramount but often were not available in the personnel area (and when they were, as with pension plans, financial managers contested with personnel managers for control).

Not surprisingly, personnel executives in the early 1960s reported more conflict with the finance department than with any other functional unit. From their perspective, the problem was that "in top management about the only thing that counts is finance." Among other senior managers, including those in finance, the personnel function was perceived as little more than "the administration of routine, maintenance, housekeeping tasks." It was criticized for being "not a risk taker" and "not business oriented." The latter accusation was not so wide of the mark. As companies became more finance-oriented and numbers-driven, personnel managers, even at the senior level, found themselves intellectually unprepared for the brave new world that corporations were entering.[29]

THE 1970s

Just when personnel managers appeared to be in trouble, several events intervened to give them a reprieve. First, the stock market began to drop in 1969, taking the wind out of the sails of CFOs and deflating their obsession with mergers, acquisitions, and conglomerations. Second, the so-called Lordstown Syndrome, or "blue-collar blues," provoked mounting concern about worker dissatisfaction. Third, companies faced increased incentives to open nonunion facilities. Finally, government regulation of the workplace proliferated along various dimensions.

Lordstown, Ohio, was the site of a celebrated strike in 1971 by young, well-educated workers in a General Motors assembly plant. They were well paid but unhappy with the rote and mechanical nature of their jobs. The strike led to a new concern with the quality of working life (QWL) and to a slew of work-enrichment "experiments," in both unionized and nonunion settings. The experiments included reorganization of tasks and technology, formation of self-directed work teams, and joint problem-solving groups. Many of these practices were based on ideas borrowed from Japan as well as Sweden. At the same time, companies were introducing related changes to management, seeking to improve communication among managers and between managers and their subordinates.[30]

These efforts caused the personnel function at corporate headquarters to acquire new professional staff that included industrial and organizational psychologists. As a result of these new hires, it developed expertise in planned organizational change and in communications. Links to university-based researchers, first established in the human-relations era, were multiplied and became commonplace. In parallel with corporate developments, the academic study of organization behavior (OB), the successor to human relations, enjoyed new funding and prestige in the 1970s. As headquarters staff expanded, however, so did the duties of line managers, who were considered a crucial element in making work reform successful. Indeed, the most innovative companies were those in which line managers had control over personnel decisions. Increasingly left out of the picture were divisional and plant person-nel departments.[31]

Several of the more advanced work-reform experiments took place in new nonunion plants—the General Foods pet-food factory in Topeka, Kansas, is an example—in part because it was easier to introduce work reform in a green-field setting, where neither workers nor first-line supervisors had traditional attitudes and ways of doing things. Another explanation is simply that compa-nies in the 1970s sought to deal with a widening union-nonunion pay gap by stepping up the pace of their union-avoidance activities such that the supply of new nonunion plants increased steadily over the decade. The innovative approach to work organization made these plants harder for unions to crack.[32]

The new emphasis on building and maintaining nonunion workplaces had several consequences for personnel managers. It further widened the divide between labor relations and employee relations: Labor relations became less centralized and lost prestige, while employee relations, which was now begin-ning to be known as human resources, gained responsibility for union-avoid-ance activities as well as for management development and other executive endeavors. Line managers became increasingly involved in union avoidance and work reform, again at the expense of unit personnel departments. Now that the key players were line managers and corporate (headquarters) HR units, friction between them increased. Line managers felt that "headquarters" was preoccupied, as in earlier eras, with the effort to ensure that "locals" com-mitted no gaffes that might entice a union to the company's facilities. Mean-while, the importance of unions, and of the threat of them, was gradually fading.[33]

On another front, though, was the myriad of new government regulations that had cropped up, and the task of complying with them was time-consum-ing. Beginning with the Manpower Development and Training Act of 1962, the federal government kept up a steady pace of regulatory innovation the likes of which had not been seen since the 1940s: the Equal Pay Act (1963), Civil Rights Act (1964), Economic Opportunity Act (1964), Occupational Safety and Health Act (1970), Equal Employment Opportunity Act (1972), Comprehensive Employment and Training Act (1973), and various executive orders, including one that established the Office of Federal Contract Compli-ance Programs.[34]

Predictably, regulation had a centralizing effect, as headquarters personnel departments took responsibility for record-keeping and the design of systems for ensuring compliance. A survey of major corporations in the mid-1970s found that the most important change in personnel activity during the preced-ing ten years was the advent of EEO and occupational-safety laws and the protocols for complying with them, much of this activity being concentrated at corporate headquarters. "Centralization," according to the report, "is the term executives and managers most often use to describe the developing trends in the organization of the personnel function. By greater centralization they mean the substantial new constraints they feel when hiring, firing, disciplining, directing, training, promoting and compensating subordinates." Lawsuits and negative publicity being a constant risk, CEOs and company presidents felt it necessary to involve themselves in many of the company's employment practices, and one result was closer contact between senior management and the corporate HR function. The net effect of the regulatory changes of the 1960s and 1970s was "an end to the 20-year trend of increasing delegation of authority over personnel matters to local [line] managers."[35]

CRISIS: THE 1980S AND 1990S

In the early 1980s, the pendulum began to swing in the other direction: HR departments shrank and lost influence in corporate affairs. All of the factors that in the earlier decades had bolstered HR's role inside the corporation now turned negative. Deregulation of transportation, communication, and other industries was initiated under President Jimmy Carter and accelerated during the Reagan years. While the employment relationship remained enmeshed in statutory complexity, federal oversight was now less rigorous. For employers, the sense of urgency about compliance faded, and that weakened HR's claim to resources it had commanded in the 1970s. Second, the strength of unions steadily declined in the 1980s and 1990s as they engaged in concession bargaining and their private-sector membership continued to fall.[36] Third, labor markets were loose. To extinguish inflation, the Federal Reserve Bank kept interest rates high for most of the 1980s and early 1990s, and that raised unemployment. Monetary stringency in the 1980s combined with increased international competition and deregulation to produce a wave of permanent job losses, which were concentrated among blue-collar workers.[37]

The 1980s and 1990s also saw a transformation of corporate governance. This was evidenced by the increased number of hostile takeovers, which were facilitated by new instruments like junk bonds. Shareholders—especially pension plans, mutual funds, and other large institutions—began to assert more aggressively their status as the corporation's sole residual claimants. Finding it now more difficult to unload their swelling equity holdings, they turned to "voice" to boost performance of their portfolios. Institutional investors also were impelled by new securities laws requiring them to disclose financial results, and thus felt pressure to seek higher returns. At the same time, corporate boards grew more assertive, seeking to hire CEOs—often from the outside—who would give allegiance to shareholders, and incentivizing them to do so through lavish stock options. Gone was the idea of balancing stakeholder interests. Not quite gone but definitely less prevalent were CEOs who had worked their way up the ranks, building loyalty to customers and fellow employees along the way.[38]

As the power balance swung, corporations found themselves having to assume greater risk in order to crank out higher returns for investors, and so sometimes they resorted to divestment of unrelated businesses. As in Japan, a firm's diversified businesses served as a hedge against risk and protected jobs and profits from cyclical and other business swings. Now shareholders insisted on higher returns—with the threat of a hostile takeover if returns did not improve. To raise performance, more risk was transferred to employees, who found the stability of their jobs and compensation growing ever more fragile.[39]

Another response to the new, shareholder-dominated environment was for firms to "reengineer" operations so as to squeeze more effort out of a smaller number of employees. Companies looking to downsize further began to focus on the managerial ranks, who had been largely immune to downsizing in the early 1980s. A sharp decline in aggregate job stability in the late 1980s and early 1990s occurred among long-tenure males in managerial occupations. Companies that had once prided themselves on offering long-term jobs and good benefits—Kodak, Digital Equipment (DEC), IBM—now sacked thousands and shredded the implicit lifetime-career contracts they had kept with their middle managers.[40]

Because HR's share of resources was partly based on headcount, job cuts throughout the corporation were devastating to the HR budget. The cuts were accompanied by a draconian contraction of training and development programs that had been designed to build firm-specific skills and to groom junior and middle managers for higher positions in the organization. HR units suffered also from a general trend toward shrinkage of corporate headquarters, as headquarters jobs in HR and in other functions were eliminated—a cost-cutting measure facilitated by decentralization and divestment.[41]

The link between corporate governance and employment relations also reflected the advancing myopia of management decision-making, that is, its focus on short-term decisions and performance measures. In the 1980s and 1990s, the turnover rate for stock rose—that is, the average amount of time a share was held fell. A variety of innovations, including discount brokerages and the Internet, induced individual investors to enter the market, trade rapidly and cheaply, and speculate on short-term price movements. With investor discount preferences working against long-term projects, one would expect to see managers adopt polices that promised a quicker payoff and that were more flexible, not only in capital projects but in other spheres of the firm as well.[42]

That, in fact, is precisely what happened with respect to employment. To a growing extent, pay and career policies emphasized short-term (market) criteria over such long-term (organization-oriented) criteria as the acquisition of firm-specific skills. Reliance on part-timers, temporary-help workers, independent contractors, and other flexible employees grew rapidly. Compensation came to depend more heavily on market criteria than on the acquisition of firm-specific knowledge and other internal organizational factors. The shift to a market orientation meant greater authority for line managers, who were closest to market signals, and less power for HR executives, who traditionally had concerned themselves with long-term, organization-wide decisions.[43]

As equity prices became the key driver of corporate decisions, CFOs rose to greater prominence within firms. Whereas in the 1960s CFOs tended to have backgrounds in accounting, now they were more likely to have been trained as MBAs and to be more creative with numbers rather than respectful of them. CFOs began to occupy the same turf—executive compensation, for example—that HR executives claimed for themselves. The growth of stock options in the 1980s and 1990s was phenomenal. Fewer than a third of CEOs received options in 1980; fifteen years later, nearly all did. During that period, the share of CEO pay deriving from options rose steadily, eventually overtaking base salary as the largest single component of executive compensation. A growing share of the compensation of many others on the company payroll, not just of CFOs, also was tied to options. HR executives often lacked the expertise that CFOs had in the designing of options packages. That had the effect of elevating CFOs over HR executives not only with respect to compensation decisions but also in the area of executive recruiting. Another area where turf conflicts took place was employee benefits. Benefits administration increasingly was in the hands of managers who had backgrounds in finance rather than human resources. A recent study finds that this shift had real consequences for corporate health-care provision: Benefits executives with a background in finance tend to be more cost-oriented and less concerned with employee morale than those with a traditional HR background.[44]

Accompanying changes in corporate governance was a host of new pressures arising from the more competitive environment of the 1980s and 1990s. Global rivalry heated up, including America's competition with Europe and Japan, while within the United States the entry of new companies was facilitated by venture capital and by technological change, particularly the personal computer and the Internet. As markets grew more competitive, product life cycles became shorter, putting a premium on speed—of decision making, product development, and business execution. The restructuring of corporations—through delayering, decentralization, and employee participation—was intended in part to make corporate bureaucracies less cumbersome. Sociologist Rosabeth Moss Kanter described it as "when giants learn to dance."[45]

While decentralization was partly a cost-cutting move, intended to shrink the size of what were now said to be bloated headquarters, it was also a way to differentiate corporate policies and thereby fit units more closely to the needs of changing and increasingly diverse markets. To achieve those ends, unit managers became more involved in hiring, evaluating, and paying their employees. Facilitating decentralization was the availability of computing power throughout the organization, allowing companies to put many of their HR systems, from recruitment through retirement, online. Power shifted from HR departments to line managers also as a result of broad-based efforts to improve product and service quality through employee involvement in business decisions. These efforts were led by line managers, not by HR staff, and that created or reinforced the perception that HR was irrelevant to operating issues. Instead of HR providing programs to line managers, the line managers were designing and executing them themselves.[46]

One of the most unsettling changes for HR was the outsourcing of HR responsibilities. Recruiting, training, compensation, outplacement—all were put up for bid to companies specializing in human resource management. In some instances, companies outsourced their entire HR function to a third party. As in Japan, outsourcing was driven partly by the desire to reduce internal headcount, which impressed investors, even when total expenses were not reduced very much. There was also a belief that the old approach—customizing HR to fit the company's idiosyncrasies and thereby deriving a business advantage—was not worth the expense because of the perception that competitive advantage increasingly depended on having low and flexible labor costs. It was thought to be cheaper and reasonably effective to go instead with the generic services offered by a third party.[47]

For HR executives, these changes were, to put it mildly, a shock to the system, affecting each of the three main roles HR departments traditionally had played: first, provider of services to career employees (benefits, training, and development, for example); second, supplier of programs to, and monitor of, line managers; and third, advocate of employee interests to senior executives and line managers. In that third role HR had stood squarely between employees and their supervisors. Now, all three roles were called into question. In the end, the size of HR staffs was reduced substantially.[48]

Corporate restructuring and tighter alignment with Wall Street created an identity crisis for HR managers. The financial approach to management meant that more and more operating decisions were based on short-term, quantifiable criteria. The age-old problem for HR programs, of course, is that the costs are quantifiable in the short term but the benefits are not. For example, the development of senior managers inside a large multinational company can take ten to fifteen years. Now employees were being viewed as costs, not assets, and line managers were assuming ever greater control.

HR managers faced a choice. They could buck the corporate trend, insist on the virtues of "employee-centered" HR policies, continue to emphasize the asset approach and the long term, and persist in being employee advocates. Or they could shift their ground, adopt a more hard-headed style, and aim to be seen as business partners with line management and strategic partners with finance, marketing, and production. For those HR managers who wanted to keep their jobs, the decision was a no-brainer. As one HR manager said, "Our role has dramatically changed from pacifying disgruntled employees to consulting with internal customers. We have moved from being focused solely on employees to a business orientation. Being here primarily to support the business is a fundamental mindset change."[49]

In theory, the new, business partner approach means that senior HR executives are more involved in business-strategy formulation at the top of the company and in the design of policies aligned to that strategy. Evidence of their new status is the growing number of HR executives who report to the CEO and participate in decisions about mergers and acquisitions, joint ventures, and other key moves. Among the most "strategic" of HR's responsibilities cited by enthusiasts of the new approach is the lead role HR plays (although, in fact, it already has been doing that for some time) in executive recruitment and promotion.[50]

In actual practice, the new approach doesn't always live up to its promise, partly because HR executives lack technical expertise and partly because they continue to be viewed as minor-league players in the executive suite. Hence HR executives find themselves shut out of the early stage of key decisions at the corporate level. HR executives tend to be least involved in finance-oriented, predator-acquirer companies, the sort that became more prevalent in the 1980s. Yet these are precisely the companies in which deals often unravel because of employee departures or clashing corporate cultures. As for tying HR to strategy, another study suggests that what links there are run from business strategy to HR policy—that HR is reactive, in other words, and does not shape corporate strategy but is driven by it. Moreover, the links are rather mundane stuff, such as adding business goals to an individual's performance criteria.[51]

Another aspect of the new HR involves decentralization, which means less authority for central HR units. Unfortunately, this leaves line managers free to do a mediocre job of supervising employees. Research shows that line managers lack the skill sets that would make them effective supervisors. They are strong at putting technical expertise to practical use and at getting things done for customers. But they are deficient as team builders and weak in selecting and motivating employees. Those are areas in which HR professionals have much to contribute, of course. The attitude of many line managers, though, is "Don't call us, we'll call you," and the phone never rings. Lacking legitimation from government, tight labor markets, or other external sources, HR is losing leverage with line managers. One report noted that "HR finds itself facing a crisis of confidence and credibility with line managers and business people."[52]

By taking the business-partner approach, HR does align itself with the dominant mind-set inside companies. As one senior HR manager said, "We want to show we are not the soft-hearted (or soft-headed) personnel directors of yore, whose only mission seemed to be making sure forms were filled out properly, taking care of the Christmas party, and sending baby gifts." However, having decided to be "harder" and more numbers-oriented, HR unwittingly sets itself up for further cuts, because the easiest figures to generate are those related to resource consumption. Moreover, the emphasis on *hard* implicitly lends credence to the cliché that there is nothing more to managing employees than a good pay-for-performance plan—precisely the formula that Frederick W. Taylor argued for back in the early years of the twentieth century! It is as if sixty years of research on the psychological and social complexities of managing employees had never occurred. Part of the blame lies with HR managers themselves. Many lack familiarity with research, and that leaves them vulnerable to outsourcing and consultants, and unable to persuasively articulate an intellectual rationale for HR.[53]

New Possibilities

In the late 1990s, it appeared that the pendulum was swinging back in HR's favor. From 1997 to 2000, the unemployment rate dropped sharply, reaching its lowest level since the 1960s. Managerial and skilled workers were in great demand. One headhunting agency reported that managers at companies announcing layoff plans often received several job offers before the layoffs occurred. Meanwhile, companies were luring new recruits with offers of traditional career opportunities. Employers dusted off and reintroduced old-style development and training programs intended to reassure managers and professionals of their prospects. Suddenly HR executives found themselves with more work and responsibility.

Although the economy began to cool in 2001 and labor shortages as a consequence disappeared, demographic pressures have not abated. The size of Generation X, the cohort behind the boomers, is relatively small. Current estimates are that the number of thirty-five to forty-four-year-olds will decline by 15 percent between 2000 and 2015. Moreover, the long-term rise in female labor-force participation is leveling off, while white-collar productivity gains remain modest. Hence labor shortages will be felt when the economy recovers.[54]

Also favorable to HR executives—and to employees—are a couple of recent shifts in corporate governance. First, in reaction to the hostile-takeover wave of the 1980s, approximately thirty states passed anti-takeover laws, which, along with a weaker junk-bond market, resulted in a slowdown in highly leveraged and hostile M&A activity in the 1990s.[55] The empirical evidence suggests that companies that are less exposed to hostile takeovers are more inclined to shift resources to employees. In states that enacted anti-takeover laws, companies pay higher annual wages, about 1 to 2 percent more each year. The interpretation is that executives who are less vulnerable to shareholder pressure are also less inclined to redistribute corporate rents from employees to shareholders. Of course, this is not pure altruism; the employees who benefit from pay increases include the incumbent executives themselves. Opposing them in this move are shareholders, who tend to be reluctant to share resources with other stakeholders or to plow funds back into the company in order to finance long-term expansion. Freed of the constraints induced by shareholder sovereignty, some managers in the 1990s shifted back in the direction of a stakeholder orientation.[56]

Second, even before the Enron implosion and corporate-governance scandals, critics were becoming more vocal about the shortcomings of shareholder sovereignty. The "irrational exuberance" of markets in the late 1990s made some economists uneasy about the claim that equity prices were a reliable indicator on which to base corporate decisions. Corporate financialization not only led to excessive short-termism, it also distorted executive incentives. Stock options, which sent executive salaries into the stratosphere, were criticized for driving a wedge between managers and shareholders—precisely the opposite of their original intent. The design of options—without indexing, reloadable, issued at the money—insured that executives would richly benefit from share-price movements unrelated to their own efforts.[57]

The mass layoffs and growing marketization of employment brought a raft of negative publicity. In 1996 the *New York Times* ran a series on "the downsizing of America." It was the longest continuous piece the *Times* had published since the Pentagon Papers in 1971. In the corporate world too, critics warned that the trend toward the expendability of employees had gone too far. Frederick Reichheld, the head of Bain & Company, a management-consulting firm, wrote a book devoted to his assertion that a stable workforce yields higher productivity, customer retention, and other benefits. He quoted the CEO of Rubbermaid as saying, "For the U.S. to compete really well in the world, we have to put more thought into our products. That's what we're really good at. What we're really bad at is handling people. When times get tough, we throw them away."[58]

In light of such criticism, some scholars and managers began to develop what is sometimes called the resource-based approach, an alternative framework for competitive strategy. The aim is to achieve competitive advantage through intellectual property, unique physical or human assets, and other inimitable resources that competitors do not possess. The resources could also include a distinctive corporate culture that supports innovation and rapid decision-making. Inimitable resources have the effect of shifting business thinking away from market factors—entry barriers, for example—toward internal factors that make a company distinctive. They also shift strategy away from purely financial considerations to those guided by practical considerations of competence. Companies cannot achieve synergy while treating business units as decentralized profit centers. Hence the resource-based approach calls for the organization to focus on one business or a few related ones; companies are assumed to do best when they stick to their knitting. This view implies a stronger role for corporate headquarters as coordinator of related, synergistic businesses.[59]

One reason for the rise of the resource-based approach to strategy is the growing importance of intellectual capital—and the relative decline of financial capital—as a source of corporate profits. Employers are becoming more dependent on skilled, creative, and technical employees. In the service industries that increasingly dominate the economy, intellectual capital is a company's chief competitive advantage.[60] As the head of HR at a software company puts it, "At 5 P.M. 95 percent of our assets walk out the door. We have to have an environment that makes them want to walk back in the door the next morning." Intangible assets are critical to competitive advantage in this new world. For that reason, career-type jobs remain prevalent in a variety of companies; the ties between employers and employees are looser than in the 1970s but far tighter than those that characterized the kind of hire-and-fire system seen at the beginning of the twentieth century.[61]

Another reason for the rise of a resource-based strategy—although it is no longer fashionable to say so—was the perception in the United States in the late 1980s that Japanese companies owed much of their success to their greater emphasis on firm-specific human capital, corporate culture, and other inimitable intangibles. Here we see a reverse flow, a kind of counter-convergence, whereby U.S. companies became more organization-oriented and more like those in Japan. Where these new strategies have been adopted, they have created important responsibilities for HR executives.

What kind of company adheres to the new approach? It tends to be willing to make long-term investments in its employees, including managers, whether through on-the-job learning or the formation of teams and other high-performance work practices. It is a company in which HR is both able to hold line managers accountable for HR-related outcomes and willing to defend employees against poor decisions made by those managers. The companywide culture tends to be strong, fostering employee morale, creativity, and commitment. To carry all this off requires an enhanced role for headquarters HR in several areas: recruitment and retention, organization culture and values, and the fitting of employment practices to business strategies.[62]

Research supports the assumption that an internally focused, resource-based approach can be profitable. Companies that combine employee participation, employee training, and employment stability exhibit high levels of productivity, and those with a strong corporate culture have better prospects for long-term economic performance. There is even evidence to suggest that, when companies emphasize the importance of multiple stakeholders—customers, shareholders, and employees—their performance exceeds that of companies whose focus is narrower, although one must treat these results with caution. Thus the resource-based approach is consistent with a stakeholder orientation. Conversely, downsizing is not associated with improved productivity or sustained share-price performance, although shareholders often applaud its short-term benefits.[63]

Beyond the small number of U.S. companies with employee ownership, however, a full-blown stakeholder approach remains rare.[64] And it is unclear just how prevalent the resource-based approach is, despite the examples of A.G. Edwards, Lincoln Electric, SAS Institute (which is privately held), and other highly visible companies. HR's history in the United States shows that internal factors have never been particularly successful at securing the profession's status and power. It is only when the environment is uncertain—when labor shortages, unions, or government are a problem—that HR is able to garner extra resources and a more influential voice in the affairs of the corporation. In that sense, HR can be said to align itself with the financial-quantitative ethos, using costs to legitimate itself. But during less turbulent periods it has had difficulty securing and institutionalizing power.[65]

It is easy to blame HR's problems on others—on the dominance of a cost-driven, mass-production mind-set in the first half of the twentieth century or on the short-term, shareholder-driven orientation of more recent years. But HR's problems are partly of its own making. It does not have strong and consistent theories that would justify its expertise inside the corporation. It has made periodic attempts at professionalization, but they have backfired because the professionalism it aspired to was not based on scientific knowledge and certifiable skills or was associated with a lack of expertise in finance, marketing, accounting, and other key business areas.

■ ■ ■

At present, there are two contending routes to power for HR executives in the United States. The first is through the business-partner model, in which HR allies itself with finance and other functions in the executive suite and provides services on demand to decentralized operating units, while employment policies are driven by market considerations. Second, there is the resource-based approach, in which skilled employees are viewed as levers of competitive advantage, employment policy is relatively organization-oriented, and HR plays the role of securing strategic outcomes based on distinctive approaches to employment that are synchronized throughout the company.

As we have seen, neither route guarantees that HR executives will have the influence they desire. The business-partner model leaves HR with little to offer that cannot be supplied by consultants, contractors, or line managers. The resource-based approach bumps up against formidable barriers, ranging from managerial myopia to the dominance of financial criteria for judging returns on soft investments like employee training programs. Data showing that HR continues to occupy a subordinate niche in the executive suite constitute indirect evidence that neither route is leading to the expected destination. A greater proportion of women and minorities, whose overrepresentation in an occupation usually indicates that its status is low, are employed in HR than in other management specialties, as was true in the past. And HR executives are paid less than most other managers.[66]

In the following chapter we explore how these two alternatives are playing out inside U.S. companies. What is HR's role in formulating business strategy, and to what extent is business strategy based on HR considerations? How are HR executives and line managers carving up their responsibilities and relationships? What happens to headquarters HR inside companies where "markets"—the stock market and the labor market—drive corporate decision-making about human resources?

Inside U.S. Companies Today

Viewed from a distance, the U.S. corporate landscape appears to be dominated by shareholder-oriented companies whose employment practices are market-based and whose HR executives rank low in the managerial hierarchy. As in Japan, however, individual corporations in the United States show considerable diversity when viewed up close. This chapter explores that diversity.

Variety comes as less of a surprise in the United States than in Japan, where the forces for standardization are stronger. The United States has fewer employer and business associations, greater decentralization, and fewer unionized employees. Pressures for conformity in the United States are not entirely absent, however. They include professional associations, periodicals, and standardized university courses that are devoted to HR managers. And while businesses in the United States are more independent from each other than those in Japan, they do communicate, rely on consultants, and occasionally reach consensus regarding what constitutes best practice.

In the United States, we conducted on-site visits with HR and other executives from five companies in industries—securities, package delivery, electronics, auto parts, and construction/energy—similar to those of our Japanese case studies. For the purpose of grouping companies, it is useful to begin by distinguishing those that are diversified from those that are more focused. It turns out that securities and package delivery, the industries that yielded the most focused companies in our Japanese sample, did so in our sample of U.S. companies as well. U.S. Securities and U.S. Package have relatively weak divisions and powerful headquarters HR departments. In the United States, however, we found that diversification is less directly related to the power of the headquarters HR function than it is in Japan. For example, U.S. Electro, a diversified company, has a strong and centralized HR function, while the HR system of U.S. Parts, a relatively focused company, is fairly decentralized.

The comparison between the HR function at U.S. and at Japanese companies is particularly complicated with respect to strategic influence. None of the HR managers of U.S. firms serves on their company's board, but at four of the firms—U.S. Package, U.S. Electro, U.S. Parts, and U.S. Securities—the senior HR executive reports to the CEO and is consulted on major strategic initiatives, typically to give implementation advice related to personnel issues. What do these companies with close CEO-HR ties have in common? Three of the four have paternalistic CEOs who are either company founders or sons of founders.[1] The CEOs are committed to treating employees as stakehold-ers—that is, to considering the impact that corporate decisions are likely to have on employees. This means not that during downturns they try to preserve jobs at all costs but that they try to avoid layoffs if possible. It also means that they are responsive to employee concerns and work to remedy policies or actions perceived as inequitable or unfair. Two of the companies, U.S. Package and U.S. Electro, also have a long history of operating all or most of their facilities on a nonunion basis, which further sensitizes management to em-ployee concerns. The result is to elevate the status of the senior HR executive, who serves in part as a kind of representative of the employees to the CEO.

The fourth company, U.S. Parts, presents a different story. It is a mature company that in recent years has had a predilection for acquiring or divesting itself of various business units. Because the HR vice president is one of the few at headquarters who has been with the company through its various incar-nations, she has established a role for herself as adviser to the CEO.

Finally, U.S. Con/Energy, a decentralized construction and energy company, is almost a caricature of a finance-driven organization. The company regularly buys and sells units, which operate autonomously. Headquarters HR has little centrality or influence; employment is market-driven and commodified.

We will see, then, great variety in the role of the HR executive in the United States; there is no single, standard "American" approach. In what follows, the industries represented by the case studies we present are in the same order as are the Japanese counterparts.

The Companies

U.S. Securities

U.S. Securities is one of the largest brokerages in the United States. Growth has been extremely rapid in recent years as the company benefited from the surge of personal investing that accompanied the U.S. stock-market boom and the growth of the 401(k) market (self-directed pension funds). Employment more than doubled between 1997 and 2000. At times during that period, the company was hiring more than one thousand employees a month. Before the stock market downturn that took hold in 2001, turnover rates were around 14 percent per month, which is very high, especially compared to the turnover rates of J. Securities. Because of rapid growth and high turnover, 68 percent of the employees, an astoundingly high figure, have been with the firm for less than three years.

The company is organized along business lines. The largest divisions are on the retail side and include walk-in branch offices, online trading, and phone centers. Retail is the heart of the company, accounting for 85 percent of revenues and 60 percent of employees. The company also has business units for retirement-plan services, capital markets and trading, financial products (including its own mutual funds), and a recently acquired bank. Backstopping all of these is a highly skilled group of "technologists"—software engineers and computer-systems specialists—who constitute about 15 percent of all employees. The firm likes to consider itself a technology company providing financial services to customers. This image, reinforced by the relative youthfulness of the employees, gives the company a "techie" aura, but, as in the case of its Japanese counterpart, its center of gravity, measured in headcount, lies in the more mundane activities of sales and account service.

The structure for HR decision making is more decentralized than at J. Securities. Each business unit has its own HR department consisting of generalist staff who report to the president of the business but have a dotted-line relationship to the central HR department. (Recall that J. Securities has few HR positions below the headquarters level.) Business-unit HR departments at U.S. Securities perform a dual function: To employees, they provide career counseling, benefits information, and other services, and to line managers they offer technical and other assistance, including coaching in performance management. The company's rapid expansion in recent years has forced it to hire hundreds of managers who lack experience in supervising employees. The local HR units are supposed to "backstop" them.

Local HR staff have to please both the line managers and employees, and the balancing act can be difficult. A line manager dissatisfied with the decision of an HR representative can appeal to the general manager of the business unit and/or to the divisional HR manager. Headquarters rarely gets involved. The executive in charge of HR says, "If somebody needs me to get involved, I will, but what I work hard to do is push decision making and accountability down the organization rather than pulling it up."

A formal complaint system is not available to employees who are unhappy with a decision made by their supervisor or who have some other grievance. What they can do is express dissatisfaction through anonymous attitude surveys that are conducted monthly throughout the corporation. Within the corporate culture, the practice of employees sending gripes via e-mail to their HR representative, their divisional HR manager, the senior vice president of HR, and the CEO is tolerated. The HR staff at U.S. Securities takes on responsibilities that in Japan lie more within the province of the enterprise union. Even the head of HR says that each year he receives "hundreds" of e-mails from employees, who suffer no reprisals and incur no stigmas. "No one gets fired, no one will ever be punished, no one will be ever be disciplined for sending an e-mail to the top of the organization."

As a result of the greater autonomy enjoyed by divisions and line managers, the quantitative and qualitative importance of divisional HR staff is greater than at J. Securities. Conversely, central HR is much weaker. There is a paradox in that: In most U.S. companies, autonomy of line managers is considered inimical to a strong HR staff function. At U.S. Securities, though, the HR staff at the divisional level and below work with inexperienced line managers to ensure that they are aware of the latest tools the company offers with respect to employee motivation and reward. Managers are assessed on their "people" skills; they are held accountable for employee development, which is counted in their performance appraisals. Staff HR find themselves performing this function in part because of rapid growth and high turnover, but there are other reasons.

The concern that U.S. Securities has for the quality of the employee-supervisor relationship is a prominent part of its corporate culture, which the central HR department has the responsibility of defining and propagating. Unlike companies that give only lip service to employee issues, U.S. Securities takes seriously the credo that people matter. The company takes great pride that in the *Fortune* magazine list of the best companies to work for, and in other similar lists, it regularly appears near the top. Its high national ranking is a measure of the company's sensitivity to employee needs, which are reflected in its generous benefits and flexible work arrangements; of the autonomy ("empowerment") of its employees; and of its emphasis on employee diversity.

Hence, despite the divisional and line autonomy that characterizes the corporate structure, headquarters HR disseminates a pervasive, pro-employee corporate culture. Indeed, the head of HR said that one purpose served by the strong culture at U.S. Securities is precisely that it provides the kind of guidance that encourages managers to solve problems without bumping them to the top of the organization. The company's management has a self-consciousness and sophistication about culture that goes back to the 1970s, when U.S. companies first jumped on the culture bandwagon, which was based in part on lessons learned from Japanese firms.[2]

FERSTT is an acronym that succinctly expresses the company's culture. Developed by the headquarters HR department, the acronym and its message are widely used and inculcated "from the time we start interviewing a new hire to the time they're hired and have gone through their [U.S. Securities] welcome, and at various points along the way." Through the use of interviews and personality tests, the company also tries to select employees who have a propensity to fit into its culture. What do the letters stand for?

F: fairness—to customers and to employees

E: empathy—understand the customer's needs and wants

R: responsive—speed of execution and speed to market are crucial

S: striving—but, recognizing that perfection may not be possible, employees should aim for "continuous improvement"

T: trust—that is, personal integrity

T: teamwork

U.S. Securities considers it a "strategic priority" that each employee understand the meaning of these concepts and the seriousness with which the company promulgates them:

> We are not like some companies where every time you turn around you have another placard that no one takes seriously. We do implementation [of culture] with a lot of accountability. The culture here is such that the king has no clothes. Senior management and the CEO are open. We are accessible to every employee, who has an inherent responsibility to challenge anytime, anyplace, anywhere . . . without any fear of reprisal. So I can tell you that every executive, all the way down to first line supervisor, had better walk the talk or the subordinate organization is really going to raise a lot of hell.

When its culture is strong, a company is easier to manage, especially during periods of rapid growth, and it can recruit and retain employees more easily. Until the stock market slump, U.S. Securities was growing rapidly while labor markets, particularly for skilled technologists, were fairly tight. The firm's national ranking as a great place to work ensures that it receives a steady stream of resumes, and its ability to retain the employees it hires is aided by its strong culture and its practice of selecting for those candidates who fit into that culture. As the senior HR executive put it, "The future of the company is all about recruiting the right talent—and having the right bench strength in place. It's about developing people, investing in our intellectual capital, and keeping it fresh and current with the state of the art."

Diversity is taken seriously. Evidence that it is ranges from the superficial (business cards with Braille superimposed on them) to the substantial. Women account for a large percentage (39) of all employees, and six of the sixteen members of the management committee are female. This has aided the company not only in recruiting in a tight labor market—U.S. Securities recently was ranked near the top of the list of best companies for working women—but also in attracting customers: 30 percent of the firm's clients are female. This is in marked contrast to J. Securities, which, while it has a strong corporate culture and pro-employee orientation, is a thoroughly masculine company, both in its values and in its employee composition; there are hardly any women in management.

The company has a twelve-person board of directors, who include the CEO and the president but no other insiders. While the board is supposed to set the company's strategic direction, in fact what happens first is that strategic analysis is conducted by the management committee, on which the president and CEO sit, along with the presidents of the seven business units and seven executive vice presidents—one each from finance, legal, strategy, marketing, administration, information, and human resources. This arrangement allows the head of HR to contribute to strategic decision-making and to trumpet how

HR helps to implement the company's chosen strategy. On the other hand, HR's strategic contributions are limited. We were told that headquarters HR does not get involved in acquisitions or divestitures until after a decision has been made, and then its role is relegated to operational HR issues.

Getting HR's point of view across can be more of an uphill battle at U.S. Securities than at J. Securities, where many more board members and senior executives have had direct experience with the HR function. The centrality of HR at J. Securities gives the head of HR there an edge, because his premises and concerns are shared by other company officers. The head of HR at U.S. Securities, even though it is a progressive company, constantly has to sell other executives on the value of HR and of pro-employee practices.

However, through his role in the selection of senior managers, the head of HR at U.S. Securities is able to affect, to some extent, executive decision-making and business strategy. For example, recently the company used a head-hunter to identify an executive to run one of the company's business units. The senior HR executive was part of a seven-person group that screened and ranked the final candidates provided by the headhunter. In the past, hiring from outside to fill senior positions was quite common at U.S. Securities, and HR took the lead role in working with headhunters to vet candidates, but two years ago the company adopted a succession plan for senior-level positions, because rapid growth and a dearth of good outside candidates made it likely that in the future the company would look first to internal candidates when filling vacancies. As at J. Securities, the central HR unit is responsible for designing appraisal instruments, collecting assessment data, and storing the information related to succession. Decisions about senior promotions are made by the management committee, with the head of HR playing an important role.

The third major responsibility of headquarters HR is to design company-wide HR systems, such as performance appraisal and reward systems. It developed the appraisal instrument, which includes feedback from subordinates and colleagues (a so-called 360-degree evaluation), in collaboration with line managers and divisional HR staff. Headquarters is usually unable to issue orders to the divisions, so the emphasis on collegiality makes a virtue of necessity. "When the product is ready to deliver, you know it's baked. Everyone agrees. Everybody's touched it. They've smelled it, they've nibbled on it, and it's ready to go. It's a very collaborative, team-driven function . . . unlike what you might find in other organizations where you know HR is turning the crank on the old printing press and stuff is getting regurgitated out into the organization."

Although the company stresses teamwork, its reward system is geared to individualized pay-for-performance plans. The emphasis on pay, combined with the heterogeneity of the occupational structure, has resulted in more than eighty incentive-pay plans, which are designed by the central HR department. Managers and financial analysts with major responsibilities can, if they are judged "stars," reap substantial rewards. Not surprisingly, then, pay inequality is greater and maximum pay rates are higher than at J. Securities. Conversely, U.S. Securities is less concerned with equity of rewards, and the involvement that headquarters has in individual pay determination is scant.

To sum up thus far: U.S. Securities has a modestly powerful headquarters HR function. It defines and propagates a pro-employee culture, influences strategy through senior hiring and the executive committee, and designs companywide appraisal and reward systems. The company is well aware that its competitive advantage is based in part on its intellectual capital. In contrast to J. Securities, however, headquarters HR has less influence at the corporate and divisional levels. While people matter at U.S. Securities, it is less concerned with internal equity, and ties between employee and employer are weaker. Consequently, the central HR function is less involved in creating and evaluating human capital and allocating it to its best use.[3]

The sharpest contrast between U.S. Securities and J. Securities is in training and career development. Headquarters HR at U.S. Securities is concerned that some managers are deficient in "people" skills and that this causes employee dissatisfaction and turnover. "Our growth has required us to promote people far faster than their life's experiences have allowed them to develop. We have hundreds of managers who really don't know how to manage." Although the problem is long-standing, the company still does not have a management-development program. To promote the establishment of one, headquarters HR recently presented to the executive committee a plan for a mandatory management-training curriculum, the justification being the high costs associated with employee turnover. Still, the level of training at all levels is well below its Japanese counterpart.

Headquarters HR used the same appeal to turnover costs when it sought the creation of a stronger internal labor market, including career "pathways" for every job and online career-development programs. "When you look at the turnover figures, it's clear: We need to invest in the development of managers. [Employees say,] 'My manager is a jerk. He doesn't know what the hell he's doing. . . . I want to know where my career goes in this labyrinth.' "

The reliance on turnover costs to justify HR expenditures is an old HR tactic, going back to the 1910s. Because turnover costs can be quantified, they register with senior executives, who generally give credence to hard numbers. The problem for HR is that, with the post-bubble slump in business, turnover rates are down, and so the turnover-cost rationale for training-and-career programs has diminished, even though such programs can still be justified on other, less quantifiable grounds. The senior HR executive still has difficulty using the company's strong, pro-employee culture to justify HR expenditures to non-HR executives.

Before the slump, U.S. Securities conspicuously valued its employees. Every employee was granted stock options and, though an ESOP, received outright grants of stock from the company. Moreover, nowhere in the company's vision statement was there mention of moneymaking; neither *profit* nor the word *shareholders* appeared there. The implication was that U.S. Securities viewed employees as a stakeholding constituency.

However, as trading and profits declined in 2001, the company's first response was to reduce its labor costs. Initially it tried to protect jobs by cutting hours, chiefly by asking employees who didn't interact with customers to take off Fridays without pay and to take unused vacation. Six weeks later, the company announced layoffs totaling 8 percent of the workforce. It was reported in the press that the reason for the depth and abruptness of the cuts was "to appease shareholders." For headquarters HR, the cuts have undermined the company's long-standing efforts to position itself as a model employer. U.S. Securities has taken some unusual steps to cushion the blow, however — partly to bolster its reputation and partly to ensure that in the future it can more easily rehire employees it has laid off. It is offering a "hire-back" bonus of $7,500 to any employee rehired within eighteen months, and it will pay affected workers up to $20,000 in tuition over two years.[4] The head of HR said, "We felt that the markets will turn at some point and that the cost of hiring people back with the bonus is small compared to what it would be to pay for recruiting and training new employees." Finally, to maintain the "Fairness" line of its corporate acronym and credo, top executives took pay cuts ranging from 5 percent for vice presidents to 50 percent for the CEO.

In sum, the HR department at U.S. Securities lacks the centrality of its Japanese counterpart and has authority over fewer operational issues. In the strategic role it plays through executive selection and the management committee, it resembles central HR at J. Securities, but its influence in strategic realms is modest. At U.S. Securities, other senior managers are less likely to sympathize with HR's role than at J. Securities, and the employee-stakeholder ethos is weaker, although strong for a U.S. company. Indeed, this remains a pro-employee company. Despite layoffs — or, rather, because of the company's adroit handling of them — U.S. Securities continues to be regarded as one of the nation's top employers. The cachet attached to this ranking insures that HR and its programs are taken seriously within the company.

U.S. Package

U.S. Package is a major provider of overnight delivery services for documents and packages. Because of the huge size of the U.S. domestic market, the company relies on air transport to insure next-day delivery. Unlike its Japanese counterpart, it employs a large number of pilots, airplane mechanics, and related personnel. In other respects, however, the two firms bear a striking resemblance to each other. Like J. Delivery, U.S. Package was founded by a visionary entrepreneur who continues to play an active role in company management. His ideas about business issues, including employee relations, have shaped the company over the years.

Until recently U.S. Package was an undiversified, U-form type of company devoted to overnight delivery. Its business was organized along functional lines: Separate divisions existed for aircraft, sorting, courier operations, and air-to-ground transport. Coordination among divisions was, and remains, close, as each is a part of a tightly organized system for delivering overnight packages. The two key divisions are aircraft and courier operations. Aircraft employs around eight thousand, most of whom are pilots. Courier operations has more than sixty thousand employees, its largest category being the drivers of the company's distinctive delivery trucks. The least skilled jobs are those of the sorters, many of whom are employed on a part-time basis, as at J. Delivery.

In the 1980s, the company expanded to the international market. After encountering some problems, it decided to run its three overseas units as autonomous entities separate from the domestic business. In the late 1990s, U.S. Package acquired several trucking companies, which led to its reorganization as a holding company, about which more in a moment. The domestic overnight business, which accounts for more than 80 percent of employees and of revenue, remains the core of the company's business,.

From its inception, U.S. Package was eager to keep its pilots, drivers, and sorters on a nonunion basis. Management feared that its highly coordinated delivery system could be held ransom by a strike at a key facility or during its busy Christmas season. Because the company defines itself as an air-transport firm, all of its employees are covered by the Railway Labor Act. Under the RLA, union representation is decided by the majority vote of an entire craft (pilots, drivers, mechanics), whereas the National Labor Relations Act requires the majority only of employees at a work site or facility. The task of organizing a geographically dispersed workforce of drivers and sorters is daunting, and few attempts have been made.

The pilots present a different story, however, because they have greater geographic and occupational cohesion. From the company's inception in the early 1970s, it offered its pilots many "unionesque" personnel policies, including a contract-like handbook that was periodically revised by the "Flight Council," a kind of in-house union that was run jointly by pilots and management. Pilots also enjoyed access to a complaint system, which was similar to the grievance procedure of a union but whose final adjudication was inside the company rather than by a neutral, third party. Finally, pilots had generous profit-sharing and pension plans. Occasional spats between the pilots and the company would break out, but by and large the system worked cooperatively. Then in the late 1980s U.S. Package acquired a freight airline whose pilots were unionized. A series of mishaps ensued, leading the original pilots of U.S. Package to form an independent union of their own. After many years of negotiation and two Christmas-season strike threats, a five-year contract was signed in 1999. The present pilots' union is independent and not affiliated with any national labor organization.

Because of the RLA's national bargaining-unit approach, it would be difficult for a union to organize nonpilot employees, but U.S. Package takes no chances. Its drivers and sorters receive highly competitive pay and benefits, extensive training, and excellent opportunities for promotion. Job security is high. Employees know that their chances of spending their entire career with the company are good, and turnover rates for full-time employees are very low. Ground employees are covered by a complaint procedure known as "guaranteed fair treatment," which management takes seriously. The company's motto, "People, Service, Profits," conveys that it regards satisfied, loyal employees as the basis of its high-quality, reliable service and of its profitability.

Some would describe U.S. Package as a leading example of a progressive nonunion company,[5] whereas critics in the pilots' union characterize it as "excessively paternalistic." Employees are told to trust management, to work hard, and that the company will take care of them. While the same can be said of Japanese companies, employees at U.S. Package are different in this important respect: They have less opportunity to participate in management decision-making, as they work in an environment in which the lines between employees and managers are sharper than in Japan. Still, most of the company's managers, from first-line supervisors to senior executives, are hired from within. Internal hiring and a clear business focus reinforce the company's strong, pro-employee culture. Management is lean, with only five ranks between the top and bottom of the company.

HR ORGANIZATION

The senior vice president for personnel has two types of individuals reporting to him: specialists in charge of companywide HR programs, and generalists in charge of HR for operating businesses. The former comprises individuals from two units—one for compensation and benefits, and another that combines training, legal, health and safety, and psychological testing. The latter type includes the heads of HR for the three international businesses and for the domestic overnight-delivery business. The total number of HR employees is large: about one thousand, of which the overnight-delivery unit (comprising several divisions) has the largest single share, with more than four hundred employees. Overnight delivery is the tail that wags the corporate dog at U.S. Package, whereas J. Delivery is a less differentiated, more unitary company—there the tail *is* the dog. However—and this is crucial—the heads of HR for the various overnight divisions report to a senior HR executive as well as to the heads of their divisions.

How does that work? Within overnight delivery's HR organization, senior managers are assigned to each of the operating divisions (sorting, driving, etc.), and each senior manager has his or her own staff servicing that division. These senior managers are responsible for all personnel systems for the employees in their respective divisions—everything from pay and benefits to training and complaint systems. What is significant and distinctive about U.S. Package is that HR is organized on a matrix. That is, the HR managers in the operating divisions report, ultimately, to the head of HR for the overnight-delivery unit; they also have a dotted-line relationship to line managers within their division. In the company's parlance, each HR manager is a direct report to another in the HR organization and is "matrixed" to a line manager. This creates a complicated dual role for the HR manager, who has to straddle the fence to keep both bosses happy.

The original idea for the matrix came from the CEO, who wanted HR to be consistent across the various divisions, which are integral parts of a common air-freight system. The fear is that coordination in the companywide HR function would be compromised if divisional HR chiefs reported to divisional line managers. "Unlike a manufacturing firm, we have a system. We're doing the same job [throughout air freight]. So you can't have a person out in Los Angeles making their own decision . . . because it will interfere with system schedules. Each operation has to mesh with every other operation." Thus the HR managers in the divisions provide a modicum of consistency that enhances coordination.

Another important reason for the matrix approach has to do with the importance of the complaint procedure ("guaranteed fair treatment"), a key element in the company's nonunion approach to employee relations. A representative of the HR organization will work with an aggrieved employee and his or her supervisor to resolve a complaint. If the employee continues to press the grievance to higher levels (the ultimate step is an appeals board consisting of employee peers), the HR department will ask its employee-relations unit to investigate the issue and make an independent judgment. Because neither the representative nor the employee-relations unit reports to line managers, they are able, if need be, to tell supervisors that they were in the wrong. Their neutrality also enhances their credibility with employees.

A third reason for the matrix approach is that it facilitates organizational learning. HR managers from the different divisions meet regularly to share "best practices" and ideas about recruitment, motivation, and employee relations, and other issues. They also form study teams to analyze what other companies are doing and to adapt those ideas to U.S. Package. The company makes little to no use of HR consultants, who, U.S. Package feels, offer only generic ideas.

Finally, the matrix approach is helpful to management development. As at a Japanese company, headquarters HR at U.S. Package considers itself responsible for the identification and development of the company's managerial talent, which, as noted, is hired almost entirely from within. For developing potential managers to fill entry-level management positions throughout the divisions, HR has a complex system that includes psychological and other forms of testing, peer evaluations, and training. For a position in senior management (i.e., in the two highest of the four ranks of management), a person has to be nominated by a manager already at that rank. Line managers make the promotion decision, but typically they request that someone from HR be present at an interview panel. "They always want us there. . . . We don't report to any of that chain [so] they know they can count on us, because we're not in that chain. Chances are I will give you a more honest opinion than will someone who works for you."

The matrix approach does entail some difficulties, however: "You want to please your core client, who is your line operator. At the same time, you have to please the personnel department." The tension involved in the effort to satisfy two bosses usually does not pose a major problem, though, since "the management and culture understand these tensions." Moreover, line managers recognize that they are receiving useful services and advice from the HR divisional managers. Having an independent HR organization is an important part of what makes overnight delivery hang together as a system and, except for the pilots, as a nonunion entity.

CHANGES

HR information systems are enabling the company to reduce the amount of paperwork passing through the HR function, as is illustrated by the computerization of the post-and-bid system for internal jobs. For positions below the third tier of management, employees are free to bid online and free to move if they are hired elsewhere in the company. At the other end, the online program permits the hiring manager to see the applicants' performance records, testing results, and other information. In the past, these promotions and transfers were routed through the HR department. The system has permitted the company to expand its employee base without proportionate growth in HR staff. The ratio of HR staff to corporate employees is considered a key measure of the HR department's efficiency, and the company benchmarks the ratio against that of other comparable organizations. Another computer system is being built that will allow computerization of vacancies and performance data for the upper ranks of management and that will include detailed information on skills and backgrounds. Finally, other information—employee records, for example, and specifics about fringe benefits—has also been put online, further enabling the HR department to contain the size of its own staff as the company grows. On the other hand, facing tightness in the labor market in the late 1990s, HR hired several hundred full-time recruiters to insure that U.S. Package would have enough employees to meet demand. The ratio of HR staff to corporate employees would be even lower had the company not taken on the recruiters. Still, the impression is that, despite efforts to use computerization to reduce HR staff, the company has a relatively staff-intensive HR department.

Another recent and important change is the acquisition by U.S. Package of four trucking companies, which will allow it to meet customers' needs for short-haul ground trucking at a lower cost than that of overnight delivery. A holding-company structure has been adopted: The new companies exist as independent entities alongside the original overnight-delivery business. For major customers, there is coordination of delivery services between the overnight-delivery company and the new acquisitions, but the pattern does not repeat itself with respect to employees. In a departure from the historic emphasis on consistency throughout the company, its HR practices and policies for overnight delivery and those of the four trucking companies are not being integrated. Each of the new companies has its own HR unit, and it remains uncoordinated with other HR units. This raises a conundrum: In a company whose systems integration drove HR integration, why is its experience with the new acquisitions proving an exception?

Part of the answer is that truck drivers in the new companies are paid less than are drivers for overnight delivery, which demands a higher level of skill and service quality. The fear at U.S. Package is that integration of HR policies would lead eventually to convergence of labor costs and to loss of margins in the new trucking businesses. "The biggest thing we have to fight is, Don't make these people look like U.S. Package. If we do, it'll take all that nice profit they are making and wipe it out." The other answer has to do with labor-relations concerns. If the new acquisitions were integrated with overnight delivery, it would be more difficult for management to claim that overnight is primarily an air-freight company subject to the Railway Labor Act. Loss of RLA coverage would allow unions to stage membership drives at individual facilities and attempt to organize the company incrementally. Meanwhile, however, that lack of integration on the HR side is hurting the ability of U.S. Package to integrate services on the delivery side. Moreover, it is unable to realize economies of scale in its use of package sorters and drivers. Critics in the investment community are questioning the company's ability to integrate the new companies effectively and to match services provided by major competitors.

Whether the explanation is labor costs or labor relations, it is clear that human resource issues are driving business strategy to an extent rarely seen in U.S. companies. HR played a key role during the initial deliberations and during the due-diligence and the post-acquisition phases of the acquisitions, a fact consistent with the close relations between the CEO and headquarters HR.

Finally, the business downturn that began in 2001 has hurt revenue growth and earnings. Despite these problems, U.S. Package is determined to avoid layoffs. To preserve earnings, it will rely instead on reduced capital spending and on creative cost-cutting. One reason it is avoiding layoffs is to prevent a replay of labor shortages when the economy recovers. Another reason is to honor its implicit commitment to protect employees' jobs whenever possible, in order both to preserve employee commitment and to prevent unions from making inroads.

In short, U.S. Package bears some uncanny resemblances to J. Delivery: Both are cohesive companies with strong, unitary cultures. Their founders either run or were recently still running the company. They have focused business strategies that are dependent on high levels of customer service and employee training. Both are "sticky" organizations, with extensive internal promotion, which, though not unusual in Japan, is far from the norm in the United States. Employees have "voice"—at J. Delivery, through the enterprise union, and at U.S. Package, to a lesser extent, through the complaint system and the pilots' union. As a consequence of all this, the HR department in each company is powerful—powerful in terms of centrality, centralization, and influence over business strategy.

U.S. Parts

U.S. Parts is a major auto-parts manufacturer headquartered in the Midwest. It has fifty plants and technical centers, mostly in the United States but also in Europe and Asia. Two-thirds of the employees are in the United States, and of those, around 30 percent of the blue-collar workers are unionized. That figure is roughly in line with what is found in the rest of the U.S. auto-parts industry. Like J. Parts, this is an innovation-driven company dominated by engineers. The company's six divisions manufacture commonplace but highly technical products, including transmissions, turbochargers, and cooling systems. The divisional presidents all have engineering backgrounds. Half are company veterans, some having up to thirty years' service, but the others are recent hires from the outside.

The company has evolved through several incarnations since the 1960s, reflecting the changing fads of corporate organization. From the 1920s through the 1950s, U.S. Parts was a paternalistic company that specialized in automotive parts. In the 1960s, it diversified out of the auto-parts business, seeking businesses—including several personal-service acquisitions—that were less cyclical and that would cushion sales during downturns. By the 1970s, U.S. Parts had become a conglomerate of related and unrelated businesses managed centrally from headquarters.

As conglomerates went out of fashion in the 1980s, U.S. Parts experienced a leveraged buyout, in which management privatized the company but took on considerable debt. To finance the LBO, many of the unrelated businesses, and even some related units, were sold to other companies. Headquarters was downsized and the central research-and-development facility was shuttered. The company became increasingly decentralized and numbers-driven. Each division competed against the other to show good numbers, secure capital funding, and remain part of the company.

In the 1990s, U.S. Parts went public again—this time, as originally, with the focus on auto parts. Strong sales in the late 1990s enabled it to make several strategic acquisitions of related parts businesses, even as it continued to shed units that it already had. In short, the buy-and-sell mentality of a conglomerate persisted at U.S. Parts after the company became more focused.

The big question confronting U.S. Parts today is how to establish cohesion and synergy among its six divisions. Other U.S. companies—GE, for example—face the same kind of challenge. Divisional autonomy is ingrained in the cultures of both GE and U.S. Parts, but U.S. Parts lacks a strong corporate identity, adequate headquarters staff, companywide personnel systems, and other resources it needs if it would knit the organization together. Moreover, as the U.S. automotive boom comes to an end, U.S. Parts finds itself going into the recession without any of the cushions it possessed when it was more diversified. Also, cash-strapped customers are increasingly reluctant to pay top dollar for U.S. Parts' innovative but pricey products.

HR ORGANIZATION

The HR department at headquarters is quite small. Its staff consists of twelve people, including the vice president and specialists in benefits and in organization development. In the past, before the leveraged buyout, central HR had more than fifty employees, as many as at all of headquarters today (itself down from nearly four hundred). The vice president of HR, a remarkably influential woman, started at the plant level nearly thirty years ago and moved into the top HR position when the company was in its leveraged-buyout phase.

Each division has its own HR vice president, who reports to the divisional president. These HR vice presidents, together with the plant HR managers, make policy for their divisions. Headquarters imposes few constraints other than safety policies, budget limits, and standardization of fringe benefits. The decentralized approach fits the company's labor-relations strategy, which is to keep unionized plants separate from each other and from nonunion plants, making it more difficult for a union to claim commonality of interest.

Some coordination of HR across divisions does exist, however. A senior HR council consisting of the divisional vice presidents meets quarterly at headquarters to discuss common concerns. Also, on an informal basis the vice president helps the divisional presidents hire their HR staff and serves as a mentor to several HR managers coming up the ranks.

The company's lean executive structure means that there is a surplus of tasks to be performed and projects waiting for someone to take responsibility for them. Because the HR vice president is full of energy and cares deeply about the company, she is quick to tackle projects that others shy away from. And because of turnover at the top—three of the division heads are new, and the CEO came from the outside in 1993—few senior officers can match the vice president's intimate knowledge of the company's history and structure, nor do they have the same network of personal relationships with operating managers. That network permits her to accomplish things that would be difficult or impossible for a newcomer working within the existing structure of divisional autonomy.

The vice president devotes her time to four main areas: corporate culture, executive selection, HR systems, and a new R&D center. Each area is distinctive, yet all are related to the larger objective of creating companywide synergy.

In the mid-1990s, U.S. Parts undertook an expensive effort in planned organizational change intended to bring various parts of the business, and the people in them, closer together. One hundred top managers from around the world met to develop a mission statement that might serve as the basis for a common organizational culture. The HR vice president, with help from outside consultants, oversaw the process. The final statement included language to the effect that U.S. Parts was a "federation of businesses" and a "commonwealth" of people, reflecting the need to balance coordination and autonomy. Five cross-business, cross-function teams were assigned to develop plans for companywide procedures in such areas as resource allocation, manufacturing systems, and talent development, about which more in a moment.

The second area the vice president focuses on is keeping track of the pay, performance, and promotion of the top two hundred executives in the company. She helps the CEO maintain the executive-succession plan and reviews it at meetings of the board of directors. The other occasion on which rankings are discussed is the president's roundtable, the biannual meeting between headquarters executives and the divisional top brass. Using a competency model developed by an outside consultant, the vice president leads a discussion about who would be ideal candidates for positions ranging from plant manager on up. Finally, when the company sought a new CEO to lead its initial public offering (IPO) in the early 1990s, the vice president, with help from an executive headhunting firm, conducted the search on behalf of the board of directors. Being involved with the selection of the new CEO gave the vice president the opportunity to establish rapport with him from the very beginning, and after taking office he relied on her knowledge of the company to help him take charge.

In the past, line managers at U.S. Parts, as at other companies, resisted the promotion and transfer of promising managers from their divisions to other parts of the company. To create a more tightly knit company—and to give managers cross-business and international exposure—U.S. Parts developed a companywide talent system. The team that worked on this project included the HR vice president, two plant managers, two divisional managers, and the company controller. They in turn hired an executive-selection consultant to work with them in creating a uniform, online performance-appraisal and executive-development system for the entire company. The tools put heavy weight on coaching, thereby pushing line managers—engineers who sometimes lack interpersonal skills—to do more in this area. The system is not particularly innovative, but its development and implementation illustrate how the HR vice president makes sure that she will contribute to the solution of the company's key strategic problems.

U.S. Parts still has much to achieve in the way of synergy and cohesion. Databases containing all payroll and employee information, except for that relating to the top two hundred managers, are on separate systems for each division. Hence the vice president's ability to affect operating decisions, or to integrate divisions, remains severely limited.

After losing its R&D center in the buyout, the company reassigned R&D staff to the plant and divisional levels. That proved to be a mistake, as the R&D staff were called on to help with daily operating problems and had little time to focus on more basic research. In the late 1990s, the idea to reestablish a corporate R&D facility began to circulate around headquarters, and the HR vice president asked the CEO to let her take charge of the project. While the vice president was not an engineer or a scientist, she had a good feel for the organizational issues posed by a new R&D center. The decision was made to locate the facility in Detroit, which is still the richest labor market for automotive innovation, and to imbue it with a Silicon Valley–like culture that would be attractive to younger engineers and designers. Unlike other parts of this still somewhat stodgy company, the R&D center has no private offices, no smoking, and other new-economy touches.

Despite her achievements, there remain areas in which the HR vice president is less influential than her peers at the other U.S. companies we examined. Because she is so removed from operating decisions, she has little ability to influence the work and pay outcomes (except for benefits) of nonmanagerial employees. Also, as the company's growth decelerates after a decade of rising sales, many younger managers must cut costs for the first time in their careers, and central HR can do little to help them. Moreover, while HR is a key part of the executive team, finance remains the most powerful function; HR becomes involved in acquisitions only after a decision to proceed has been made, and then its role is merely to gather data for due diligence. The data are important, but at that point it is too late for HR to influence the decision even if it detects that integrating two disparate companies would pose serious problems.

The HR vice president does wield influence and is respected by other executives, but not entirely by virtue of her position, as she puts to good use her personal talents, company experience, and positive relationship with the CEO. The small staff at headquarters forces the company to regularly call on outside consultants to develop HR products and systems, leaving U.S. Parts with little in the way of employee policy that is distinctive or original. When the vice president retired in 2002, she left to her replacement a culture in which HR-related issues still do not receive high priority, and that still has far to go before the company becomes a "commonwealth of people."

U.S. Electro

With more than one hundred thousand employees, six divisions, and dozens of business units, U.S. Electro is an extraordinarily complicated organization. Founded before the Second World War, the company, like J. Electronics, today sells technology-intensive products to consumers but also, like J. Electrical, to industrial users. Although the company is publicly owned, a significant share remains in the hands of the founding family, and the founder's grandson until recently was the company's CEO.

U.S. Electro's long history and close identification with the founding family give it a corporate culture that is notably different from that of the smaller and newer technology companies against which it competes. Like U.S. Package, it is and always has been a nonunion company. In the 1930s and 1940s it successfully avoided unionization at its domestic manufacturing plants; in fact, it enjoyed a growth spurt by handling struck work for unionized companies. Staying nonunion became part of the corporate tradition. U.S. Electro offered its manufacturing employees unionlike working conditions: employment security, generous benefits, and a complaint system that it also made available to professional and managerial employees. It also tried to develop a strong bond between the founding family and employees.

Today, less than 20 percent of the workforce consists of domestic production workers; the bulk of the employees are either engineers or overseas production workers. Still, the nonunion legacy continues to be felt. Despite enormous losses in the late 1990s, the company, wishing to honor its long-standing promise to protect jobs, was slow to lay workers off. For years, the founding family promoted "constant respect for people" and "uncompromised integrity" as key corporate values. To the annoyance of some executives who have wanted to expedite corporate restructuring, the CEO cared deeply about how employees would perceive and be affected by any acquisitions or divestitures. Finally, the company began to shutter plants and lay off large numbers of employees—more than thirty thousand in the last three years. The layoffs were vetted through the employee-complaint system, a complicated process that stands in contrast to employment "at will," the legal norm prevailing in the United States.

Company benefits have an old-fashioned feel to them. Like traditional welfare-capitalist companies, U.S. Electro still provides recreational and leisure activities for employees. Though employees come and go, a substantial number have spent most of their career at the company; a service club holds banquets for ten-year, fifteen-year, and quarter-century employees. Unlike most high-tech companies, U.S. Electro offers a generous defined-benefit pension plan, although in the late 1990s it also began to offer a cash-balance plan for employees who thought that they might not spend the rest of their career at the company.

For years U.S. Electro was dominated by its engineers; in a tradition associated with the founder, many senior managers rose from their ranks. The company prided itself on its innovative and reliable products but sometimes failed to attend to consumer needs. In the 1990s — as technology shifted from analog to digital, and when competition heated up domestically and abroad — U.S. Electro gradually developed a stronger consumer orientation. More managers were hired from outside the company and more of them came from non-engineering backgrounds. But U.S. Electro is still run largely by lifers, people who have devoted their careers to building the company.

As at U.S. Securities, the pro-employee culture contributed to a strong company brand. U.S. Electro regularly appears on lists of the top U.S. companies to work for. Now that its smaller high-tech competitors have shed workers and seen their stock plummet, the "bricks and mortar" solidity of U.S. Electro makes it a relatively attractive place to work, despite layoffs of its own.

HR ORGANIZATION

In light of the above, news that the corporate HR function is large, powerful, and central to corporate decision-making is hardly surprising. The global HR organization has more than three thousand employees, around 10 percent of whom are based at corporate headquarters. The HR staff has shrunk in recent years, but at the same rate as has the number of employees in other headquarters units.

One feature of the HR organization is its matrix structure, which is similar to that of U.S. Package. HR employees throughout the organization report to the headquarters HR department, although some of them have dual-reporting relationships whereby they also report to divisional and business-unit managers. Despite the matrix, the HR function is highly centralized and is somewhat independent of line management. There are two reasons for this. First, divisions are autonomous — the company is sometimes described as group of "warring tribes" — and HR, providing some of the glue that holds the divisions together, fosters the sense of a strong, unitary culture. The second reason can be traced to the company's ethos, which was forged in the era of union avoidance, according to which HR is to serve as a "third force," mediating between employees and managers and running the complaint system. Even today, the CEO and president

> want an independent set of eyes and ears. They [the HR managers] are the eyes and ears, the CEO's eyes and ears in all units. It reaches all of [the company], so that if we do have situations where managers aren't performing well or where our code of

business conduct is not being adhered to as religiously as it should, they have an independent voice that will come to them, and help them realize what is expected of them.

The HR organization has three main parts. Around 30 percent of the staff are "in business" and operate alongside line management. They handle employee relations (including communications and complaints) and are assigned to the divisions. They report, ultimately, to the senior HR executive, not to the divisional line managers. However, they are funded entirely by the divisions, who are viewed as the HR staff's customers. The in-business HR staff also handle issues specific to the businesses they serve. For example, in their human resource planning for an individual unit, they will look at long-range business needs to help it decide in which job categories it needs to add or drop employees. Another important role of the in-business staff is to integrate the services provided by the other two parts of the HR organization: shared services and the geographic teams.

Shared services, comprising 40 percent of HR staff, is the largest part of the HR organization. Shared services has two subdivisions. The first maintains core systems that are universal throughout the company. These include HR information systems, employee benefits, and employee transactions. The staff in this subdivision work at headquarters and report to the senior HR executive. The second subdivision handles global staffing, training, leadership, and compensation on an integrated basis, trying to maintain a balance between company-wide uniformity and sensitivity to market conditions facing the business units.[6] For example, the merit-review process is similar throughout the company, reinforcing the understanding that all employees work for the same company, but the HR staff in global compensation tailor the merit budgets to fit divisional and unit needs. The global staff have varied reporting relationships. Some report to headquarters HR only; others report both to headquarters and to the heads of HR in the business units they service, in which case part or all of their salary is paid by the local unit.

Country and regional teams, the third main part of the HR organization, comprise around 30 percent of the staff. They handle the legal and compliance issues encountered by units operating in different parts of the world. The North American regional team is based at company headquarters, along with shared services and the in-business team for a major division likewise based at headquarters. The ensuing HR presence at company headquarters is sizable, and reminiscent of that at J. Electrical.

CAREERS AND COMPLAINTS

In contrast to smaller high-tech companies, U.S. Electro sells itself to potential recruits as an organization at which a person can enjoy an interesting and lifelong career. Today the "company man" is less common than in years past:

About 70 percent of the top 1,500 people in the company have risen through the ranks, down from about 95 percent twenty years ago. Still, the portion is sizable, and the firm devotes considerable resources to employee development.

As at some of the Japanese companies we visited, the headquarters HR unit ranks all persons at or above the level of senior director and grooms candidates for the top two hundred positions in the company. In the past, headquarters did not interfere when the divisions gave preference to candidates from inside their division, but in the last few years it has made a conscious effort to transcend divisional barriers in order that U.S. Electro might realize the competitive advantage stemming from its being a large, diversified company with a pool of internal talent. As a result, central HR now plays a more active role in executive selection, and, where for years the trend had been toward the decentralization of career development, it fosters centralization. The move toward centralization was born not only of the wish to encourage synergy across divisions but also of the realization that the most effective way for the CEO to influence divisional strategies is not through diktats but through talent management. U.S. Electro says it learned that lesson from IBM's turnaround in the early 1990s.

The company's internal complaint system permits employees to challenge management actions and press their grievances all the way to the CEO level. The system is used in all its divisions around the world and is available to all employees, even though its original intent was to deter unionization of the company's domestic production workers. The employee meets first with his or her direct manager and then, if necessary, with the manager's boss. If the issue is not resolved at that point, the in-business HR staff become involved, serving as the employee's representative. As the complaint moves up the hierarchy, the employee is represented by members of successively higher echelons of the HR organization.

It is a policy of U.S. Electro that, if employees with at least ten years of service are terminated, they can ask that the CEO and the senior HR executive review that decision. The result is that employees recently laid off have flooded the complaint system with requests for reviews. Line managers understand that a case for terminating a senior employee must be well documented, whether the reasons are related to the employee's poor performance or, as is the case more recently, to the company's economic constraints. Since the company began laying off employees, it has received about two thousand appeals, and of those about fifty have reached the CEO level, meaning that the employee received an audience with the CEO or the HR director. A handful of those approximately fifty dismissals have been overturned. For the company, the benefit of the reviews is that it leads most employees to perceive the dismissals as fair, and U.S. Electro has been the object of no class action or other lawsuits related to the force reduction. In the company's view, its nonunion status permits a faster and less contentious layoff procedure than would be the case in a unionized organization.

BUSINESS DECLINE

Just as in better times the central HR function allocated hiring slots across divisions, so now, as human resource planning shifts into reverse, the function plays an important role in mapping strategies for personnel cuts. What complicates matters is that the company is laying off some workers while hiring others. Although there are internal transfers from declining to growing divisions, these placements are less common than in a typical large Japanese company. HR facilitates movement of talent across divisions, through employee transfers and through solutions that are more complicated and require interdivisional cooperation. For example, the senior HR executive proposed that a high-performing design center be shifted from one division to another and, to accommodate the move, that some relatively ineffective employees be shed from the receiving division. That kind of balancing act is typical for HR. This is not to say that the downsizing process is dominated by the HR organization. Layoff decisions are deliberated by the senior management committee, in which divisional heads have a voice, as does the CFO. The CFO has urged deeper and faster cuts than others in the company—the CEO, some of the divisional heads, and the HR director—were willing to make.

HR performs a balancing act also with respect to compensation, as it tries to preserve internal equity while making adjustments in light of diverse market conditions. Recently, several divisions wanted to defer merit increases, while healthier divisions said they could not delay without running the risk of losing employees. According to the senior HR director, there simply is "no artificial system that you can put in to stop movement across boundaries." The HR director visited all of the divisional offices, explaining the need to do "the right thing for the corporation." The decision they reached was to impose a six-month deferral for all divisions.

Another problem related to the business downturn is the company's stock price, which is far below its peak, leaving most stock options under water. An initial response was to issue new—relatively low striking price—options with a short exercise time. These were intended to raise morale and motivate employees to turn the organization around. Although the company's business has improved, its stock is still languishing. Still, the underwater options are creating fewer retention difficulties for U.S. Electro than for some of its smaller rivals that historically relied far more heavily on options. With the dot-com crash and shrinkage of smaller competitors, U.S. Electro is finding that options are not nearly so important to retention as they once were. Employees have other reasons—benefits, career opportunities, a sense that they will be fairly treated—to remain at U.S. Electro. In short, over the last twenty years employment policies and the centrality of the HR function have changed less at U.S. Electro than at many other U.S. companies, leaving HR with a level of influence that approximates what it held at this paternalistic company back in the 1960s and 1970s.

U.S. Con/Energy

This company grew rapidly in the 1990s, transforming itself from a modest natural-gas wholesaler to a diversified, multinational energy and construction company. The largest and most profitable part of the company is its energy-trading business, which in the 1990s came to dominate the original gas-pipeline division. Although not a general contractor like J. Alpha and Beta, Con/Energy has units engaged in the construction of major energy projects both in the United States and overseas. It has more than twenty thousand employees and, because of its pioneering trading practices and capacity to enter new businesses, is consistently ranked as one of the most innovative companies in America.

To understand HR at Con/Energy, it is necessary to distinguish among three periods: the 1980s and early 1990s, when the company was still a quasi-regulated public utility; the heart of the 1990s, when the original business was eclipsed by energy trading and other new ventures; and the period since 1999, when the headquarters HR office was reorganized.

THE WAY IT WAS

In the 1980s and early 1990s, Con/Energy was a modestly diversified company with a top-down, traditional management style. Headquarters HR handled recruitment, compensation, training, and benefits for the entire company. Employees brought in for management jobs came from regional colleges; many had backgrounds in engineering or undergraduate degrees in business. Employees tended to remain with the company a long time, and it emphasized internal stability and equity. Pay was systematized through a companywide job-evaluation plan. This environment required a sizable central HR staff, which at its peak, in the mid-1990s, comprised about 350 employees.

After 1990, the company's center of gravity shifted to its trading units, which, developing their own approach to HR, diverged from the existing model administered by headquarters. Eager to let the new units grow and prosper, the CEO permitted them to set their own policies. The units hired employees with backgrounds in finance and consulting; many were freshly minted MBAs from elite business schools. The new hires did not always get along with veteran employees in the gas-pipeline business, where the culture was more conservative and rule-oriented.

The new approach to HR was an attempt to deregulate the internal labor market. Employees were completely free—in fact, encouraged—to consider jobs elsewhere in the company and to transfer to them if they found them interesting. In a move that irked the headquarters HR staff, the trading unit, to facilitate movement, eliminated job descriptions and job evaluations. Employees were told that they should "have a resume on file at all times" and that, if they were at the top of the performance curve, they could switch to new positions easily. The company's phenomenal growth created opportunities for movement and facilitated the flow of people across different projects. Company managers kept track of the labor flows and, on the assumption that employees had the best information on which projects offered the greatest potential, poured resources into areas toward which employees gravitated.

To provide an incentive for employees to search out the best opportunities, the trading units relied heavily on performance-based pay, which included generous stock options. The trading businesses were rife with managers who had made wise career moves, worked extremely hard, and ended up as millionaires while still in their thirties. To encourage maximal effort, the lion's share of the options went to the top performers. The bonus multiples between those judged outstanding and those seen as only mediocre were considerable. Money—and the quest for more of it—was the key motivator.

Early on, the trading units developed a consistent metric for evaluating employee performance. It lay at the heart of the units' approach to HR: the so-called 360-degree evaluation overseen by a "performance appraisal committee" or PAC. Employees were reviewed twice a year by their immediate superior, their subordinates, and their colleagues, all of whom used standardized forms on which they took into account innovativeness, teamwork, leadership, and other qualities. A committee (the PAC) consisting of key line managers appointed by the unit president reviewed the appraisals of all employees in the same category (commercial, technical, or other) and at the same level (there were four levels). The task of the committee was to compare the employees to each other. For each of the twelve categories, the PAC ranked all employees on a curve, rating the top 5 percent as "outstanding," and so on down the list. In the early days of the trading unit, the bottom 10 percent were given a second chance and then terminated if they failed to improve. An employee's dossier contained his or her PAC rankings, which helped hiring units screen internal transfers.

The appraisal-and-reward system reflected trading's freewheeling but meritocratic approach to HR. A notable advantage of the PAC system was that the consistency of the metric it used in its evaluation of employees permitted easy transfers across projects. On the other hand, the PAC system was fairly cutthroat, leading to intense competition among employees as they strove to secure the highest ratings.

Over time, tension between headquarters staff and the trading units developed. The president of the trading division insisted on, and received, enough autonomy to set strategy for the division, and enough latitude to operate in whatever way he deemed necessary to make his targets. Headquarters, and particularly central HR, had little control over the trading division. The president of the division disdained HR—both at the company and more generally—because he thought it stifled creativity and performance, and he frequently bad-mouthed its bureaucratic approach. Both the implementation of the PAC and the shredding of standard job descriptions were done without approval by headquarters HR. Even the trading division's vacation policy was at variance with companywide rules. Its managers could take as much vacation as they wanted as long as their performance did not suffer. That frustrated and enraged headquarters HR—and may have been intended to do so. By the late 1990s, the friction between headquarters and the trading units had grown conspicuously more intense.

In 1997 the head of the trading division became the company's president. One of his first actions was to extend the PAC system to vice presidents and managing directors throughout the company. It was a controversial move that required cross-calibration, a complicated process of cross-divisional comparisons. In practice, cross-calibration often meant that managers automatically received credit or blame—halos or dunce's caps—for a unit's performance, even when it was the result of market forces beyond the manager's control. This created an incentive for managers, and other employees, to transfer to hot units, replicating within the internal labor market some of the "irrational exuberance" seen in financial markets.

The system introduced in 1997—it is still used today for assessing the 430 vice presidents—stipulated that each business unit as well as headquarters do its own, separate ranking, and then that a grand PAC appointed by the company president arrive at a combined ranking. The seventy-five managing directors are also ranked by the grand PAC.

Other divisions began to adopt the PAC approach for employees below the level of vice president. If they needed HR expertise, they turned to outside consultants or to staff from the trading division. Because each division's HR staff considered their customer to be the divisional head, coordination of HR policy across the company suffered. Divisional staff duplicated many of the functions performed by headquarters and "didn't listen to corporate." At this point, divisional HR staff comprised 250 employees, almost as many as at headquarters HR. Something had to give.

THE NEW SYSTEM

In 1999, the president and the CEO appointed as the new head of corporate HR an employee who had been with the company for over twenty years. She had no experience in HR—her background was in accounting. Indeed, it was in her role as head of the accounting operation for the trading division that she gained the president's confidence. In a move that cleared the way for the dissemination of the trading division's HR model to the rest of the company, the president asked her to help dismantle the headquarters HR office.

The new HR executive's first move was to shrink the central HR staff. All recruiting employees were moved down to the divisions, as were those who worked in nonexecutive compensation. Payroll was shifted to accounting, compliance experts to the legal office, and so on. Because the divisions were already performing many of these functions, some of the employees who had worked in central HR were dismissed. Duties that were traditionally part of HR—such as recruitment of MBAs into the executive-development program—are now handled by the president's office because it was felt that association with HR would send a negative signal to new recruits. The president's office, along with the CEO, also handles succession planning. Headquarters HR has been pared down to a staff of seventy-five people who handle employee benefits and also have responsibility for community relations. Little is spent on training programs anywhere in the company.

Under orders from the president, headquarters HR is helping the divisional HR staff extend the PAC system to everyone in the company. In 2001, 35 percent of employees were covered by the PAC approach; the company's goal is 100 percent coverage in a few years. This will entail the dissemination of stock options to all employees, which will surely feed an existing obsession with the daily fluctuations of Con/Energy's share price. At headquarters, the lobby and the employee parking garage feature electronic boards that flash the value of the company's stock. The head of HR says that "it's fun to watch people always looking at the stock prices."

Most of the PAC rollout effort is being handled by the divisions, although the head of central HR does try to coordinate and share information. The divisions send her their PAC rankings of vice presidents and directors, and she forwards them to the grand company PAC. She holds weekly telephone meeting with the divisional HR heads, although there are no plans to leverage this group beyond information sharing. Because the PAC rankings in practice tend to place heavy weight on revenue generation—the trading model—headquarters staff in HR and other units feel pressured to show that they are capable of bringing money into the company. The head of HR is looking into the possibility of commercializing the PAC system and selling it to other companies.

PROBLEMS

The CEO and the president jointly hired the head of HR, but they hold different views on what her mandate should be. The CEO, with whom she has a close relationship, is a folksy "people person" who values good employee relations and wants the new HR head to help the company become one of the nation's best companies to work for. The president, on the other hand, "doesn't see a value in HR," as she reported, "and said that to me before I even came into this job." The head of HR thinks the modicum of respect that the president pays her is a reflection of his respect for her accounting skills and for her *lack* of prior HR experience. She feels that her powers are too limited and does not want to continue in the position for more than a year or two. Whoever replaces her, she says, will also have to be a non-HR person, someone who will show the president—as she has not been able to—"the hard-number piece of how HR can add value."

Because of HR's perceived irrelevance, the president does not include HR on his acquisitions team. Somewhat plaintively, the HR head said, "I'm not involved in anything." She thinks she could make a contribution here, since under the current process "we focus on the hard stuff, getting the balance sheets right and all that stuff . . . but we do not do a good job of integrating our cultures." As a result, after an acquisition "a lot of it walks." She is doubtful she can persuade key officers in the company—the CFO and the president—to listen to her.

The impotence of headquarters HR has ramifications for other aspects of the organization. While the PAC is the glue that holds the company together, the PAC process has problems, which are escalating as an increasing number of the company's employees come under the PAC's coverage. Because central HR is weak, different divisions are handling the PAC differently. That creates headaches when executives from different divisions are "cross-calibrated" by the headquarters PAC. Some business units do absolute ratings and then convert them to a ranking; others do only the absolute rating and leave the ranking to the PAC. The head of HR isn't capable of reconciling the discrepancies because "HR is more administrative than it is about policy setting, and [the president] firmly believes that the business should set policy."

How the various PAC committees—they number around 150 and meet twice a year—interpret the ratings and rank employees raises some thorny issues. For example, executives from international management positions feel at a disadvantage with respect to traders, whose contributions are easier to quantify. Despite lip service paid to teamwork and leadership, the PACs tend to focus on hard numbers. Referring to employees who might have bad people skills, the head of HR admitted that "if they make a lot of money for the company, they will still be at the higher levels of the performance curve. I guess that's anti-HR, isn't it?" Those who sit on PACs, including the top PAC appointed by the president, consist of managers with no particular skill for judging diverse talent. PAC members have received no coaching or training, either from headquarters or business-unit HR staff, nor are there plans that they receive any in the future. At Con/Energy, said the HR head, "You jump in and learn by fire."

Not surprisingly, unhappiness with the PAC approach is growing. Some employees feel that the system is political, not meritocratic, and that it is poorly administered. The head of HR receives complaints from employees but doesn't want to intervene. "I support, I recommend, I encourage, but I can't make decisions." Lacking a formal complaint system, the best she can tell disgruntled employees is to rely on exit, not voice, as they attempt to address their job-related issues. "We tell people, 'You know, if you don't like who you're working for, go work for somebody else.' And that entails the open market for talent. . . . Eventually the crummy manager will find that they're not going to have good people want to come work for them."

In practice, however, the company's free-market approach to employee allocation had its own share of problems. Until now, dissatisfied but competent employees could transfer to new jobs because the company was steadily expanding—hiring more than one hundred new employees each week—but slower growth has put a crimp on the use of transfer as a relief valve. Moreover, while the theory persists that employees have the best information about where their talents can best be put to use, the head of HR and some divisional managers disagree. They find that employees tend to jump on and off bandwagons as they pursue the situation that seems to promise the best opportunity to make the most money. They also find that divisions raid each other's talent, behavior exacerbated by the use of companywide PACs, which make public the identity of those who have been rated as the best performers in each division. Given that units "don't work together," they give no consideration to what might be in the company's best interest. The problem is especially severe for headquarters. "No one wants to work here," said the head of HR.

The company's huge increases in share price in recent years have created an atmosphere that borders on arrogance, according to the head of HR. Recently, however, the stock declined, and "No one believed it could happen. Us go down?" The arrogance, reinforced by rich rewards for individual achievement, has created what she sees as a somewhat dysfunctional culture. She is concerned that the failure of divisions to cooperate with each other and with headquarters could hinder the company's growth, and so she would like the company to "focus HR at the corporate level more around culture." A well-defined culture, she believes, would serve to impose "soft" controls and make it easier to align individual, divisional, and corporate objectives. HR at Con/Energy cannot drive strategy, she said, but could drive culture. If she goes that route, however, she will suppress any reference to the HR function as such and call her department instead the "corporate culture office." Otherwise, "no one will take it seriously."

CONCLUSIONS

The first observation to make about the U.S. case studies is that the diversity in the organization of the headquarters HR function is remarkable. Companies range from those with a powerful HR function, as at U.S. Electro, to their polar opposites, exemplified by Con/Energy. Of the factors driving diversity, several are the same as in Japan: variations in business conditions and production technology, and the presence or absence of a strong corporate culture bearing the mark of a founder for whom fairness to employees was a core value (recall J. Delivery). What seems characteristically American is that the nature of the HR function in a given company can be defined by either the presence of the progressive nonunion model—in which HR plays a role as employee advocate—or by its absence. This is in marked contrast to the Japanese norm of ubiquitous enterprise unions. While the U.S. nonunion model distinguishes U.S. corporations from their Japanese counterparts, it has its roots in 1920s-style welfare capitalism, which in turn was an important element in the formation of Japanese welfare corporatism.[7]

The commonality of diversity-generating factors provides parallels between several of the U.S. and Japanese pairs—between, for example, the package-delivery companies (whose HR systems are built around a key occupation group, the drivers) and the diversified electrical companies (whose key occupational group is the engineers). Global producers (e.g., J. Electronics and U.S. Electro) not only face similar technical exigencies and customers but also look to similar multinational companies as models for their internal organization. As for U.S. Securities, its efforts to propagate a distinctive corporate culture hark back to the late 1980s, when U.S. employers venerated Japanese companies and regarded them as exemplars. In short, the view that the Japanese and the U.S. models of HR organization are each monolithic, and that each is distinct from the other, is distorted. What our case studies demonstrate is closer to the "converging divergences" story, according to which industry-specific effects that span different nations are superseding national models.

Strong national patterns persist, however. The U.S. companies are more market- and shareholder-oriented than their Japanese counterparts; they spend far less on training; and their employees are weak stakeholders at best. The U.S. cases also exhibit more variability. There is a broad spectrum of relationships between the corporation's power center and the HR executive, whose role ranges from that of business partner and CEO confidant to that of occasional consultant and even to nonentity. Variability is less pronounced in Japan, where the tracks between the president, the board, and the senior HR position are more uniform across companies. In a similar vein, U.S. companies show great variety in the internal status of the HR function—that is in its role in strategic decisions and its relation to line management. The forces favoring standardization in Japan—tight intercompany linkages, peak business associations, common sources of information on best practice—are notably weaker in the United States. Hence, in the United States the consensus about the appropriate role of human resources in a company's business strategy is thinner.

The U.S. companies appear to fall into a two-humped distribution. Some firms follow a resource-based business and HR strategy, relying on employees with firm-specific skills to generate competitive advantage; this is true of U.S. Package and U.S. Electro. HR policies there tend to be relatively organization-oriented and imbued with a mild stakeholder ethos. Other companies—U.S. Parts and Con/Energy—tend to let HR policy be driven by market considerations. They rely on workers with relatively general skills and they have a stronger orientation to short-term shareholder concerns. U.S. Securities sits somewhere in the middle of the two groups, leaning in the resource-based direction.

What drives this divergence is not clear, although CEO values (the first group is run by founders) and diversified M-form financialization (high in the second group) are possible factors. Financialization requires resource flexibility that is inconsistent with substantial investments in firm-specific human capital.

However, there is no clear relation between HR's standing inside the executive suite and the company's choice of either a resource-based or market-oriented strategy. At U.S. Securities, the headquarters HR function is not especially influential, despite the premium the company places on its reputation as an attractive employer. Conversely, the HR executive at U.S. Parts, a market-oriented company, is a key player in the company's top management decisions. Teasing out these relationships is difficult. One reason is that in the United States the influence of the HR executive depends heavily on his or her personal relationship to the CEO; another reason is that we have only a handful of case studies to generalize from. If we expand our ambit to include a larger and more diverse group of companies, what will we find?

Comparative Survey Data

THE CASE STUDIES DEMONSTRATE considerable diversity in the role of the HR executive in both Japan and the United States. By some measures, the Japanese and the U.S. companies that we have paired resemble each other as much as their national counterparts. Now we turn our attention in the other direction, to national tendencies and to the "gap," if any exists, between Japan and the United States.

Our window on this issue is a unique dataset derived from a survey of senior HR executives in U.S. and Japanese companies. We asked about a company's HR organization, HR's involvement with operating and strategic decisions, and relations between HR and other functions. Some of our questions replicate those in surveys conducted earlier by other researchers, and that allows for longitudinal perspective, as do questions we asked in which respondents had to estimate change over the past five years. Many of the questions in our U.S. survey occur as well in the Japanese survey and were composed so as to be commensurate, although a few questions (chiefly on corporate governance) are country-specific.

We mailed the survey in the first half of 2001, requesting that it be answered by the senior executive in the company's headquarters HR unit. The Japanese sample consisted of firms listed on major stock exchanges in Japan (Tokyo, Osaka, Nagoya, Fukuoka, and Sapporo) for whom the name and address of the senior HR executive were available from a commercial database. The U.S. sample consisted of firms that were listed on the New York Stock Exchange and for which the names of both the senior HR and the senior finance executives were available in an online database. Among the U.S. sample only, we conducted a small survey of the CFOs as well as the larger survey of the HR executives.

Out of about 1,000 companies contacted in each country, we had usable responses from 229 Japanese and 145 U.S. firms, yielding response rates of 23 and 17 percent, respectively.[1] While those figures may seem low, bear in mind that this is an elite survey — of senior corporate executives — in which response rates typically are modest. Response rates probably also were affected by the size of the questionnaire, which contained 124 items. The possibility of response bias exists, although we did not find any difference in the industry distributions of the respondents and nonrespondents. For the CFO survey, the number of respondents was very low, as we conducted only a single survey round, because of limited funds. Of the eighty-one CFO replies, twenty-two were from companies whose HR executive also replied, allowing for some interesting comparisons.

At the time of the survey, each country was at a different stage of the business cycle. The United States was at the tail end of a boom, with labor shortages, low unemployment, and high share prices—precisely the conditions in which HR is likely to flourish. Japan was in the tenth year of the "lost decade," during which employment, real output, and profits grew slowly or, in some instances, contracted.

OVERVIEW OF THE RESPONDENTS

Senior HR executives in the United States hold various titles (vice president, senior vice president, director), but the important distinction is between those who report to their CEO and those who report to someone else, either a chief operating officer or another executive. An important change from twenty-five years ago is that fully 65 percent of the senior HR executives report to the CEO; in 1977, only 30 percent of senior HR executives of similar companies did.[2] This change has been confirmed by other researchers and is not limited to HR executives. There has been an increase in CEO reporting by other staff executives, such as chief information officers (CIOs), and a sizable increase in the number of group and divisional managers reporting to the CEO.[3]

Reporting to the CEO has real consequences. A close relationship to the CEO can give the HR executive influence over corporate strategy. CEO reports are more likely than nonreports to say they are involved in final decision-making on senior appointments (93 percent versus 55 percent) and on mergers and acquisitions (59 percent versus 22 percent). At the same time, as we saw in the U.S. Parts case, reporting to the CEO also inclines the HR executive to conform to the dominant (i.e., finance-driven) corporate mind-set. In fact, we did find that CEO reports are less likely than nonreports to say that they care about safeguarding employee jobs.[4]

CEO reports are more likely to work in companies with lean headquarters HR departments and decentralized operations in which line managers make relatively more operating decisions than does headquarters. This is consistent with other studies finding that an increase in CEO reporting by line and staff managers is associated with flatter organizational structures.[5] HR executives who report to the CEO belong to the senior management team, and their role is more consultative than operational.[6] As compared to other HR executives, the CEO reports say that HR has more power relative to other functions such as finance and marketing, an issue to which we will return.

We did not ask whether Japanese respondents reported to the CEO but asked instead for their rank. Japanese companies tend to use standardized nomenclature for the hierarchy of senior management positions. About a fifth of the respondents were managing directors, meaning that they served on the board of directors. Three-fifths were general managers of the headquarters HR unit, the highest nonboard rank, and the remainder held positions lower than that.

In the United States, HR continues to be a specialty more open to women than other executive functions. Of the HR respondents, 33 percent were female, while the figure for CFO was 11 percent. In Japan, however, senior management—regardless of the function its members are employed in—remains an all-male preserve. Finally, with respect to age, the U.S. respondents were a tad younger than their Japanese counterparts (forty-eight versus fifty-two).

HR executives in the United States tend to be specialized professionals who, on average, have spent 77 percent of their careers in the HR field.[7] As professionals, they keep up with the latest developments in HR and identify with their occupation, this in addition to their corporate loyalties. Still, they are quite mobile. Mean tenure with the current employer is nine years. In Japan, the HR executives are a blend of specialists and generalists. The specialists, though, who predominate in manufacturing, are not "professionals" in the American sense. Because of lifetime employment, the average tenure that senior HR executives in Japan have with their current employer is long—twenty-six years, almost triple the U.S. figure. Consistent with weak HR professionalism in Japan is the finding that few Japanese executives (9 percent) there had planned a career in HR while still in college, compared to more than a quarter (28 percent) of U.S. executives.[8]

The advantage of professionalism in the United States is that it permits high job mobility, which allows HR managers to be on the lookout for better jobs and better pay. A disadvantage of specialization, however, is that it leads to complaints from other executives that HR executives don't know enough about business fundamentals in finance, sales, production, and accounting. Conversely, those Japanese companies that utilize the HR-generalist model don't have this problem; as we have seen, HR executives there are well rounded. However, the trade-off is that some of those Japanese HR executives are unfamiliar with U.S. and European HR techniques grounded in organizational and industrial psychology.

Another striking difference has to do with labor relations. Of those companies we surveyed, the percentage of employees who belong to a union is 65 in Japan and only 16 in the United States. Managers in both countries reported that the figures represent a decline from five years ago. Yet even though U.S. companies are lightly unionized, some remain concerned about unions. Thirty percent of the U.S. companies said they spend *more* time on union issues now than five years ago; these companies tend to be more heavily unionized.[9] Interestingly, these companies also are more likely to make labor-relations decisions at headquarters than are companies for whom labor relations are not consuming more time. The desire to coordinate collective bargaining across the company and/or to prevent union inroads at unorganized facilities leads to greater centralization.

TRENDS AND COMPARISONS

In the following section we look at recent trends in Japan and the United States and compare the two countries along eight dimensions:

1. resources flowing to the HR function (resource allocation)
2. operating authority of headquarters HR units (centralization)
3. HR's strategic influence
4. employment practices
5. corporate governance
6. executive power
7. size and diversification
8. values of executives and their companies

Resource Allocation

To cut costs, large Japanese companies are shrinking their headquarters HR units and decentralizing operating decisions. The number of employees in headquarters HR units has fallen 22 percent during the past five years, and in very large firms (those above the 90th percentile in total employment) the cuts have been even deeper. Headquarters staff has fallen more steeply than total employment, and so the number of headquarters staff per employee (1:129) is smaller than it was five years ago (1:106).

In the United States, where most companies experienced employment *growth* from 1996 to 2001, the average number of staff in headquarters HR units rose by 4 percent during this period.[10] When we calculate staff per employee, however, we find that U.S. companies failed to add staff as quickly as they added employees (and, in the case of some large firms, staff was cut more rapidly than employees). Hence the ratio of staff to employees fell from 1:144 in 1996 to 1:185 in 2001, representing a leaner HR function than in Japan. In fact, the staffing gap between the two countries *widened* during this period. In the United States, as noted earlier, the staffing ratio is considered to be a key quantitative indicator of HR efficiency, so there is pressure on HR departments to reduce the ratio even when times are good.

Are staff cuts taking place across the board or are companies singling out their HR units? To find out, we asked respondents, "Is HR's current share of

TABLE 6.1
Outsourcing: Percentage of Firms

	Japan	U.S.
Welfare and benefits management	41	35
Training	35	22
Payroll administration	19	21
Recruitment/hiring	13	10
HR information systems	20	12

total headquarters employment larger, smaller, or about the same as its share five years ago?" In Japan, 5 percent (in the United States, 24 percent) reported that HR's share was somewhat larger or a lot larger; 47 (in the United States, 35) percent said there had been no change; 36 (29) percent said somewhat smaller; and 11 (11) percent said a lot smaller. Thus the tendency for HR to be singled out for cuts is stronger in Japan.

Another reason for staff cuts is outsourcing. We asked about outsourcing of HR activities such as benefits (including welfare programs), training, recruitment, pay systems, and HR information systems (see table 6.1). In Japan, the HR functions for which outsourcing is most prevalent are training and welfare activities. However, by "outsourcing" many of the Japanese respondents have in mind something different from what the term means in the United States. In Japan, as we saw in the case studies, companies often spin off welfare or training departments and then purchase services from them. This is a way to cut costs, make headcount appear smaller, and boost the parent company's financial performance. However, these spin-offs represent a lower level of marketization than does third-party outsourcing, because they involve former company employees and typically there is no competitive bidding for their services.[11]

Diverging from the traditional Japanese view that HR (and other expertise) should be provided from within, some Japanese firms are adopting U.S.-style outsourcing to entirely independent third parties—partly to acquire expertise and partly to shift funding from capital investments to operating expenses. Foreign as well as domestic companies are active in this market, with the result that HR practices are becoming more generic.[12]

Table 6.1 shows outsourcing levels in the United States to be somewhat lower than in Japan. This is odd, since experts in the field indicate that in Japan the outsourcing market is newer and smaller.[13] The discrepancy can probably be attributed to the tendency of Japanese respondents to conflate spin-offs and third-party relationships, whereas the U.S. figures represent only the latter.

In both countries, then, we see that the prevailing tendency is for the headquarters HR unit to be changing size at about the same rate as are other functional units and for staffing ratios to be shrinking. Also, firms in both

TABLE 6.2
Change in Line Involvement over Five Years: Percentage of Firms

	Increased		Same		Decreased		N		χ^2
	Japan	U.S.	Japan	U.S.	Japan	U.S.	Japan	U.S.	
Introduce or modify participation plans	23	44	66	52	11	4	213	132	19.38***
Develop policies toward unions	18	15	75	76	6	9	212	102	1.27
Decide on business unit head count	21	46	72	46	8	8	213	132	27.83***
Assign jobs to managers	29	40	63	52	8	7	213	132	5.11†
Evaluate performance of managers	39	53	57	43	4	4	213	132	6.42*

† $p < .10$.   * $p < .05$.   *** $p < .001$.

countries rely considerably on outsourcing. These trends are occurring in tandem in both countries, so their positions relative to each other have not changed. Staffing ratios in the United States, for example, continue to be leaner than in Japan. However—and this is worth noting—the absolute size of that gap has widened during the past five years.

Centralization of Operating Authority

Another reason that headquarters is shrinking is that decision making is becoming decentralized. We asked respondents to tell us how the role of line and operating managers had changed over the previous five years. We focused on five areas (see table 6.2): the introduction or modification of employee-involvement plans such as TQM or quality circles, the development of policies towards unions, decisions on headcount (hiring, layoffs, accelerated retirement), job assignment, and performance evaluation of managers.

In Japan, what once was a core headquarters responsibility—the assignment and evaluation of managers—is undergoing decentralization in roughly a third of surveyed companies. Divisions and business units now have more control over the rotation and promotion of rank-and-file managers, and individuals enjoy a greater choice of assignments. Consistent with this development is the smaller role that headquarters is playing in managerial evaluation, and that in turn is a result of the proliferation of individualized pay-for-performance systems, about which more in a moment.

While some Japanese companies are experiencing change, the central tendency is stasis. The level of line involvement in decision making has remained constant for the majority of Japanese companies. The media's attention is often riveted on how companies have changed, but most have not. On questions of hiring, career rotation, transfers, and the like, headquarters HR units still hold substantial power relative to that of line managers.

U.S. firms are decentralizing significantly faster than those in Japan—a surprising fact, as U.S. firms in the 1980s already were relatively decentralized.[14] Change-rate gaps between the United States and Japan are especially wide in decisions over business-unit headcount: Line managers in the United States have much more freedom to make hiring and layoff decisions than do line managers in Japan. In the decentralization of decision making, then, as in the ratio of HR staff to employees, the gap between the two countries has widened, even though they are moving in similar directions.

It is possible that some of the authority being relinquished by headquarters HR is being transferred not only to line managers but also to HR staff elsewhere in the organization. Therefore we asked respondents to assign weights for the five activities previously analyzed and to distribute those weights (which would sum to 100) across four categories of decision-maker—line managers, unit HR departments, divisional HR departments, and headquarters HR departments. The results are shown in table 6.3.[15]

Here, notice several points. First, despite decentralization, operating decisions remain significantly more centralized in Japan than in the United States.[16] This is a key finding. In fact, only in the area of participation plans do U.S. and Japanese companies show similar levels of centralization. In the United States these plans were introduced in the 1970s and 1980s and patterned after the Japanese approach, which traditionally gives substantial authority for quality control to line managers and frontline workers.[17] Second, in neither country do units at the subheadquarters level have a substantial measure of operating authority; they are squeezed between headquarters and line management. Third, in Japan there is a strong positive correlation between headquarters operating authority and HR staff per employee. That is, centralization is associated with greater resources for headquarters, as one would expect. In the United States, the relationship is also positive but not statistically significant, meaning that centralization yields no assured payoff in HR-staff intensity.[18]

HR's Strategic Influence

Senior management periodically makes strategic decisions that affect an organization's future. To assess the strategic influence of the headquarters HR department, we posed two types of questions. First, we asked respondents to tell us at what stage(s) they were involved in five different business decisions related to growth and restructuring: mergers and acquisitions, investing in new locations, creating spin-offs, expanding existing sites, and closing existing sites. The stages of involvement—they are not mutually exclusive—were drawing up the proposal, evaluating its financial consequences, final decision-making, and implementation. Respondents also indicated if they were never involved or if the event did not occur.[19]

TABLE 6.3
Division of Responsibility for HR Activities, Japan and United States

	Line Managers		Unit HRD		Divisional HRD		Headquarters HRD		t-test	N	
	Japan	U.S.	Japan	U.S.	Japan	U.S.	Japan	U.S.		Japan	U.S.
Introduce or modify participation plans	52	45	11	12	13	17	25	27	-0.529	203	125
Develop policies toward unions	11	17	7	9	9	16	73	58	3.589***	209	103
Decide on business unit head count	19	50	12	9	18	14	50	28	6.693***	220	140
Assign jobs to managers	23	62	5	9	16	14	57	16	15.771***	220	140
Evaluate performance of managers	41	65	5	8	15	12	38	15	8.589***	221	140
Operating Authority Index value[a]	28.9	50.5					48.9	26.6	10.262***	221	140

Note: Respondents were asked to apportion responsibility for various HR activities across the four different levels such that the weights summed to 100. Because of rounding, numbers may not sum to exactly 100.
[a] The index is the mean of the items in the column above it.
*** $p < .001$.

Second, we asked respondents to tell us what part they played in two other decisions that are more closely related to HR concerns but that have strategic consequences: the allocation of payroll budgets across corporate divisions, and the selection and remuneration of senior executives. The responses—again, not mutually exclusive—from which they could choose were: that they were limited to providing information, that they regularly offered advice on the basis of the information, that they regularly took part in decisions, and that they had no role. For the U.S. sample only, we also asked CFOs to tell us about HR's role and about their own role in these decisions.

What is interesting about table 6.4 is it shows the high involvement in strategic decisions of U.S. HR executives as compared to their Japanese counterparts. Somewhere between a quarter and a half of Japanese HR executives are not involved in such decisions, except those relating to plant closures. Noninvolvement rates for U.S. executives average only about 10 percent. These are sizable and statistically significant gaps.

One explanation for that gap is that the issues at the heart of restructuring decisions are less salient in Japan, where, as shown in the righthand column of table 6.4, there is less M&A activity and less new-site investment than in the United States. On these two issues, the involvement gap is wide, especially at the earliest and most strategic stage of drawing up a proposal. Perhaps as an issue becomes more prevalent and routine, HR is more likely to be involved. Conversely, the rate of site closures was about the same in the two countries, while spin-offs were more prevalent in Japan. On these two issues, the involvement gap is smaller, again, especially at the earliest stage of drawing up a proposal, although the U.S. executives still wield more influence.

Similarities across borders do exist, however. U.S. and Japanese executives alike are less involved in the decisional phases of strategic events—drawing up a proposal and making final decisions about it—than they are in its implementation.[20] Also, U.S. executives who report to the CEO are more involved in the decisions, as are Japanese respondents who hold the rank of managing director, although there remains an involvement gap even between managing directors in Japan and CEO reports in the United States.

One should not, however, simply accept the U.S. findings wholesale. When we asked CFOs in the United States about the involvement of their HR executives, we received a notably different pattern of responses, including when we matched CFO and HR respondents from the same company. For example, while 50 percent of HR executives said they were involved in final decision-making on closures, only 26 percent of the CFOs from the same companies corroborated that claim. On other strategic issues we found similar discrepancies between HR and finance.[21] We suspect that these discrepancies can be explained by the HR executives being simply unaware of the early stages of M&A activity (which typically involve the CEO, the CFO, and investment bankers) or being out of the loop when crucial decisions are actually made.

TABLE 6.4
Role of HR in Strategic Business Decisions in Japan and the United States: Percentage Checking Stage

	Drawing Up Proposal		Evaluation of Financial Consequences		Final Decision		Implementation		HR Not Involved			Event Did Not Occur		
	Japan	US	Japan	US	Japan	US	Japan	US	Japan	US	χ^2	Japan	US	χ^2
Merger or acquisition	10	32	7	61	14	47	41	85	38	3	29.46***	66	18	51.63***
									(29)	(115)		(85)	(141)	
Creation of spin-off	43	42	14	56	7	46	48	72	24	11	3.71†	32	58	14.90***
									(58)	(57)		(85)	(137)	
Invest in new site	9	33	8	45	11	38	34	62	47	22	10.93***	37	21	6.35*
									(53)	(110)		(84)	(140)	
Expand existing site	14	27	12	43	11	36	38	64	42	18	11.97***	24	18	0.95
									(65)	(117)		(85)	(143)	
Closure of existing site	42	48	16	56	10	55	54	77	16	3	9.49**	22	19	0.35
									(67)	(116)		(86)	(143)	

Note: "Event did not occur" column gives percentage of all respondents. Other columns show the percentages for those companies where the event occurred. N (shown) in the last column is all respondents. N shown in the "HR Not Involved" column is the number of companies indicating that the event occurred. Respondents could check more than one stage if the event occurred. Note that, due to an error in the original survey, we had to resurvey the Japanese companies on this question. Hence the Japanese total available sample size is 86 for this question versus 143 for the U.S.

† $p < .10$.   * $p < .05$ ** $p < .01$ *** $p < .001$.

Moreover, despite assumptions that the involvement of U.S. HR executives marks a new, more strategic era for HR and a departure from past practices, the historical data suggest otherwise. In 1966, the percentage of HR executives who were involved in M&A decisions was 71, while the corresponding figure for 2001 was 79 percent, which is an increase, but not a dramatic one.[22]

A different type of strategic decision lies in the domain where HR strategy interacts with business strategy. This includes the selection and remuneration of senior executives (a process that affects the future management of the organization) and the allocation of payroll budgets across divisions (a process that determines how quickly divisions will grow). We asked respondents what role they played in these decisions: whether to provide information, offer advice, take part in the final decision, or some combination of those (see table 6.5). Here the involvement gaps between Japan and the United States are smaller and less significant. In fact, Japanese involvement significantly surpasses U.S. involvement in more than half of the table's cells.

One possible explanation is that U.S. HR executives are viewed as lacking the financial acumen necessary to make budgetary decisions or that, unlike Japanese HR executives, they must compete with CFOs for authority over budgetary and executive-compensation issues. In our CFO survey, we asked who was involved in decisions to review business-unit performance. The CFO was reported to be personally involved in 90 percent of these decisions and line managers in 85 percent, but the senior HR executive in only 53 percent. Again, a comparison of assessments—this time of HR involvement in key personnel and budget decisions—shows discrepancies between the prevailing perception among HR executives and that among CFOs.[23]

Another explanation is that differences in involvement stem from distinctive national approaches to business structure. Japanese companies tend to be less divisionalized, so it is more likely that they make budgetary decisions at the headquarters level.

In short, there are multiple dimensions of strategic influence. HR executives in Japan and the United States both play strategic roles in executive decision-making, although the roles are expressed differently in each country.

Employment Practices

A striking similarity between Japan and the United States is the proportion of full-time employees in the workforce of the sample companies. It stands at around 85 percent, part-time and temporary employment accounting for the remainder (and being distributed similarly in both countries). In both, full-time employment is positively correlated with education level (as indicated by the percentage of employees who are college graduates) and with membership in a union.[24]

TABLE 6.5
Role of HR in Strategic Personnel Decisions: Percentage Checking Role

	Provide Information			Offer Advice Based on Information			Take Part in Final Decisions			Not Involved			N	
	Japan	U.S.	χ^2	Japan	U.S.	χ^2	Japan	U.S.	χ^2	Japan	U.S.	χ^2	Japan	U.S.
Selecting and remunerating senior managers	15	8	4.27*	62	25	49.15***	67	80	6.44*	1	7	8.41**	227	142
Determining size and allocation of payroll budgets across divisions	10	20	6.44*	32	33	0.01	74	45	30.74***	8	16	5.1*	214	141

* $p < .05$.   ** $p < .01$.   *** $p < .001$.

TABLE 6.6
Preferred Methods for Filling Vacancies: Percentage of firms

	Managers		Nonsupervisory employees	
	Japan	U.S.	Japan	U.S.
Only consider internal candidates	35	0	30	1
First priority to internal; recruit outside only when needed	54	41	54	59
Consider both internal and external candidates	11	59	15	40
Prefer recruiting external candidates	0	1	1	0
χ^2	122.52***		64.27***	
Mean ILM index value[a]	1.238	.392	1.121	.604
t-test	13.819***		8.066***	
N	227	143	223	144

[a] Considering internal candidates is coded as 2; giving first priority to internal candidates and recruiting outside only when needed is coded as 1; considering both internal and external candidates is coded as 0; and preferring to recruit external candidates is coded as –2, for both managerial and nonsupervisory positions. Coding the latter as –1 does not affect the relative differences.
*** $p < .001$.

These parallels between the employment picture in Japan and in the United States exist alongside divergent national approaches to structuring employment. When asked how they would fill vacancies for either managerial or nonsupervisory employees, the Japanese companies, showing a strong preference for internal candidates, were significantly less inclined than U.S. companies were to consider external candidates (see table 6.6).[25] Note the startling finding that hardly any U.S. employers give strong preference to internal candidates, whereas in Japan about a third of companies do. Also, in Japan the preference for internal candidates is only slightly greater for managerial than for nonmanagerial positions, reflecting the persistence of single-status employment policies. In the United States, though, not only is the cleavage between managerial and nonmanagerial employees significant, but it is the managerial positions that actually receive fewer benefits from incumbency. Indeed, this is consistent with reports that, in large U.S. companies, recent downsizing has been concentrated among salaried rather than hourly employees.[26]

Other data we gathered support the finding that employment practices in the United States are more market-oriented than in Japan. For example, we asked respondents to estimate what percentage of an average middle manager's annual salary was determined by the individual's job performance versus other factors such as job classification and seniority. Despite the increased emphasis on performance in Japan, the Japanese mean for performance-based pay was 30 percent; in the United States, it was 55 percent.

Centralized decision-making in Japan is associated with a strong internal labor market. Where incumbent managers are employed "for life," headquarters is more likely to be involved in managerial rotations and pay decisions—that is, they are more centralized (as defined in table 6.3).[27] Strength of the internal labor market for nonsupervisory employees also is positively associated with HR centralization, but the relationship is weaker. However, the Japanese companies with the highest levels of insider hiring and HR centralization have also seen the greatest shrinkage of HR staff during the past five years—a kind of regression to the mean.[28]

In the United States, national patterns are less evident. Few of the measures of the internal labor market are significantly related to HR variables such as degree of centralization or staff intensity. One exception—and it is intriguing—has to do with corporate governance. As the number of persons on the board who have HR backgrounds increases, so does the practice of favoring incumbent employees in hiring decisions.[29] The other significant relationship concerns pay for performance: Firms in which managers receive a large share of compensation based on individual performance—that is, where compensation is market-oriented—have lower levels of control by headquarters and greater involvement of line and operating managers over the past five years.[30] Some have argued that this reduction of hierarchy indicates a shift to a partnership-type model for managerial employment.[31] But it also may signal a defect in corporate governance. The lack of central control over managerial salaries mirrors the lack of board control over CEO salaries, the problem that gave rise to the corporate scandals that first emerged in 2001.[32]

Corporate Governance

As we saw in the case studies, one recent change in Japanese corporate governance is the advent of the Sony-style corporate-officer system (*shikkō yakuin*), which has caught on in the past five years. Under this system, a small U.S.-style board is created, consisting of insiders and one or two outsiders, while the other (now former) board members, all of them incumbent executives, are relegated to a management committee ostensibly focused on operating, not strategic, issues. Twenty-eight percent of respondents said their firms had adopted the system, a figure consistent with other surveys.[33] Because of this development, and because of investor pressure to reduce board size, Japanese boards are smaller, on average, than in past years. Respondents report a mean board size of fifteen persons: eleven in companies with the corporate-officer system and sixteen in other firms. Only ten years ago, some boards had as many as fifty or more persons, and the mean was about thirty.[34]

The changes in corporate governance have not, however, diminished HR's influence. Between companies with and those without the corporate-officer system, we found no difference in the perceived power of the headquarters

HR unit or in its influence over strategic decisions.[35] One explanation may be that reforms in Japanese corporate governance are symbolic, signaling to investors that management has become sensitive to shareholder interests, thereby forestalling the adoption of more radical reforms. There is evidence that U.S. companies act in this fashion—making changes to achieve legitimacy rather than efficiency—so to see Japanese companies exhibit the same behavior would not be surprising.[36]

Even under the corporate-officer system, boards continue to include individuals with HR experience. When respondents were asked how many board members had prior executive experience in HR, 58 percent said one or two, 19 percent said three or four, and 4 percent said five or more, so a total of 80 percent of the Japanese companies we surveyed had at least one board member with previous experience as an HR executive.

The enterprise union also plays a role in grooming managers for the board. When respondents were asked how many board members previously held a leadership position in the enterprise union, 25 percent said one or two, 14 percent said three or four, and 6 percent said five or more, yielding a total of 45 percent. While there may be some overlap between companies whose boards reflect HR executive experience and those whose boards reflect experience in union leadership, half of the companies that fit the former definition had zero board members with a union background. Hence a total of 85 percent of companies have at least one person on their board with either experience in HR and/or union leadership.

Far fewer U.S. respondents, only 34 percent, reported that their boards had at least one member with HR executive experience. Moreover, major U.S. companies rarely appoint their own HR executive to the board. Data from Korn/Ferry for the nine hundred largest U.S. companies show only six whose boards include an in-house HR executive. While one might attribute this to the tendency of U.S. companies to seek outsiders to serve on their board, it is interesting to note that ninety-two of the companies gave a board seat to their CFO.[37] Also indicative of the CFO's influence is that, within the same company, finance reports to the CEO in more cases (95 percent) than does HR (72 percent). That is, in nearly a quarter of the matched HR-CFO pairs, the CFO reports to the CEO but the HR executive does not, despite the rise in the number of HR executives reporting to that level.

Executive Power

We asked executives to tell us about the relative power of different headquarters departments to influence strategic decisions (see table 6.7). While we did not define *power*, the results here and in other studies suggest that respondents had a consistent understanding of the word.[38] Rated on a scale of 1 to 10, with 10 being "most influential," the top department in the United States was

Table 6.7
Perceived Power of Headquarters' Functions

	Japan HR Mean (rank)	U.S. HR Mean (rank)
Finance	5.7 (3)	8.4 (1)
Human Resources	5.7 (3)	6.1 (5)
Marketing/Sales	6.7 (2)	7.1 (2)
Planning/Strategy	8.2 (1)	6.3 (4)
Production/Operations	5.2 (5)	6.4 (3)
R&D	5.4 (4)	5.4 (6)

Note: Spearman's rank correlation = 0.203 (p = 0.6998).

finance, followed, in order, by marketing, production, planning/strategy, and HR. Only R&D ranked lower. Answers to this question when posed to CFOs yielded similar rankings: Finance rated itself as the strongest department and HR as the weakest, weaker even than R&D. Among the matched-pair companies, CFOs and HR executives alike rated finance as the most powerful function, and, again, finance gave HR a lower rating than HR gave itself.[39]

However, when asked which departments have gained or lost power to influence strategic decisions over the past five years, U.S. HR executives were most likely to include in the former category their own function: 77 percent said that HR and 50 percent that finance, ranking second in this measure, had gained power. This view is not shared by CFOs, 70 percent of whom cited finance as having gained power but only 27 percent of whom said the same of HR. One check on finance's power arises through board composition: In the United States, the power of finance is moderated by the presence of board members with an HR background. As the number of these board members rises, the perceived power of finance declines.[40] This suggests yet another link between board composition and HR outcomes in the United States.

In most U.S. companies, however, HR and finance executives agree that finance rules the roost. This is hardly surprising, given the prevalence of the M-form type of corporate organization, the pace of M&A activity, the salience of the shareholder ethos, and the stratospheric level of equity prices during the study period. One point on which HR and finance do not agree, however, is HR's status. The CFOs see HR gaining and holding less power than the HR executives think is the case. Unfortunately, there is no way to determine whose perception of HR power is correct, but it is plausible that HR, the underdog, has greater reason to overstate changes in its influence than finance has to understate them.

The decision-making process in Japanese companies is different. When asked about power, Japanese respondents said the top department was planning, which typically is a small unit that is attached to the president's office and handles spin-offs and other issues related to strategy and organizational design (see table 6.7). Marketing ranks second, and finance and HR are tied for third, while production and R&D are farther down the list. Even if Japanese and U.S. HR executives are equally prone to hubris, it is still the case that the former are more inclined to assess themselves as powerful.[41]

However, on a related measure—of which departments had gained or lost power during the past five years—the percentage of Japanese respondents who said HR had gained was 40, which is lower than the percentage recorded by their U.S. counterparts. At the same time, most Japanese HR executives did not rate their departments below finance: Only 37 percent said finance had gained power. Again, it is the planning department, identified by 54 percent as having gained power, that emerged as the leader in this category.

Finance, then, is not the top function in Japan, nor does it dominate HR. Rather, the planning department, which specializes in corporate organization from a strategic rather than a financial perspective, holds the largest share of power, and its share is gaining.[42] In other areas as well, no strong evidence exists to support claims of a trend toward the financialization of corporate strategy in Japan. Stock options—in the United States, a key mechanism for aligning management decision-making to shareholder interests—remain uncommon. Only 19 percent of the surveyed companies reported using options; an additional 10 percent said they were considering them. Firms offering options tend to limit them to their most senior executives. Other studies have found that, when Japanese companies do offer stock options, they account for a trivial portion of total compensation.[43] In the United States, options are used by nearly all companies (97 percent). The majority (60 percent) though, pay them only to their managerial employees and then usually only to senior and divisional executives, the upper crust of management.[44]

The perceived power of the headquarters HR function does have consequences: for the unit's strategic influence, for its role in the organization, and for employment outcomes such as the strength of internal labor markets. Table 6.8 breaks out Japanese and U.S. companies in the lower and upper quartiles of perceived HR power, with HR power normalized on a respondent's mean rating for all functions. (We call this "relative power.") In both Japan and the United States, high relative HR power is associated with stronger internal labor markets for managers; greater centralization of operating decisions; and greater HR influence over executive career decisions, budgetary allocations, and strategic business decisions. While HR power is associated with larger staffs, it is *not* associated with higher staffing ratios (staff per employee). Power is related to the sheer number of employees—which makes HR more salient—while staffing ratios are affected by economies of scale, an issue to which we turn next. Note, however, that most of these relationships, while they have the expected signs, are not statistically significant, with the exception of our measures relating power to strategic influence.[45]

TABLE 6.8
Relative Power of the HR Function and Corporate Outcomes (N in parentheses)

	Japan			United States		
	Lower Quartile, Relative HR Power	Upper Quartile, Relative HR Power	Correlation with Relative HR Power	Lower Quartile, Relative HR Power	Upper Quartile, Relative HR Power	Correlation with Relative HR Power
Index, internal hiring, managerial employees[a]	1.21 (52)	1.25 (63)	.00	.31 (35)	.44 (39)	.15†
Index, internal hiring, nonsupervisory employees	0.96 (52)	1.15 (61)	.06	.66 (35)	.56 (39)	−.02
Number of headquarters staff	18 (52)	23 (65)	.04	25 (35)	75 (40)	.10
Staff per employee	1:121 (52)	1:140 (60)	−.02	1:212 (35)	1:211 (40)	−.04
Operating authority index value[b]	47.4 (52)	50.3 (61)	.03	24.5 (34)	26.5 (38)	.02
Strategic influence:[c]						
—Senior executives and payroll allocation	5.85 (46)	6.38 (61)	.03	4.47 (34)	5.73 (37)	.27**
—Other business decisions	1.44 (18)	2.39 (23)	.19†	3.13 (34)	4.80 (38)	.26**

Note: Relative power is the power value for the HR function in a firm divided by the mean power value for all other functions in the firm.

[a]This is the same index shown in table 6.6, only here we break out managerial versus nonmanagerial employees.

[b]See table 6.3.

[c]"Senior executives and payroll allocation" is the sum of the cells in table 6.5, where 1 point is given for each instance of providing information, 2 points for offering advice, 3 points for being involved in the final decision, for a total maximum of 12 points. For "Other business decisions" it is the mean across rows (events) in table 6.4, where 3 points is given for drawing up the proposal and final decision-making, 2 points for evaluating financial consequences, and 1 point for implementation, for a maximum of 9 points for each event.

† p < .10.   ** p < .01.

Size and Diversification

What have been recent trends in firm size? In the United States, the size of nonmanufacturing corporations increased steadily in the 1990s, especially in the service and retail sectors, while the share of employment accounted for by the top one thousand firms held steady (after a decline in the 1970s and 1980s). The reasons, though not clear, may include improvements in the ability of large firms to realize economies of scale in technology, distribution, and global trade.[46] Similar trends can be found in Japan, albeit for different reasons. Because the recession of the 1990s hit smaller firms harder than large ones, the employment share of large firms has risen since 1986 (after falling in the period 1978–86) and now stands at a higher level than in 1978.[47]

Does size affect the organization of the HR function? Indeed, we found that the HR function in large firms (measured by employment) in both Japan and the United States is more decentralized, has fewer HR staff per employee, wields greater strategic influence, and contains HR executives who are more powerful (see table 6.9).[48] As noted, the association may be due to a link between the amount of corporate resources a department is responsible for managing and its perceived power.[49]

What about trends in diversification? The received wisdom is that Japanese companies were slow to adopt the M-form model of organization, subsequently overdiversified into unrelated industries in the late 1980s (partly to eliminate surplus cash and partly to create employment opportunities for permanent employees), and since then have been divesting unrelated businesses.[50] Actual data on diversification at the company level are scarce, however. Consistent with the assumption about de-diversification, one study found a decline in the 1990s in the average number of industries handled by a single company. But the study also showed a decline in the percentage of sales based on a company's core business—a finding consistent with greater diversification in the 1990s.[51]

The received wisdom about the United States goes something like this: An emphasis on shareholder value led to huge divestment of unrelated businesses in the 1980s, and less diversification meant higher risk but also higher returns. In the early 1990s, some companies adopted a new rationale for de-diversification, as the move away from diversification was fueled now by the resource-based (or core-competency) approach to strategy.

Again, however, the aggregate data tell stories that are more complicated. From 1985 to 1992, company-level diversification increased, at least among the five hundred largest U.S. companies.[52] While no corporate-level studies for the post-1992 period yet exist, we do have data on concentration ratios at the industry level. We would expect to see a rise in those ratios if companies were shedding unrelated units and selling them to companies whose business profiles they more logically fit. Prior to 1995, concentration ratios fell. That

TABLE 6.9
Diversification, Size, Centralization, and Power

	Mean HQ Operating Authority Score		HR Staffing Ratio		Influence in Stategic Business Decisions		Relative Power of HR Unit		Mean Firm Size	
	Japan	U.S.	Japan	U.S.	Japan	U.S.	Japan	U.S.	Japan	U.S.
Sales > 90 percent in same industry	55	28	1:129	1:177	2.3	3.9	.93	.89	4,662	17,863
Sales 70–90 percent in same industry	48	25	1:103	1:139	2.2	4.7	.98	.87	3,780	14,980
Sales < 70 percent, related and unrelated	44	18	1:144	1:483	1.4	5.0	.92	.93	6,137	25,864
Size below median	54	32	1:93	1:138	1.4	3.6	.92	.82		
Size above median	44	21	1:208	1:270	2.4	4.6	.95	.95		

TABLE 6.10
Indicators for Evaluating the Corporate HR Function

	Japan (rank)	U.S. (rank)
Level of direct and indirect labor costs	3.2 (3)	2.5 (3)
Revenue or sales per employee	3.0 (4)	1.8 (5)
Retention and turnover rates	2.1 (5)	3.0 (2)
Employee attitudes & morale	3.7 (1)	3.1 (1)
Cooperative relations with union (if any)	3.4 (2)	1.8 (5)
Union avoidance in unorganized facilities	–	2.2 (4)

Note: 0 = not used, 1 = not very important . . . 4 = very important.

is consistent with greater diversification, but since 1995 they have risen only slightly, providing weak support for the notion that U.S. companies are becoming more focused.[53] Experts believe, however, that at the company level there is now, as in the past, more unrelated diversification in the United States than in Japan. This remains a question into which additional research is needed.[54]

Recall from the case studies that Japanese companies demonstrate a relationship between diversification and HR's corporate status: True to resource-based theories, the role that headquarters HR plays in focused Japanese companies is more influential. Also recall, though, that we did not find a consistent relationship in the case of the U.S. companies. The aggregate data (see table 6.9) corroborate these inferences. Operating authority—that is, centralization—declines with diversification in both Japan and the United States. That makes intuitive sense, since focused companies, because of similarity in processes and technologies across units, can achieve economies of scale through centralization. Presumably these focused companies operate more like U-form than M-form organizations. The data also show that, in Japan, HR's strategic role is greater in focused companies, although this is not the case when we consider HR's strategic influence in the United States. Here the largest strategic role that HR plays is in diversified companies. Again, that may be related to the greater salience of M&A-type decisions in diversified U.S. companies as compared to U.S. and Japanese companies that are more focused.

Another way of identifying the role of HR in business strategy is to determine how companies evaluate the performance of their headquarters HR department (see table 6.10). Two of the measures—labor costs and revenue per employee—suggest a commodity approach to labor that is consistent with maximizing shareholder value in the short term. Two other measures—employee morale and union relations—suggest a human-capital-investment approach that is reflective of a resource-based business strategy.[55] The significance of turnover is ambiguous: It can fit with either approach, since turnover is both a transaction cost as well as an indicator of asset retention. We also asked about union avoidance but only of the U.S. respondents.

The data in table 6.10 suggest that in Japan the human-capital-investment approach is more prevalent, this due to the high absolute value assigned to

employee morale and the high ranking given to union-management cooperation, Turnover is more important in the United States, where traditionally it
has been a key quantitative indicator of the HR unit's efficiency. In Japan,
where voluntary turnover is low, it has less meaning.[56]

Somewhat surprisingly, we did not observe national differences in the emphasis placed on labor-cost minimization. Remember, though, that the survey
was conducted at a time when Japanese companies were struggling to cut
costs and U.S. companies were coming off a boom during which the importance of cost minimization was more likely to be scanted. One important
difference between Japan and the United States is this: In Japan, an emphasis
on labor-cost minimization is positively associated with an emphasis on employee morale and good union relations. This can be interpreted as evidence
of the emergence of a hybrid Japanese model, in which market principles
are being grafted onto a traditional base. In the United States, however, the
association between cost concerns and human-capital concerns was negative,
suggesting that the two strategies are substitutes for, rather than complements
to, each other in the American case.[57]

Values of Executives and Their Companies

One would expect, and studies have found, that Japanese and U.S. managers
hold different values as a result of differences in career patterns, corporate
governance, and culture.[58] Table 6.11 presents results from four surveys that
asked similar questions concerning executive values. The 1993 data, from a
Japanese survey of corporate directors, gives some perspective on changes in
Japan during the 1990s. However, we expect this group to be less inclined to
hold stakeholder values, even in 1993, so any gap between the directors and
current HR executives is probably an understatement of change in executive
values since 1993. We also compare HR executives in the United States and
Japan, and CFOs and HR executives in the United States.

First, with respect to Japan during the period 1993–2001, what is significant
is the change in executive attitudes: The importance of share-price value has
risen and that of market share has fallen. Part of this no doubt is the result of
secular changes in corporate governance and reflects a new shareholder-value
ethos in Japan. Part may also be related to cyclical economic factors: Japanese
managers stress dividends and market share less now than in 1993 because
their markets are shrinking and profits (to pay dividends) are thin or nonexistent, while in the United States the case is the opposite (or was until 2001).
Nevertheless, the national difference in the emphasis placed on stock prices
is sizable and significant. In the United States, HR executives rank share price
the second most important measure (fair treatment is ranked first) of what is
important to them in their jobs, while in Japan HR executives rank it seventh.

TABLE 6.11
Executive Values

	1993 Japanese Directors[a]	Japanese HR Executives[b]	U.S. HR Executives[b]	U.S. CFOs[c]	t-test Japanese vs. U.S. HR Executives
Raise dividends	2.6	2.2 (225)	2.6 (139)	1.7	−3.328 ***
Raise share price	2.0	2.3 (225)	3.3 (141)	3.6	−11.873 ***
Raise market share	2.9	2.2 (225)	2.9 (142)	2.7	−6.564 ***
Diversify & expand into new markets	2.9	2.5 (226)	2.4 (144)	2.5	1.079
Improve employee morale	NA	3.6 (226)	3.3 (143)	2.7	5.013 ***
Ensure employees are treated fairly	NA	3.0 (225)	3.4 (144)	2.7	−5.557 ***
Safeguard employees' jobs	3.3	3.2 (225)	2.1 (142)	1.8	12.662 ***
Increase number of management positions	1.3	1.2 (224)	1.2 (144)	1.1	−.491
Increase my department's budget	1.5	1.4 (225)	1.3 (144)	1.1	1.585
Coordinate with other departments	2.4	2.8 (226)	3.2 (144)	NA	−4.101 ***
Make contribution to society	2.6	2.5 (225)	2.4 (144)	2.2	1.641

Note: Respondents were asked, "What is important to you in your job?" 1 = not important, 4 = most important.
[a] 1993 data courtesy of Fujikazu Suzuki, RENGO Research Institute for Advancement of Living Standards (RIALS), Tokyo. (N) = 2246.
[b] N in parentheses.
[c] (N) = 81.
*** $p < .001$.

Among U.S. CFOs, who are closer to the highest echelons than are HR executives, share price outranks all other measures, including fair treatment.[59]

Conversely, Japanese HR executives give greater weight to job security, ranking it their second most important concern; their U.S. counterparts rank it ninth. That difference is big, and emblematic of the distinction between the stakeholder (organization-oriented) and the shareholder (market-oriented) visions. In the relative importance they assign to internal management issues (increasing department budgets and the number of management positions), though, Japanese and U.S. HR managers are close to each other and the gaps are not significant. In short, there are striking national differences with respect to share prices and job security, the values that relate most directly to philosophies of corporate governance, and smaller differences with respect to other values.[60]

Are these normative concerns related to the structure of the HR function? Table 6.12 examines two key values: maximizing share price and safeguarding employee jobs. For each country and each value, we identify what number cite the value as being of low or of high importance, and we display the means for four variables associated with each category.

For the U.S sample, we hypothesized that strong HR career backgrounds, a measure of professionalism, would be associated with weaker support for shareholders and stronger support for safeguarding employees' jobs.[61] The first but not the second part of the hypothesis is supported by the data in table 6.12. We also expected that a strong union presence would affect the values of an HR executive much as the professionalism criterion would, but no relationship between a firm's unionization level and the values of its executives was demonstrated.

However, there *is* a relationship between executive values and power. In both countries, HR executives who hold "shareholder" values (either to maximize share prices or to minimize the safeguarding of employees' jobs) rate their own central HR unit as relatively powerful. (The size of this group is much larger in the United States than in Japan.) Recall also our earlier finding that, in the United States, CEO reports are more likely to hold shareholder values and to rate their departments as relatively powerful. It is reasonable to posit that the causality runs from values to power: that HR executives who put shareholders ahead of employees gain power for their units, and themselves, by demonstrating allegiance to the financial mind-set dominant among senior management. Another possibility is that shareholder-oriented CEOs (who increasingly are outsiders with sole allegiance to the board that hired them)[62] select HR executives whose values match their own; HR's perceived power is an offshoot of reporting to the CEO. Either pathway is consistent with the new "business partner" model being proposed for HR executives in the United States.

TABLE 6.12
Correlates of HR Executive Values (N in parentheses)

	Maximize Share Price				Safeguard Employees' Jobs			
	Japan		U.S.		Japan		U.S.	
	Low Importance	High Importance	Low Importance	High Importance	Low Importance	High Importance	Low Importance	High Importance
% career in HR	43 (137)	36 (88)	82 (20)	76 (117)	41 (36)	40 (189)	78 (99)	72 (39)
		$r = -.07$		$r = -.15$†		$r = -.01$		$r = -.02$
% union	64 (127)	66 (83)	15 (19)	16 (114)	58 (34)	66 (177)	17 (94)	12 (39)
		$r = .03$		$r = -.02$		$r = .10$		$r = -.07$
Relative HR power	.92 (131)	.95 (84)	.80 (19)	.90 (118)	1.03 (35)	.92 (180)	.94 (97)	.77 (41)
		$r = .06$		$r = .17^*$		$r = -.09$		$r = -.27^*$
Influence in business strategy	1.8 (57)	2.0 (22)	3.2 (18)	4.3 (119)	1.7 (15)	1.9 (63)	4.3 (97)	3.8 (41)
		$r = .17$		$r = .15$†		$r = .07$		$r = -.15$†

Note: "Low importance": respondent rated the value as not important or somewhat important; "high importance": respondent rated the value as very important or most important.
† $p < .10$. * $p < .05$.

It may well be that a similar emphasis on the shareholder is now gaining ground inside Japanese corporations and that those HR executives who align themselves with it will be able to boost their power. However—and this is key—the power differential associated with a shareholder orientation is smaller than in the United States and not statistically significant—so that Japanese HR executives have less incentive to adopt these values as a way to maximize their power.

As for strategic influence, again the U.S. pattern is for HR executives with shareholder values to have significantly more influence than managers with stakeholder values. Among Japanese executives, however, there is little evidence of this effect. In fact, those Japanese executives who care more about safeguarding employee jobs tend to have *greater* strategic influence, although the relationship is not statistically significant.

■ ■ ■

As we close this chapter, three points bear repeating: First, there is a split in the U.S. sample between HR executives who hold stakeholder values and those with shareholder values, the latter tending to be more influential, more likely to report to the CEO, and more likely to be found in diversified companies. Second, Japanese HR executives, as compared to their American counterparts, receive a smaller payoff—in terms of power and influence—from adopting shareholder values, and that fact slows the process of U.S.-centric convergence. Why the payoff is smaller is not clear, though it very likely is related to the Japanese corporation's insulation from fickle investors and, at a more micro level, to the persistence of business strategies based on long-term cultivation of a firm's internal resources, including its human and social capital. There is evidence that a powerful new concern with minimizing costs has taken hold in Japan, although as yet it has not changed fundamental business strategies.

Our third point draws from the other two: In both countries there is a relationship between features of corporate governance like board composition and HR outcomes. In other words, employment relations are very much at stake in current debates in Japan and the United States about corporate responsibility and corporate governance.

Taking Stock and Looking Ahead

THE HEADQUARTERS OF LARGE CORPORATIONS is precisely where one would expect to see evidence that globalization is eroding national differences, but the senior HR executive in Japan continues to play a significantly different role from that of the senior HR executive in the United States. In Japan, decision making and large HR staffs remain centralized, reflecting the persistence of organization-oriented employment practices. The HR function ranks relatively high in the corporate hierarchy and influences strategic decisions related to executive careers and budgetary allocations. Many senior HR executives participate on company boards, where they join others with HR backgrounds. As the majority of Japanese executives still espouse "stakeholder" rather than "shareholder" values, enterprise unions and employment security—two of the three pillars of the Japanese employment system—remain in place, at least in large public companies. The relative importance of seniority, the third pillar, is declining, but that is a long-term trend—it was in 1965 that Nikkeiren first recommended the de-emphasis of seniority—and, as we saw in the previous chapter, the share of pay based on individual performance remains below U.S. levels.[1]

Still, Japanese corporations have not been immune to change. Total HR staff has been cut back, as have staffing ratios, and HR activities are being outsourced. While to some extent this reflects companywide belt tightening, there are signs that the HR function is being singled out. More than ever in the past, unions are weak and independent investors are strong, and that affects HR's clout. True, HR departments are in charge of implementing the transition to performance-based pay, but the shift itself entails a transfer of operating authority to line managers. In other areas, too, line managers and business units are being given more authority.

Other aspects of corporate governance also are changing, both in law and in practice. Nearly a third of Japanese companies utilize the corporate-officer system, and a smaller number rely on stock options. The effects of these innovations are modest, but a beachhead for a shareholder-sovereignty approach has been established nevertheless. A minority of Japanese HR executives hold shareholder values, and it is reasonable to speculate that such executives will grow more numerous in the future. Eventually, HR executives might have to choose between loyalty to shareholders and loyalty to the *shain,* the lifetime employees, and in so doing create a tectonic shift in values and practices.

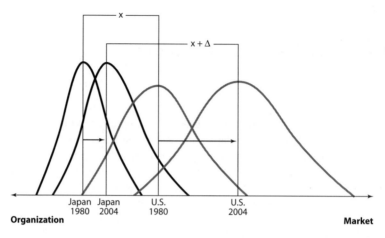

Figure 7.1 Corporate Employment Systems in Japan and the United States: Contemporary

As for strategy, the survey data suggest that, while a resource-based approach to business strategy remains dominant, Japanese companies have come to emphasize a more commodified view of labor. On the market-organization continuum, Japan is moving, albeit slowly, toward the market pole. It is doing so by creating a hybrid employment system that combines making as well as buying skills (see figure 7.1). The new hybrid is more focused on individual performance and, at the margin, relies more heavily on mid-career mobility and signals from the external labor market. Conversely, it is less concerned with internal equity, regardless of whether that equity arises from seniority, single-status personnel policies, or the enterprise union. It bears repeating, though, that the hybrid constitutes an incremental shift. New performance and hiring policies are being grafted onto a traditional base consisting of intensive training, lifetime employment, cohesive corporate cultures, and a relatively powerful headquarters HR unit—not as powerful as thirty years ago, but still a force to be reckoned with.

In their effort to cut costs while preserving the traditional model, Japanese companies are pursuing a variety of courses. Dispersion is driven by differences in technology, diversification, and economic performance. Companies, whether in services or manufacturing, with a large proportion of foreign ownership are in the vanguard of adopting corporate-governance practices that tilt toward investor concerns. They are at the market- and shareholder-oriented end of the continuum and are lauded in the business press, but the mainstream of Japanese management does not necessarily view them as models to emulate. Much respect is still accorded to firms like J. Securities—and like Canon and Toyota—that are globalizing their operations but not their organizational philosophies. That is to say, change is more modest in companies whose shares are in patient hands. For now, we can expect to see some competition between governance models in Japan.

Among large U.S. companies, while there *is* internal hiring and attention to organizational factors, there is less of it today than twenty years ago, so that employment and pay remain more market-oriented than in Japan. The market emphasis means a shift in operating decisions from central HR to line management. Headquarters HR does have a say in strategic decisions, although just how much influence it exerts depends on whether one listens to CFOs or to HR executives themselves. Despite an upgrading of headquarters HR, at least in terms of reporting relationships, its rank in the corporate hierarchy remains low. Like Japan, the United States is decentralizing and cutting headquarters staff, only more extensively than in Japan, even though the United States started from a more market-oriented position. Thus, on the organization-market continuum shown in figure 7.1, the gap between the United States and Japan (x) is *widening* $(x + \Delta)$ not narrowing.

The same divergence is occurring with respect to corporate governance.[2] Ten years ago, U.S. corporations already were more finance-oriented than Japanese firms were. Since then, the United States has financialized aggressively, to the point that finance has become the key unit in the executive suite. Its logic dominates other functions and fosters the marketization of employment. U.S. boards embrace the principles of shareholder sovereignty, and some even have the company's own CFO serving on them. HR, on the other hand, is almost never represented on corporate boards, either directly or indirectly, although, as we saw in this study, the presence of board members with HR backgrounds does make a difference to corporate decision-making.

One feature of the U.S. scene is the relatively high dispersion of corporate practices, as is shown in figure 7.1.[3] The case studies demonstrated a range of relationships between the HR executive and other top managers, in addition to a range of choices regarding employment practices. Boiling the dispersion down to distinct modes, we find two contemporary paradigms for the HR-executive role in the United States: the business-partner model and the resource-based model.[4]

In the business-partner model the HR executive reports to and advises the CEO, partners with other functions and with line management, and maintains a lean headquarters staff through decentralization and outsourcing. It emphatically eschews the concept of HR as the employee advocate. It tends to be found in diversified, predator-acquirer companies and is associated with shareholder values, with a relatively powerful HR function, and with HR executives having a voice in strategic decisions on business restructuring. Our case-study exemplar was U.S. Parts. The business-partner model calls for HR to work closely with the CEO on decisions such as mergers and acquisitions and to help with executive hiring, the importance of which has grown in recent years as executive turnover has risen. The continuing shift of U.S. corporations toward the market has not erased but actually augmented some of the responsibilities of the senior HR executive. Headquarters HR now oversees parts of the outsourcing process, often working closely with IT staff and vendors to design companywide information and contractor systems. But the objective of HR's involvement is to minimize labor costs rather than to secure a competitive advantage based on distinctive employee resources.

The other paradigm for the role of the HR executive in the United States is the resource-based model, which favors a focused business strategy, a larger headquarters staff, an emphasis on firm-specific training, and a corporate culture that supports stakeholder values; think of U.S. Delivery and U.S. Securities. This model is a hybrid that, like its Japanese counterpart, reflects the effort to strike a new balance between organization and market and between centralization and autonomy. It tends to be associated with relatively egalitarian personnel policies, such as the distribution of stock or stock options to rank-and-file employees. It is also associated with the adoption of team-based, participative work practices. The conundrum is that, despite the productivity advantages of these practices, they remain relatively uncommon in the United States.[5] This is another way of saying that HR executives in resource-based companies in the United States have less power than either Japanese HR executives or American HR executives in companies that follow the dominant business-partner model.

One explanation, based on our research, is that corporate boards act as a brake on HR power and a resource-based approach in many (but not all) companies seeking to cultivate human capital. Although the presence of board members with HR backgrounds may incline a company in the stakeholder and resource-based direction, a critical mass does not yet exist on most U.S. boards, which fail to offer much support for a resource-based approach. Also, the financialization of corporate decision-making in the United States is ubiquitous, leaving HR fighting an uphill battle for legitimacy and for funds to support employee training programs and other resource-based strategies. Not until corporate boards and shareholders are willing to cede some kind of governance role for those who would represent employee interests will the resource-based approach take hold in the United States.[6]

Contributing to American diversity are companies that do not conform to either of these two ideal types and so lie "off the diagonal." On one part of the off-diagonal are resource-based companies in which the senior HR executive *is* powerful and does have a close relationship to the CEO; examples include U.S. Electro, Southwest Airlines, and Men's Wearhouse.[7] What is revealing about these three companies is that they are under the influence of the founder or a member of the founder's family. This suggests that private ownership can create a bond between the CEO, the employees, and the HR executive that counteracts the effect of shareholder-oriented boards and CFOs.

On the other part of the off-diagonal are companies whose emphasis on shareholder values and market-based employment do not yield much power or influence for the HR executive. This was true of U.S. Con/Energy, where HR was not a business partner but entirely peripheral to key decisions. As we descend the hierarchy of American companies—to those that are smaller, less visible, and less profitable—this approach becomes more prevalent.[8]

The business-partner model, then, should not be taken for granted, but it does represent an unstable equilibrium. It is based on systemization and cost minimization, the competencies for which are widely available outside the executive HR department. This leaves open the possibility for further outsourcing of the HR executive function, for the movement of finance-trained managers into the HR domain, or both. As we have seen, a rising number of managers in charge of health-care benefits have finance, rather than HR, backgrounds. Managers with HR backgrounds care more about employee retention and morale; those with finance backgrounds are more cost-oriented and presumably were selected for this reason.[9] One thing is clear: In the United States, finance has influenced the values and attitudes of HR executives more than the other way around.

Compounding this problem is the professional orientation of American HR executives, who spend most of their careers in the HR field. Professionalism is a two-edged sword. It was originally intended to elevate HR's status, both in the labor market, where it created career opportunities for HR specialists, and inside the corporation, where it provided legitimacy for the HR executive as the practitioner of a new managerial specialty. Much of that legitimacy derived from HR's early ties to the emerging behavioral and social sciences. Today, though, HR professionalism is mostly about the building of career options (i.e., networking), while the technically sophisticated parts of HR— selection, development, organizational change—are handled by consultants with Ph.D.'s. Deep but narrow career paths in HR fail to build familiarity with accounting and finance, the lingua franca of the business world. The professional associations do little to remedy this problem or to ground HR in a research base. An indication of HR's low status in the business world is that few MBAs choose the field as a career option.

A solution to HR's uncertain role is provided by the business-partner model, in which HR is positioned closer to the executive mainstream. That, though, carries the risk that HR will lose its distinctive identity, competencies, and values. The Japanese generalist model is an alternative, but it is not a realistic option for the United States. What is needed to boost HR's influence in U.S. corporations is a greater number of HR executives trained in business fundamentals but at the same time grounded in the technical and ethical parts of the profession. It is a feasible solution but not one that American corporations or business schools have yet adopted. For their part, professional HR organizations should work more closely with their academic counterparts to identify a set of HR competencies grounded in behavioral and social-scientific research. They should be familiar with research that analyzes the impact of employment policies on corporate performance and on shareholder value.[10] As a model, they might look to CFOs, who owe their authority, in part, to their mastery of an increasingly technical knowledge base.

Finally, all professional organizations have social obligations, and in this case HR organizations need to be stronger advocates for employees and for an ethical approach to employment issues. Given the current loss of confidence in U.S. corporate governance, that kind of advocacy is hardly a far-fetched idea.[11] There is even the possibility of professional organizations taking a more nuanced position on the employee role in corporate governance and on employee representation, which in the past was a vehicle for elevating the HR function. While the main forces driving HR's status will always lie in the external environment—that is, outside the profession's control—the HR profession, by adopting a more assertive approach, could advance its own cause and help its members play a more effective role inside their companies.

WHAT'S AHEAD FOR THE UNITED STATES?

Any discussion of what the future holds for HR in the Unites States is bound to be affected by the recent debacles at Enron, Global Crossing, Tyco, WorldCom, and other stars that burned brightly in the 1990s but have since imploded. The recent corporate governance debates constitute the kind of environmental event that can trigger a shift in the balance of power inside and outside large U.S. corporations. At the very least, these incidents have punctured share prices and investor confidence, and deflated hyperbolic claims that U.S.-style corporate governance is as good as it gets. The Enron case appears to signal an event of fundamental importance. The claim that CEO-appointed boards, even small boards composed of outsiders, are capable of monitoring managements is today greeted with skepticism. So is the assertion that generous CEO salaries and ubiquitous stock options are necessary incentives. Not a few journalists and even some respected academics argue that U.S.-style corporate governance promotes "rent extraction"—greed, in plain English—and is not, as was alleged back in the 1990s, a system of "optimal contracting."[12]

The current regulatory wisdom is to insist that corporate boards will be more effective if they are made up of outsiders. The New York Stock Exchange and other regulatory bodies like the Securities Exchange Commission (SEC) are requiring companies to move in this direction. I happen to think that this "one size fits all" approach is a mistake that forecloses the option of having an HR executive or other informed insider—such as an employee representative—serve on the company board. The preference for outsiders is based on a purely theoretical presumption that agency costs are best minimized by appointing independent directors. Yet some of these independent directors, even those who have no relationship to the CEO, are unfamiliar with a company's problems (and thus prone to being mesmerized by a CEO), and others are unfamiliar even with basic business principles.[13]

Nevertheless, there are other ways that HR executives can affect corporate governance. First, HR executives can work with boards to select future directors. In so doing, they will be able to influence the board's premises regarding the kinds of experiences, values, and ethical backgrounds considered appropriate to board membership. Second, HR executives are well placed to help train and socialize persons who have been appointed to the board. Third, HR executives may take a page out of the Japanese corporate governance book and help boards fashion term limits for members. In other ways, too, they can make corporate boards more effective. They can define and clarify roles and devise payment schemes for board members. They can work with boards in finding and selecting new CEOs, although, of course, this requires political skills of the highest order. Finally and most importantly, persons with HR backgrounds should be among the outsiders appointed to boards. They will bring with them the team-building, selection, and compensation skills necessary for effective functioning of the board, and will likely appreciate the contribution of employees to the larger corporate team.

In the wake of the Enron phenomenon, the mystique of the CEO superstar has been greatly diminished: There is no longer an automatic assumption that a charismatic outsider can easily boost profitability and shareholder value by being incentivized with truckloads of stock options.[14] In the future we can expect to see a greater number of CEO insiders, people who have been vetted by their peers and are more attuned, and loyal, to a corporation's stakeholders. In theory, there is strong reason to believe that effective corporate governance is promoted when there is competition between insiders for top executive positions and when boards are sensitive to stakeholders whose economic welfare is affected by the firm's performance. In practice, this has been the experience of companies in other parts of the world, including Japan.[15]

It is also less likely that in the future CEOs will come from finance, another rose whose bloom has faded. The drop in share prices and the mixed record of M&A activity have begun to undermine the centrality of finance to corporate decision-making. So has the perception that some of corporate America's difficulties—exemplified by the decline of the 'Big Three' automotive producers—can be traced to the dominance of a finance rather than an engineering mind-set at corporate headquarters.[16]

The diminishment of finance creates opportunities for those with different perspectives on the creation of corporate value. The business-partner model, in which finance is first among equals, may in the coming years give way to an approach in which HR, as well as other functions, will have greater influence on strategic decision-making. Shareholders, at least for the moment, appear chastened by the collapse of the equity bubble. Unrealistic demands for share-price gains have subsided, and that opens the possibility for a longer-term approach to resource-allocation decisions, a development that would be a boon to training, employee development, and other HR programs. A decline in emphasis on stock options—due, in part, to requirements that options be expensed and properly accounted for—suggests a return to more organization-oriented and less finance-driven forms of executive compensation.

The sullied reputations of CEOs like Al Dunlap and Jack Welch, who were among the leading practitioners of the "slash and burn" philosophy of corporate restructuring, have called into question whether, as was claimed at the time, the job cuts of the 1990s were driven by a single-minded search for efficiency.[17] There is an alternative view that some of those cuts were distribu-tionally motivated—that they were an attempt to put into the pockets of top executives and shareholders money that otherwise would have been reinvested or paid to other stakeholders.

If the pendulum does begin to swing and the CEO position is awarded to a greater number of insiders, the impact will be felt further down the ranks. More care will be devoted to the grooming of internal talent, and the reliance on headhunters will decline. Both of those developments would entail an enhanced role for HR. Use of financial incentives would decline, while reli-ance on implicit contracts—long-term understandings built up over time through employee development—would rise. HR executives would have greater opportunity to influence the selection of CEOs, both by grooming possible candidates and by working with boards in helping to select future CEOs. As in Japan, more weight would be attached to the company-specific skills of the candidates.

Of course, it is possible that the scandals will fade before they have had any real impact on the power balance between shareholders and other stakehold-ers. The governance reforms of the SEC, the New York Stock Exchange, and the Bush administration thus far have been timid.[18] Few voices are advocating changes in corporate governance that are so far-reaching as to widen the defi-nition of stakeholders to include employees. The only mainstream employee-related proposals are those seeking to protect employee pensions from being overinvested in the employer's stock.

But there are straws in the wind which suggest that the scandals are pro-voking a reconsideration of the shibboleths of shareholder capitalism. The AFL-CIO has been urging companies to refuse the renomination of former Enron directors who might sit on their boards. Having thus positioned itself as a player in the governance-reform debates, the AFL-CIO has joined institu-tional investors in pressing for changes—including provisions for more inde-pendent directors, eliminating poison pills, expensing options, and separating the CEO position from the chairman of the board—that would make boards more independent and would limit executive-compensation levels.[19] The AFL-CIO has been quite prominent in its efforts to criticize stratospheric levels of CEO compensation, as with its popular "Executive Paywatch" website. It has joined with other investors in an effort to give shareholders the right to place their own director choices on a proxy card. This would make it easier for investors to elect alternative directors, an effort that companies have protested but which the SEC has approved in limited form.[20]

To some progressives, it may seem that the labor movement's alliance with shareholder activists is the wrong way to go. Critics contend that organized labor's stance in reforming corporate governance gives too much weight to the interests of union pension funds—to workers as shareholders rather than as employees. But keep in mind our finding that in the United States an increase in the number of board members with an HR background is associated with less power for finance and with stronger career-type employment policies. It may well turn out that proposed changes in the board nomination process, if fully implemented, eventually will have a beneficial effect on corporate decisions that affect employees and other stakeholders. At scandal-ridden and bankrupt WorldCom, the court-appointed monitor, Richard C. Breeden, has issued a variety of recommendations intended to make the new WorldCom a model of corporate governance. These include the appointment to the corporate board's compensation committee of persons who possess experience with human resource issues. These directors would meet with the senior HR executive at least twice a year to go over compliance issues, consider employee complaints about compensation, and otherwise provide a counterweight to a strong CEO. Still, this is a more indirect path than is being pursued by British trade unionists, who have been calling for employee representatives to have seats on corporate boards.[21]

At the same time, heretical ideas about the importance of human capital to the economy are beginning to crop up in influential and unlikely places. *Business Week* recently told its readers that "Corporate finance as it's taught in business schools takes for granted that shareholders are king. . . . But theory doesn't match reality. At many companies, shareholders are no longer the owners in a conventional sense. That's because key employees are not simply hired help brought in to run the assets of the company. . . . They *are* the company."[22]

If notions like that take hold, the business-partner and shareholder-sovereignty models will retreat and the resource-based and stakeholder models will advance. Without doubt, this would boost HR's status in U.S. companies. Evidence that corporations are moving somewhat away from market and back to organization includes the deceleration in the outsourcing industry, which is growing more slowly than was anticipated in the 1990s. Routine corporate services, including human resources, are staying in-house.[23] Another sign of a growing emphasis on organization as opposed to market is the partial recentralization of large multinational companies, which, in an effort to achieve economies of scale, are reining in country managers and investing more power in the hands of headquarters staffs. Even high-tech companies are rethinking their old market-oriented models. Cisco Systems, which is in the midst of a successful comeback, initially responded to the tech downturn by laying off workers. But recently it shifted gears, cutting back on acquisitions, centralizing its operations, and changing the internal culture to emphasize teamwork and employee retention. Ninety percent of its employees expect to be there in five years, versus 50 percent at other Silicon Valley companies.[24]

But the United States still has a long way to go before stakeholder models supplant investor capitalism. At U.S. companies, mass layoffs remain a primary response to declining sales. Although employers have discretion in how they organize the employment relationship, they are tending to choose the low-cost, low-commitment option. Corporate-governance reforms face an uncertain future. Business decisions continue to be finance-driven, making it difficult to secure funding for long-term investments in firm-specific skills. And in many companies, the HR function is perceived as a non-revenue-generating frill that, like the workforce, is a logical place to cut when resources are tight. As one HR executive complained recently, "You can't find loyalty to HR folks in the corporate world."[25]

JAPAN AT A CROSSROADS

The collapse of U.S. equity prices has had an impact on Japan. Five years ago, norm entrepreneurs in Japan—foreign investors, the financial press, economics pundits—confidently asserted that the Dow-Jones level reflected the strength of the U.S. economy, whose vitality they attributed to a risk-loving culture, venture capital, and a superior system of corporate governance. Those voices are more subdued now that the shortcomings of the U.S. system are apparent and Japan enters a recovery phase. With the clarity of hindsight, observers are discovering how widely the U.S. economy in the late 1990s was driven by bubble expectations—from Silicon Valley to Wall Street, both of them wounded and weakened in the years since then. Proponents of a gradual route to the reformation of Japanese institutions are now receiving a more respectful hearing. These are the incrementalists mentioned in chapter 2. They do not think that shareholder sovereignty and its accoutrements, like stock options, are feasible in Japan, so instead they advocate modest adaptations to improve transparency and facilitate bankruptcy.

Those who think that the large Japanese corporation will gradually morph into its American counterpart are mistaken. Radical norm entrepreneurs are minorities inside the ranks of Japanese business. The (mostly) silent majority look at recent U.S. economic difficulties not with institutional envy but with a sense of schadenfreude, and of determination not to follow suit, just as today many Europeans are increasingly assertive of an identity separate from that of the United States.[26] Japanese executives are pragmatists, interested in what works, not in what impresses ideologues. They are skeptical that the corporation, as opposed to macro factors like monetary stringency, is (or was) the main source of Japan's economic problems. On corporate governance, the pragmatists believe that, like the U.S. system, the Japanese system has benefits as well as costs. As one critic recently put it: "The particular form of corporate governance — [for example], whether a company has outside directors or statutory auditors — does not have a direct bearing on a company's performance. I am skeptical about claims that American companies respect shareholders' rights and interests substantially more than Japanese firms do."[27]

Such skepticism is echoed at the highest levels inside Japanese management. A majority of large companies is expected to remain with the postwar governance system rather than adopt American-style outsider boards, with the exception of firms that have a relatively high proportion of foreign shareholders. Of the one-fourth of public companies that have appointed outside directors, more than half have only one external director, and many of these individuals are actually executives from within the *keiretsu*.[28] These facts reinforce an observation made in earlier chapters: that there is a symbolic motivation behind some of the governance reforms being adopted by Japanese companies, who wish to appear sensitive to foreign shareholders even when — or because — the reforms do not cut deep. Important as foreign investors were in the 1990s, however, their influence now is waning. Overseas investment banks are shrinking their Japanese operations, and there has actually been a slight decline in the percentage of Japanese corporate shares held by foreign investors.[29]

Although unions are weaker and layoffs more prevalent than at any time since the Second World War, what is striking is how much of Japan's distinctive approach to human resource management has been preserved, at least in the large companies discussed in this book. As we saw in the case studies and in the survey data, movement to a market orientation has been modest. The central tendency is to focus employment systems on a core group of employees, who spend a lifetime with the company, receive extensive training, are part of an enterprise union, and are paid and promoted with some attention paid to internal criteria. While headquarters HR is not as powerful as in its heyday, it continues to occupy a privileged position. Even in manufacturing, where the pragmatists running Japan's corporations are moving facilities and jobs to mainland Asia, there is reluctance to widen the scope of downsizing. One reason is that employers are responsive to the constraints imposed by law, by unions, and by concern for public image. The legacy of the postwar years — when large companies functioned as a kind of private welfare system — is still felt as a sense of social obligation, albeit to a shrinking core of regular employees.[30]

A related reason is that the pragmatists are themselves "lifers" who believe in the system that created them. Recently, Fujio Mitarai, the president of Canon, said: "The advantage of lifetime employment is that employees absorb the company's culture throughout their careers. As a result, team spirit grows among them—a willingness to protect the corporate brand and stick together to pull through crises. I believe that such an employment practice conforms to Japanese culture and is our core competency to help survive global competition."[31]

Mitarai's point is that Canon derives an advantage from the difference between it and its global competitors—that is, from the distinctiveness (the "brand") of its products and from the underlying business structure that helps produce them. Mitarai is the latest in a very long line of Japanese businessmen who have asserted a close fit between Japan's cultural matrix and the practices of its private employers.[32] While a measure of skepticism is warranted here, so is recognition that Mitarai's comment affirms that big companies like Canon are sensitive to social norms and that they seek to make the best of them. And the Japanese corporate system has other features—business strategy, the role of headquarters, and corporate governance—that, while they may be more mundane, provide further support for organization-oriented practices and a strong HR function. In fact, Mitarai is a staunch defender of Japanese corporate governance practices.[33]

Consider strategy, for example. Some observers claim that Japanese companies don't know how to effectuate business strategy.[34] What we found in the companies we visited, however, as well as in the survey data, is that the modal Japanese company does formulate and pursue strategies, but that its approach is different from that of its U.S. counterparts. First, Japanese firms are more inclined to "make" talent and technology than to buy them through mergers and acquisitions. Second, they are less inclined to keep unrelated divisions inside the company, preferring instead to spin them off into *kogaisha* affiliates that retain relational ties to the parent company via *shukkō*, coordination of employment policies, and other mechanisms. Making talent and managing *kogaisha* relationships are key HR responsibilities related to strategy, whereas in the United States the strategic levers—buying or selling units and managing an empire of diversified businesses—are essentially financial decisions. With respect to strategic decisions, HR executives in the United States end up playing second (actually fifth) fiddle to CFOs.

Generally speaking, headquarters in every large corporation serves three main functions: It manages business units as profit centers, creates synergies across those units, and provides centralized services to them.[35] In this case too, the modal Japanese and the modal U.S. company operate differently from each other. In its relations with business units, headquarters in Japanese companies supplements financial controls with tacit knowledge of local units and the people working in them. (Think of the HR staff at J. Securities visiting every employee around the world.) This nonfinancial approach to control is supported by career rotation and the prevalence of homegrown executives, both of which foster informational networks within the company. These features also make it easier for headquarters to foster synergies across units; top executives know the idiosyncrasies of their processes and markets. In HR's case, that means it knows the people working in the local units. Also, as we have seen, Japanese firms are not classic M-forms: Divisions tend to be weaker or are managed from headquarters, again reducing the distance, both organizational and informational, between units and headquarters. Finally, Japanese headquarters provide a vast range of services to their local units. Systems and decision-making are centralized, not only for human resources but for other functions as well (marketing, for example, and R&D), and economies of scale and scope are thereby achieved.

Headquarters in the United States tends to be different: smaller, more distant from local units, and more likely to be staffed with outsiders or newcomers. Partly out of necessity, decisions are based more heavily on quantitative, financial indicators. Synergies are harder to establish when, as is the U.S. tendency, units are purchased rather than grown from within. That's one reason for the mediocre performance associated with U.S. mergers and acquisitions. For the period 1995–2001, an astounding 61 percent of U.S. mergers resulted in a subsequent reduction of share-price value.[36] In the United States, central HR's reason for being has less to do with the objective of realizing synergies and creating internal resources than it does with servicing the needs of headquarters and providing companywide systems for benefits, records, and the like.

None of this is to say that the Japanese corporate system is better. The strength of Japanese headquarters operations, in combination with the strategy of generating talent and technology in-house, promotes consistency, information sharing, synergy, and speed of execution. As for the dominant U.S. approach, it promotes local experimentation and achieves flexibility through reliance on decentralization and general (rather than firm-specific) skills, which in turn permit rapid cost reductions and reshuffling of corporate units. A company like U.S. Parts can sell a plant in a heartbeat. Also, the U.S. system promotes start-ups that can hope to be acquired, eventually, by a larger company. In the Japanese and the U.S. system alike, there are institutional complementarities—the parts have interdependent relationships that strengthen the overall system—so it is difficult to effect more than piecemeal change in either system.

Corporate governance remains a contentious issue in Japan because its characteristic institutions—inside directors, cross-holdings, and a stakeholder philosophy—are intertwined with so many other parts of the Japanese corporate system, including the *keiretsu*, banks, customer and supplier relationships, and even central HR units. The elimination of inside directors might seem an innocuous change, but it cuts to the heart of current methods for strategic decision-making—which are based on tacit knowledge—and for incentivizing senior managers. Similarly, cross-shareholding is related, among other things, to a company's wage structure (via spin-offs to reduce labor costs) and to layoff avoidance (via *shukkō*, the transfer of employees to affiliated companies), both of which require a centralized system of HR administration. Again, interdependence should not be taken to imply Japanese superiority, in this case of its corporate governance. Many of the Japanese flaws that were in the spotlight during the 1990s have yet to be remedied. Compared to the United States, Japanese corporate governance is less transparent and less adept at facilitating bankruptcy, and it generates less equity capital.

Tempting as it may be to tote up the costs and benefits of the Japanese and U.S. corporate systems and declare one of them "the winner," the fact of the matter is that no one has any idea how to conduct such a reckoning. The Japanese corporate system, despite its faults, supports cross-unit synergies, high-quality products, and steady improvements in products and processes. Conversely, the U.S. system, despite *its* flaws, supports new venture creation, rapid cost-cutting, and risk-taking. These complementarities constitute what economists call "multiple equilibria"—different yet equally effective ways of organizing economic institutions—and result in sluggish and path-dependent change in both countries. Moreover, when there are multiple equilibria and bounded rationality regarding what constitutes an institutional optimum, we are operating in the world of the second best.[37] In that world, there is no reason to believe that revamping a corporate system will necessarily move an economy closer to an economic optimum. The economic case for the superiority of the Japanese *or* the American system is actually rather weak.[38]

Finally, what is sometimes forgotten in discussions of convergence is the point implicit in Mitarai's remark: that Japanese companies derive advantages from being different. The Japanese corporate system—governance, strategy, HR, and much besides—facilitates organizational learning and allows companies to specialize in products and processes that are difficult for other companies to imitate. By contrast, the U.S. emphases on flexibility and mobility require general, not firm-specific, skills to facilitate rapid allocation of resources to emergent industries. Each country occupies a niche carved out by its business institutions. Overall gains are reaped from the sustenance of institutional difference between the two countries and from their competing internationally on that basis. That is the comparative-advantage logic of trade between advanced countries. A globalized world economy does not inevitably produce convergence—formal or functional—at the industry or national levels.[39]

Is history destiny? The theory of path dependence is based on the evolutionary idea that starting points may be random but have lasting consequences, and that over time institutions will evolve in patterns that are related to initial conditions. Countries with different initial conditions will develop differently and respond differently to similar environmental pressures. As long as the outcomes generated by their separate paths are comparably efficient, the pressure for convergence will be minimal. If efficiency gaps are wide and persistent, however, the laggards will eventually have to imitate the leader, either formally or with functionally equivalent adaptations, or risk extinction. Thus competition provides a check on historical determinism—paths *can* change— although path change requires sustained economic problems and even then may be difficult to effect if institutions are interdependent and related to comparative advantage.[40]

What does this mean for Japan? In the late 1990s, after nearly a decade of slow growth, it appeared to many that Japan was destined to veer off its postwar path and converge with the decade's high-flyer, the United States. But with the U.S. stock market having gone through its worst slump since the 1930s, and with yawning current-account and budget deficits, the promise of enduring U.S. superiority is not unambiguous enough to elicit institutional imitation and dominant-model convergence. Some, like economists Paul Krugman and Fed chairman Alan Greenspan, see ominous parallels between recent problems in the U.S. economy and the deflationary stagnation that set in after the bursting of Japan's bubble. At this point, Japan's uncritically imitating America would only be—like history repeating itself—a farce. So the dominant model is no longer a model, if it ever was. Meanwhile, the Japanese economy is in better shape than at any time since the late 1980s, with positive growth, strong profits, and solid equity returns. Increasingly Japanese prosperity is based on trade with East Asia, especially China, and depends less on trade with—and guidance from—the United States.[41]

National economies generate, in addition to "efficiency" outcomes, such as productivity and growth, "distributional" outcomes—the slices of the wealth and income pies. In continental Europe and Japan, overall wage inequality is less than in the United States, and the gap between the pay of executives and that of front-line workers is much narrower.[42] Contrary to conventional wisdom about an equity-efficiency trade-off—that is, that the Japanese and the Europeans are indulging a taste for equity whose cost is inefficiency and slower growth—the evidence in fact shows that equity is associated with higher long-term growth rates.[43]

The distributions of income and wealth can be exogenous to an economy, because government often steps in to reallocate through transfer programs— negative income taxes, for example, or social security. Efforts to change the distribution of income, to reslice the pie, are in fact what politics is often about. Alternatively, distribution can be endogenous, as in the case of European corporatism, in which collective bargaining constrains the income streams going to workers and employers; these bargaining systems are endogenous because other economic institutions—training, price setting, product competition—are interrelated with, and dependent on, them.[44] One sees some of these same effects in the Japanese case. Endogeneity can also reflect the power of social norms. A country that values egalitarianism will embed that norm in its economic institutions. It is one explanation for the existence of modest pay differentials and stakeholder governance in continental Europe and Japan.[45]

Just as persistent economic problems can cause a systemic path shift, so can efforts to reallocate the returns from economic activity. It can take the form of conventional politics—the bolstering or bashing of unions, the selling of tax cuts—or of more subtle shaping of public opinion so as to cause a shift in social norms. One effective agent for the change of distributive values is the norm entrepreneur who takes care to appear altruistic ("the nation needs to be more competitive"), cloaking his distributional objectives in efficiency garb. Sometimes norm entrepreneurs really do think that they are altruists whose proposed reforms will bolster efficiency, even though the evidence for efficiency gains from redistribution is lacking or at best ambiguous.

My own interpretation of what transpired in corporate America in the 1980s and 1990s is that, while changes in governance and in employment were to some extent an effort to improve efficiency in response to heightened competition,[46] the rationale for corporate restructuring included significant distributional objectives: the transfer of risk from employers to employees, of corporate resources from retained earnings and ordinary employees to executives and shareholders, and the replacement of managerial capitalism with shareholder sovereignty. Whether the events of the 1990s qualify as a path shift for the U.S. economy is not yet clear. But they do represent a break with the New Deal system established during the 1930s and 1940s, a system in which markets did not strictly determine employment outcomes, social norms were somewhat egalitarian, and inequality declined from previous levels.[47] Today, as during previous periods of distributional reshuffling—the Gilded Age, for example, and the 1920s—the distribution of income and wealth in the United States has grown extremely lopsided.[48] Hence changes in corporate governance must be added to the standard explanations for the growth of American inequality—technology, trade, government policy, and declining union strength.[49]

Like the New Deal, the postwar Japanese social contract had distribution as its focus. Its aim was to make adult-male employees permanent stakeholders in the enterprise and limit executive pay and dividends in favor of retained earnings. In the 1950s and 1960s, Japan's large companies adjusted their business strategies and employment practices to create a smooth fit with those distributional objectives. Now, like their U.S. counterparts, Japan's norm entrepreneurs claim to be concerned with efficiency, but many are really concerned with obtaining higher salaries or dividends for themselves. Here's the rub: Normative change is proving difficult in Japan. Its institutions are more tightly linked and embedded in shared social values than are those in the United States. Ultimately the future of corporate Japan will depend as much on political and normative developments as on competitive imperatives.

■ ■ ■

Executive decision-making, employment practices, and corporate governance form a totality of interrelated parts whose arrangement situates a company on an organization-market continuum. Aggregating across companies in each country, we get national distributions like those shown in figure 7.1. Japan continues to have a more interwoven corporate system than does the United States, and that results in the narrower variance of its curve. The national distributions overlap, however, as they have in the past, due to industry-specific factors, such as common technology, and to bidirectional trading of ideas and practices. We often hear about Japan adopting U.S. practices, but it is not well appreciated that the converse—U.S. companies adopting various Japanese practices (quality methods, high-performance work sytems, focused business strategy)—is also occurring and that it has contributed to the strengthening of a resource-based model in the United States.

Japan in recent years has seen a shift to the market, to shareholder corporate governance, and to a smaller role for the executive HR function. But movement in that direction has been slow because of inertia, institutional interdependencies, social constraints on the change process, and a reluctance to give up the competitive advantage that accrues from having distinctive institutions. In large Japanese corporations, HR executives are less powerful but still important, while the traditional employment and corporate governance systems are weaker but still intact. It is difficult to characterize the hybrid that is emerging in many Japanese companies in part because the changes that have been adopted often are faddish add-ons rather than fundamental reforms.

The United States has also moved toward the market pole, but the shift there has been more far-reaching. HR executives have created new roles for themselves as business partners with line managers and as advisers to CEOs, but the declining importance of employees to corporate strategy and to corporate governance has left HR executives in a precarious position. Countervailing efforts to establish a quasi-Japanese, resource-based model have made only modest headway, much like efforts to establish the U.S. model in Japan. In the United States, what was already a relatively shareholder-oriented system has strengthened itself over the last twenty years.

What all this points to is that the gap between the two countries is not narrowing but gradually widening. That explains why the change that has occurred in Japan in recent years has impressed Japanese observers, who compare the present to the Japanese past, while U.S. visitors to Japan, whose reference point is different, see a system that is changing at maddeningly slow speed. Of course, these trends could change if the future brings a drastic worsening of either the American or Japanese economies. Also, the excesses of some U.S. executives during the late 1990s have, at least for the moment, tempered American exuberance for free markets. Public disenchantment with the business system—and the introduction of a raft of new regulations—sets an outer limit on how far towards the market pole the United States is capable of moving.

Thus we have a paradox: In Japan and the United States alike, firms have become more market-oriented, which is consistent with convergence theory. Also consistent with convergence is the adoption by some U.S. companies of a Japanese-style approach to managing internal resources. Yet at the same time, national differences—as measured by central tendencies—not only persist but, in fact, have been widening, which is a repudiation of convergence.

In short, there is evidence to support the conclusion both that convergence is occurring *and* that varieties of capitalism endure and remain significant in the modern global economy.

▮ Acknowledgments

THE ORIGINS OF THIS BOOK go back to the late 1970s, when I was a graduate student at Berkeley. In those days, doctoral students in economics were advised against reading articles outside the discipline. Doing so was believed to be a distraction from absorbing the neoclassical canon, an intrusion into the discipline's autarky. Reading books was considered a waste of time—the only economists who wrote books were fuzzy thinkers like John Kenneth Galbraith—and it delayed progress through the doctoral program, this in an era when economics emulated engineering and receiving the Ph.D. in three years was considered "optimal." Yet I was sorely tempted. My advisor, Lloyd Ulman, not only read but wrote books. And I had after-hours access to the library of the Institute of Industrial Relations, where I could explore its holdings in sociology, history, and political science. I remember coming across Ronald Dore's *British Factory, Japanese Factory*, a book on industrial relations unlike any I had seen before. It was readable yet erudite, based on field research yet historically grounded. It opened my mind to the possibility that, along with the usual universalist factors considered by economists, market institutions were produced by contingencies of time and place. This whetted my appetite to learn more about what we today would call "the varieties of capitalism" and specifically to learn more about Japan.

I spent the next year or so studying Japanese economic history and industrial organization. Eventually I formed what I thought would be my dissertation topic: a comparative historical study of employment relations in Japan and the United States. There was only one problem: I couldn't speak Japanese. I visited various faculty, asking them how long they thought it would take for me to acquire facility in reading primary Japanese documents. The consensus was: about five years. This was not good news. I agonized over which road to take and ultimately decided to forego the comparative thesis and to write only about the United States (although I did publish an article—my first publication—summarizing what I had learned about Japan).[1]

In retrospect, this was both a good and a bad decision. Good, because unbeknownst to me, a young historian at Harvard, Andrew Gordon, was writing his dissertation on the development of the modern Japanese employment system, covering much of the terrain I had hoped to explore. Bad, because I never managed to shake a sense of regret that I had not pursued the Japanese road. Over the years, I kept up my interest in Japan through study and travel. In 1987, Professor Takashi Mori, then of Hokkaido University, visited me and proposed translating my first book into Japanese. As a result of that and subsequent translations, I acquired a circle of friends and colleagues in Japan.

In 1998, Andy Gordon, knowing of my interest in Japan, suggested that I apply for an Abe Fellowship. The proposal I wrote formed the basis of what was to become this book. The fellowship—administered by the Center for Global Partnership and the Social Science Research Council—permitted me to travel to Japan several times and to conduct much of the U.S.-based fieldwork. Still not speaking much Japanese, however, I needed a collaborator. I was very fortunate when a friend suggested that I get in touch with Professor Kazuro Saguchi of the University of Tokyo's economics department. I proposed this project to him and he agreed to work with me. It was a lucky match. We jointly conducted the Japanese field interviews and Saguchi single-handedly managed the mechanics of the survey in Japan. He contributed many ideas to this project. Without him—and his wisdom, reliability, and generosity—the project would never have been completed.

In addition to the Abe Fellowship, support came from the University of California's Institute for Labor and Employment, the Center for International Business Education and Research at UCLA's Anderson School, the UCLA Academic Senate, the University of Tokyo Center for International Research on the Japanese Economy, and Doshisha University's Institute for Technology, Enterprise, and Competitiveness. Among other things, these funds permitted me to hire an outstanding research assistant, Emily M. Nason, who coded the questionnaires and helped prepare the tables. In Japan, my field interviews were translated into English by Lai Yong Wong, then a graduate student at Yokohama National University. Also providing research assistance was a terrific group of UCLA undergraduate and graduate students: Keiju Minatani, Jenna Allen, Rosemary Eap, Kim Nguyen, and Sarah Prehoda. Thanks also to Nick Frankovich, and Richard Isomaki, who helped copyedit the manuscript.

Many, many people have contributed their time and ideas to this project. First to thank are the dozens of executives—they must remain anonymous—who were interviewed during the fieldwork. They graciously took time out from busy schedules to answer odd questions from a skeptical academic. Thanks also to hundreds of other executives who responded to our unconscionably lengthy questionnaire. I appreciate the generosity of other persons who made this project possible, including Takashi Araki, Barak Berkowitz, Frank Baldwin, Vickie Chen, Chris Erickson, Eve Fielder, Nate Furuta, Andrew Gordon, Takeshi Inagami, Kenichi Ito, Mariko Kishi, Archie Kleingartner, Kazuo Koike, Leo Lawless, John Logan, Dan Mitchell, Don Morrison, Caroline Nahas, Keisuke Nakamura, Yoshifumi Nakata, Michio Nitta, Marleen O'Connor, Naoto Ohmi, William Ouchi, Jennifer Riss, Eric Rutledge, Hiroki Sato, Teiichi Sekiguchi, Hiromichi Shibata, Haruo Shimada, Fujikazu Suzuki, Yoshiji Suzuki, Kazuo Takada, Masayasu Takahashi, Satoshi Takata, Yoko Tanaka, Yuji Tsutsumi, Kenji Wada, Yoshihiko Wakumoto, Bruce Willison, Yoshiaki Yamaguchi, and Hironori Yano. And a special thanks to Peter Dougherty, whom I am lucky to have as my editor. He is a wise counselor.

My family—Susan, Alexander, and Margaret—put up with my periodic absences, both physical and other kinds. I am ever grateful for their tolerance and love.

This book is dedicated to my teachers, from my earliest days as a student (Florence Kaiden, Harris Weinstein, Gloria Cioppa) to my undergraduate years (the late David Gordon and Bennett Harrison, Michael Wachter), to graduate school (David Brody, Clair Brown, Michael Burawoy, Nicholas Crafts, Michael Reich, George Strauss, and Lloyd Ulman). There were many others. As the Chinese proverb puts it, "Good teachers open the door. You enter by yourself."

▮ Notes

Preface

1. The classic modern statement of this view is Mark Granovetter, "Economic Action and Social Structure: The Problem of Embeddedness," *American Journal of Sociology* 91 (1985), 481–510. Also see Geoffrey M. Hodgson, *How Economics Forgot History* (London, 2001), and, for an institutional classic on corporate governance, Adolph A. Berle and Gardiner C. Means, *The Modern Corporation and Private Property* (New York, 1932).

Chapter 1
Management and the Varieties of Capitalism

1. Peter A. Hall and David W. Soskice, eds., *Varieties of Capitalism: The Institutional Foundations of Comparative Advantage* (New York, 2001); Mark J. Roe, *Political Determinants of Corporate Governance* (New York, 2003).
2. For example, Mauro F. Guillén, *The Limits of Convergence* (Princeton, 2001); Rafael LaPorta, Florencio Lopez-de-Silanes, and Andrei Shleifer, "Corporate Ownership around the World," *Journal of Finance* 54 (April 1999), 471–517.
3. Robert Freeland, *The Struggle for Control of the Modern Corporation: Organizational Change at General Motors, 1924–1970* (Cambridge 2001).
4. For exceptions see Jeffrey Pfeffer, *Power in Organizations* (Marshfield, 1981) and Neil Fligstein, "The Intraorganizational Power Struggle: Rise of Finance Personnel to Top Leadership in Large Corporations," *American Sociological Review* 52 (1987), 44–58; James G. March, "The Business Firm as a Political Coalition," *Journal of Politics* 24 (November 1962), 662–78; Lucian Arye Bebchuk and Jesse M. Fried, "Executive Compensation as an Agency Problem," NBER Working Paper no. 9813 (July 2003).
5. For an early statement of this view, see Reinhard Bendix, *Work and Authority in Industry: Ideologies of Management in the Course of Industrialization* (New York, 1956).
6. Susan Helper, "Economists and Field Research: 'You Can Observe a Lot Just by Watching,'" *American Economic Review* 90 (May 2000), 228–32; Kathleen M. Eisenhardt, "Building Theories from Case Study Research," *Academy of Management Review*, 14 (1989), 532–50.
7. Todd D. Jick, "Mixing Qualitative and Quantitative Methods: Triangulation in Action," *Administrative Science Quarterly* 24 (December 1979), 602–11.
8. Michael Porter, Hirotaka Takeuchi, and Mariko Sakakibara, *Can Japan Compete?* (London, 2000); Chalmers A. Johnson, *MITI and the Japanese Miracle: The Growth of Industrial Policy, 1925–1975* (Stanford, 1983); Ulrike Schaede, *Cooperative Capitalism: Self-Regulation, Trade Associations, and the Antimonopoly Law in Japan* (Oxford, 2000).
9. Ronald Dore, *Flexible Rigidities: Industrial Policy and Structural Adjustment in the Japanese Economy* (Stanford, 1986).

10. Richard Katz, *Japanese Phoenix: The Long Road to Economic Revival* (Armonk, N.Y., 2002).

11. Masaru Yoshitomi, "Whose Company Is It? The Concept of the Corporation in Japan and the West," *Long Range Planning* 28 (August 1995), 34.

12. Yashiro Naohiro, *Jinjibu wa Mō Iranai* (Tokyo, 1998).

13. Marie Anchordoguy, "Japan at a Technological Crossroads: Does Change Support Convergence Theory?" *Journal of Japanese Studies* 22 (Summer 1997), 363–97.

14. Robert J. Ballon and Keikichi Honda, *Stakeholding: The Japanese Bottom Line* (Tokyo, 2000); Nobuo Tateisi, "Corporate Governance in Tomorrow's Japan," *Glocom Platform* (August 2001).

15. Toyohiro Kono, "A Strong Head Office Makes a Strong Company," *Long Range Planning* 32 (April 1999), 225–36. Also see Margarita Estevez-Abe, Peter Hall, and David Soskice, "Social Protection and the Formation of Skills: A Reinterpretation of the Welfare State," in Hall and Soskice, *Varieties of Capitalism*, 145–83.

16. It is worth noting that after a decade of being a laggard, Japan's GDP growth rate at the end of 2002 was the fastest among the world's fifteen richest nations, and it surpassed the United States and the Euro area in 2003. On the other hand, although real growth has been positive for eight consecutive quarters, deflation has caused slower growth in nominal terms. OECD, *Quarterly National Accounts*.

17. Sanford M. Jacoby, *Modern Manors: Welfare Capitalism since the New Deal* (Princeton, 1997).

18. William G. Ouchi, *Theory Z: How American Business Can Meet the Japanese Challenge* (New York, 1981); Robert Hall, "The Importance of Lifetime Jobs in the U.S. Economy," *American Economic Review* 72 (September 1982), 716–24.

19. Peter Cappelli, "Rethinking Employment," *British Journal of Industrial Relations* 33 (December, 1995), 1563.

20. Louis S. Csoka, *Rethinking Human Resources*, Conference Board Report No. 1124–95-RR (New York, 1995), 31.

21. Jay Barney, "Firm Resources and Sustained Competitive Advantage," *Journal of Management* 17 (1991), 91–120; Nicolai J. Foss, ed., *Resources, Firms, and Strategies* (London, 1997).

22. The concept of "efficiency wages" is helpful to understanding the resource-based approach.

23. Jeffrey Pfeffer, *The Human Equation: Building Profits by Putting People First* (Boston, 1998).

24. Robert Wade, "Globalization and Its Limits: Reports of the Death of the National Economy Are Greatly Exaggerated," in Suzanne Berger and Ronald Dore, eds., *National Diversity and Global Capitalism* (Ithaca, 1996).

25. Leonard Schoppa, "Japan: The Reluctant Reformer," *Foreign Affairs* 80 (September–October 2001), 76–90.

26. Ronald Dore, "Where Are We Now? Musings of an Evolutionist," *Work, Employment, & Society* 4 (December 1989), 425–46; Albert O. Hirschman, *Exit, Voice, and Loyalty: Responses to Decline in Firms, Organizations, and States* (Cambridge, Mass.,1972). Other terms for labeling these poles are 'status' and 'contract.' Sir Henry Maine's oft-quoted "law of progress"—"the movement of the progressive societies has hitherto been a movement from Status to Contract"—was an apt description of the

Anglo-American experience of the nineteenth century. But later it was qualified by the organizational revolution of the twentieth century, which shifted the pendulum back from contract to status through citizenship rights and membership rights of corporate employees. Now it appears that the pendulum is swinging again. Sir Henry Sumner Maine, *Ancient Law* (London, 1931), 141; Frank Tannenbaum, *A Philosophy of Labor* (New York, 1951); Wolfgang Streeck, "Status and Contract as Basic Categories of a Sociological Theory of Industrial Relations," in Streeck, ed., *Social Institutions and Economic Performance: Studies of Industrial Relations in Advanced Capitalist Economies* (Beverly Hills, 1999).

27. Alexander Gerschenkron, *Economic Backwardness in Historical Perspective* (Cambridge, Mass., 1962).

28. D. Eleanor Westney, *Imitation and Innovation: The Transfer of Western Organizational Patterns in Meiji Japan* (Cambridge, Mass., 1987).

29. Andrew Gordon, *The Evolution of Labor Relations in Japan: Heavy Industry, 1853–1955* (Cambridge, Mass., 1985); Sanford M. Jacoby, "Pacific Ties: Industrial Relations and Employment Systems in Japan and the United States since 1900," in Howell J. Harris and Nelson Lichtenstein, eds., *Industrial Democracy in America* (Cambridge, Mass., 1993), 206–48.

30. Jonathan Zeitlin and Gary Herrigel, eds., *Americanization and Its Limits: Reworking US Technology and Management in Postwar Europe and Japan* (Oxford, 2000).

31. Clark Kerr, John T. Dunlop, Frederick Harbison, and Charles Myers, *Industrialism and Industrial Man: The Problems of Labor and Management in Economic Growth* (Cambridge, Mass., 1960); John W. Dower, *Embracing Defeat: Japan in the Wake of World War II* (New York, 1999).

32. William Tsutsui, *Manufacturing Ideology: Scientific Management in Twentieth Century Japan* (Princeton, 1998); William B. Gould, *Japan's Reshaping of American Labor Law* (Cambridge, 1984).

33. Lester Thurow, *Head to Head: The Coming Economic Battle among Japan, Europe, and America* (New York, 1992); Michel Albert, *Capitalism vs. Capitalism* (New York, 1993).

34. Ezra F. Vogel, *Japan as Number One: Lessons for America* (Cambridge, Mass., 1979); Ronald P. Dore, *British Factory, Japanese Factory: The Origins of National Diversity in Industrial Relations* (Berkeley, 1973); William G. Ouchi, *The M-Form Society: How American Teamwork Can Recapture the Competitive Edge* (Reading, Mass., 1984).

35. Robert E. Cole, *Managing Quality Fads: How American Business Learned to Play the Quality Game* (New York, 1999).

36. Henry Chesbrough, "The Organizational Impact of Technological Change," working paper, Harvard Business School, 1999.

37. Alan Hyde, "The Wealth of Shared Information: Silicon Valley's High-Velocity Labor Market, Endogenous Economic Growth, and the Law of Trade Secrets," unpublished ms., Rutgers University Law School, Newark.

38. Richard B. Freeman, "The U.S. Economic Model at Y2K: Lodestar for Advanced Capitalism?" NBER Working Paper no. 7757 (2000); U.S. Bureau of Labor Statistics, various; "The 'New' Economy," *Economist* (13 September 2003), 61–63.

39. Leonard H. Lynn, "Technology Competition Policies and the Semiconductor Industries of Japan and the U.S.: A Fifty-Year Retrospective," *IEEE Transactions* 47 (2000), 200–210; Jeffrey Macher, David C. Mowery, and David Hodges, "Reversal of Fortune? The Recovery of the U.S. Semiconductor Industry," *California Management Review* 41 (1998), 107–36.

40. Freeman, "The U.S. Economic Model at Y2K," 9; "Waiting for the New Economy," *Economist* (14 October, 2000), 70–77; "A British Miracle?" *Economist* (25 March 2000), 57; "Desperately Seeking a Perfect Model," *Economist* (10 April 1999), 67–68; "Debating the New Economy," *Business Week* (12 July 1999), 26.

41. Richard B. Freeman, "Single-Peaked vs. Diversified Capitalism: The Relation between Economic Institutions and Outcomes" NBER Working Paper no. 7556 (2000); Frank Dobbin; *Forging Industrial Policy: The United States, Britain, and France in the Railway Age* (Cambridge, 1994), 233; Andrei Shleifer and Robert Vishny, "A Survey of Corporate Governance," *Journal of Finance* 52 (1997), 755.

42. Harry C. Katz and Owen Darbishire, *Converging Divergences: Worldwide Changes in Employment Systems* (Ithaca, 2000).

43. Masahiko Aoki, "Unintended Fit: Organizational Evolution and Government Design of Institutions in Japan," in Masahiko Aoki, Hyung-ki Kim, and Masahiro Okuno-Fujiwara, eds., *The Role of Government in East Asian Economic Development: Comparative Institutional Analysis* (Oxford, 1997), 233–53.

44. David Soskice, "Reinterpreting Corporatism and Explaining Unemployment: Coordinated and Non-coordinated Market Economies," in R. Brunetta and C. Dell'Arringa, eds., *Labour Relations and Economic Performance* (London, 1990). The United States is *not* considered a coordinated market economy; coordination is primarily achieved through market relations.

45. Chesbrough, "The Organizational Impact of Technological Change"; Steven N. Kaplan, "Top Executive Rewards and Firm Performance: A Comparison of Japan and the U.S.," *Journal of Political Economy* 102 (1994), 510–46; Kaplan, "Top Executives, Turnover, and Firm Performance in Germany, *Journal of Law, Economics, and Organization* 10 (1994), 142–59.

46. Paul David, "Path Dependence, Its Critics, and the Quest for 'Historical Economics,'" in P. Garrouste and S. Ionnides, eds., *Evolution and Path Dependence in Economic Ideas: Past and Present* (Cheltenham, 2001).

47. Steven K. Vogel, *Freer Markets, More Rules: Regulatory Reform in Advanced Industrial Countries* (Ithaca, 1996); Trevor Bain, *Banking the Furnace: Restructuring of the Steel Industry in Eight Countries* (Kalamazoo, Mich., 1992); Robert E. Cole, *Small Group Activities in American, Japanese, and Swedish Industry* (Berkeley, 1989).

48. Richard R. Nelson, *National Innovation Systems: A Comparative Analysis* (Oxford, 1993).

49. Aoki, "Unintended Fit"; Lucian Arye Bebchuk and Mark J. Roe, "A Theory of Path Dependence in Corporate Governance and Ownership," *Stanford Law Review* 52 (1999), 127–70; Michael Storper, "Boundaries, Compartments, and Markets: Paradoxes of Industrial Relations in Growth Pole Regions of France, Italy, and the United States," in S. M. Jacoby, ed., *Workers of Nations: Industrial Relations in a Global Economy* (New York, 1995). Of course, if economic results are not meeting threshold—as

in the former Soviet Union—there might be a case for more drastic institutional change, that is, for punctuating an equilibrium.

50. Mancur Olson, *The Rise and Decline of Nations* (New Haven, 1984).

Chapter 2
Human Resource Departments in Large Firms

1. Hideo Inohara, *The Japanese Personnel Department: Structure and Functions* (Tokyo, 1990).

2. As mid-career hiring declined and employee mobility fell, employers did not have to worry about the possibility of losing their training investments in general or firm-specific human capital. Kazuo Koike, *Human Resource Development* (Tokyo: Japan Institute of Labor, 1997).

3. On the (fairly recent) origins of the three pillars and other ostensibly "traditional" practices, see Andrew Gordon, *The Evolution of Labor Relations in Japan: Heavy Industry, 1853–1955* (Cambridge, 1985) and Tetsuji Okazaki, "The Japanese Firm under the Wartime Planned Economy," *Journal of the Japanese and International Economies* 7(1993), 175–203. Japanese courts in the 1950s and 1960s espoused the doctrine that layoffs to maintain profitability were an abuse of employer power. This made it difficult to conduct mass layoffs, thus rigidifying corporate practices. See Takashi Araki, "Japan," in Roger Blanpain, ed., *The Process of Industrialization and the Role of Labour Law in Asian Countries* (London, 1999), 4–83.

4. Note that, prior to the 1990s, Japanese HR departments, like those in the United States, were called either labor relations, industrial relations, or personnel management departments. However, I will use the term HR in referring to these units.

The advent in the 1950s of a regularized system for hiring school graduates into blue-collar jobs boosted the role of central HR departments (who designed the new approach) and cast them in the role of "helpers"—working with the young graduates to socialize and train them.

5. W. Mark Fruin, *The Japanese Enterprise System* (Oxford, 1994), 220; Toyohiro Kono, *Strategy and Structure of Japanese Enterprises* (Armonk, N.Y., 1984), 108; Rodney Clark, *The Japanese Company* (New Haven, 1979).

6. Fruin , *Japanese Enterprise System*, 220.

7. Hideki Yoshihara, "Dynamic Synergy and Top Management Leadership: Strategic Innovation in Japanese Companies," in Kuniyoshi Urabe, John Child, and Tadao Kagono eds., *Innovation and Management: International Comparisons* (Berlin, 1988).

8. Hiroyuki Odagiri, *Growth through Competition, Competition through Growth: Strategic Management and the Economy in Japan* (Oxford 1994).

9. Yoshifumi Nakata and Ryoji Takehiro, "Joint Accounting System and Human Resource Management by Group," *Japan Labour Bulletin* 40 (1 October 2001), 5; "Corporate Spinoffs Becoming More Popular," *Japan Labour Bulletin* 40 (1 December 2001), 1. Prior to 1999, Japanese accounting rules did not require consolidated performance statements, allowing companies to shift losses to their subsidiaries.

10. Kiyohiko Ito, "Japanese Spinoffs: Unexplored Survival Strategies," *Strategic Management Journal* 16 (September 1995), 431–46; Kiyohiko Ito and Elizabeth L.

Rose, "The Genealogical Structure of Japanese Firms: Parent-Subsidiary Relationships," *Strategic Management Journal* 15 (Summer 1994), 35–51.

11. Tadao Kagono, Ikujiro Nonaka, Kiyonori Sakakibara, Shiori Sakamoto, and J. K. Johansson, *Strategic versus Evolutionary Management: A U.S.-Japan Comparison of Strategy and Organization* (New York, 1985), 40.

12. Personal correspondence from David J. Collis, September 2000; Michael Goold, David Pettifer, and David Young, "Redesigning the Corporate Centre," *European Management Journal* 19 (February, 2001), 83–91; Sumantra Ghoshal and Christopher Bartlett, "Matsushita Electrical Industrial Co., Ltd.," Harvard Business School, 1988. Of course, when comparing headquarters staff adjusted for revenue and employment, one has to somehow control for the fact that Japanese parent companies involve themselves in the affairs of their affiliates, effectively raising the employee base and revenues managed from the parent's headquarters staff. Nevertheless, even when this is taken into account, Japanese firms have larger headquarters than Western companies.

13. Tomohiko Noda, "Determinants of Top Executives' Promotion and Remuneration," in Toshiaki Tachibanaki, ed., *Who Runs Japanese Business: Management and Motivation in the Firm* (Cheltenham, U.K., 1998); Kono, *Strategy and Structure*, 296.

14. Hiroyuki Itami, *Mobilizing Invisible Assets* (Cambridge, Mass.,1987).

15. Toyohiro Kono, "A Strong Head Office Makes a Strong Company," *Long Range Planning* 32 (1999), 225–36.

16. W. Mark Fruin, *Knowledge Works: Managing Intellectual Capital at Toshiba* (Oxford, 1997).

17. Ghoshal and Bartlett, "Matsushita."

18. Michael E. Porter, Mariko Sakakibara, and Hirotaka Takeuchi, *Can Japan Compete?* (New York, 2000), 171; personal communication from Tadao Kagono, 2001; Ronald Dore, *Stock Market Capitalism, Welfare Capitalism: Japan and Germany versus the Anglo-Saxons* (Oxford, 2000), chap. 4. The criticism—that Japanese firms engaged in excessive unrelated diversification in the late 1980s as a result of which the economy became mired in recession—seems wide of the mark. The companies that are cited for becoming too diversified—chiefly the general trading companies (*sōgō shōsha*) and electronic conglomerates (*sōgō denki*)—were already highly diversified in the 1960s and 1970s. Precisely, what constitutes "excessive" diversification and when it is problematic is not well explained by the critics. In the United States, diversification, both related and unrelated (conglomerates), became more prevalent in the 1960s and 1970s, when it was associated with profitability at lower risk. Even with the divestitures of the 1980s, as a result of which U.S. industrial concentration rose modestly, the United States still has more unrelated diversification than Japan. (Some studies actually show an increase in U.S. diversification in the late 1980s and early 1990s.) Companies like General Electric and Berkshire Hathaway were lionized in the U.S. business press in the 1990s, yet they are every bit as diversified as Hitachi or Mitsui. Julia Porter Liebeskind, Tim Opler, and Donald Hatfield, "Corporate Restructuring and the Consolidation of U.S. Industry," *Journal of Industrial Economics* 44 (1996), 53; Cynthia A. Montgomery, "Corporate Diversification," *Journal of Economic Perspectives* 8 (Summer 1994), 163–78); Itami, *Mobilizing Invisible Assets*.

19. Kagono et al., *Strategic versus Evolutionary Management*, 40.

20. Dore, *Stock Market Capitalism*, passim.

21. Kenichi Imai and Hiroyuki Itami, "Interpenetration of Organization and Market," *International Journal of Industrial Organization* 2 (1984), 285–310; Oliver Williamson, "Corporate Governance," *Yale Law Journal* 93 (1984), 1197, 1225.

22. Kagono et al., *Strategic versus Evolutionary Management*, 40.

23. Hideyoshi Itoh, "Japanese Performance Management from the Viewpoint of Incentive Theory," in Masahiko Aoki and Ronald Dore, eds., *The Japanese Firm: The Sources of Competitive Strength* (Oxford, 1994), 232–64.

24. Lola Okazaki-Ward, *Management Education and Training in Japan* (London, 1993), 170.

25. John Storey, Paul Edwards, and Keith Sisson, *Managers in the Making: Careers, Development, and Control in Corporate Britain and Japan* (London, 1997).

26. John C. Beck and Martha N. Beck, *The Change of a Lifetime: Employment Patterns among Japan's Managerial Elite* (Honolulu, 1994); Masahiko Aoki, *Information, Incentives, and Bargaining in the Japanese Economy* (Cambridge, 1988).

27. Andrew Kakabadse, Lola Okazaki-Ward, and Andrew Myers, *Japanese Business Leaders* (Boston, 1996); Jonathan Clarkham, *Keeping Good Company: A Study of Corporate Governance in Five Countries* (Oxford, 1995).

28. Andrew Gordon, *The Wages of Affluence: Labor and Management in Postwar Japan* (Cambridge, Mass.,1998); Charles Weathers, "Japan's Fading Labor Movement," Japanese Policy Research Institute Working Paper no. 25 (July 1997). Second unions were management-initiated entities intended to undermine the existing enterprise union.

29. Gordon, *Wages of Affluence*, 2; Kazuro Saguchi, "The Japanese Employment System and Meritocracy in Historical Perspective," working paper, Tokyo University, 1996. However, many firms also engaged—and still do engage—in joint consultation on a wide range of issues in both unionized and nonunion companies. Joint consultation typically occurs at the unit level, although in unionized firms it is coordinated with companywide collective bargaining. Robert A. Hart and Seiichi Kawasaki, *Work and Pay in Japan* (Cambridge, 1999), 50–51; Motohiro Morishima, "Use of Joint Consultation Committees by Large Japanese Firms, "*British Journal of Industrial Relations* 30 (September, 1992), 405–23.

30. Mari Sako, "Shunto: The Role of Employer and Union Coordination at the Industry and Intersectoral Levels," in Mari Sako and Hiroki Sato, eds., *Japanese Labour and Management in Transition* (London, 1997), 236–64; William Tsutsui, *Manufacturing Ideology: Scientific Management in Twentieth Century Japan* (Princeton, 1998); Osamu Koyama, "Flexibilization of the Human Resource Management in Japan," working paper, Sapporo University, 1997.

31. Hiroshi Okumura, *Corporate Capitalism in Japan* (New York, 2000), 99–100.

32. Data from a recent survey of very large companies show that 28 percent of all corporate directors had once been officers at some level of the enterprise union. The figure is not comparable to the Nikkeiren survey, which included a larger proportion of small and mid-sized firms. Nikkeiren data in Inohara, *Japanese Personnel Department*; Research Institute for the Advancement of Living Standards (RIALS), Fujikazu Suzuki, and Takeshi Inagami, "How Top Managers See the Japanese Corporation: An Interim Report of the Survey of Corporate Governance," in International Industrial Relations Association, 12th World Congress, Special Seminar Proceedings, *Corporate Governance and Industrial Democracy* (Tokyo, 1 June 2000), 99. Also see Takeshi

Inagami and RIALS, *Gendai Nihon-no Kōporēto Gabanansu* (Corporate governance in contemporary Japan) (Tokyo, 2000), table 3–4.

33. Sanford M. Jacoby, "American Exceptionalism Revisited: The Importance of Management," in Jacoby, ed. *Masters to Managers: Historical and Comparative Perspectives on Employers* (New York, 1991).

34. Richard Freeman and James Medoff, *What Do Unions Do?* (New York, 1984); Nobuhiro Hiwatari, "Employment Practices and Enterprise Unionism in Japan," in Margaret M. Blair and Mark J. Roe, eds., *Employees and Corporate Governance* (Washington, D.C., 1999), 275–311.

35. Takao Kato, "The Recent Transformation of Participatory Employment Practices," NBER Working Paper no. 7965 (2000).

36. Kono, *Strategy and Structure*, 33.

37. Tachibanaki, *Who Runs Japanese Business*, 4. Because of rotation, the organizational location of a manager's early postings is much less important as a predictor of executive promotion than where the manager is working at mid-career.

38. Inohara, *Japanese Personnel Department*, 12.

39. The generalist career pattern characteristic of HR executives is most pronounced in nondiversified companies, especially in services, while diversified manufacturing firms have a mixture of HR generalists and specialists. In Japan, however, being an HR specialist does not connote the semi-professionalism that it does in the United States or the United Kingdom. Paradoxically, Japanese HR specialists focus on the practices of a single company, whereas HR professionals in the West tend to have broad knowledge of practices in a variety of industries. The former is more appropriate for a career-type labor market and the latter for the high interfirm mobility associated with Western careers. Takao Kato, "The Nature and Scope of Career Development of Managers of Large Firms in Japan and the United States," in Japan Institute of Labor (JIL), *Human Resource Development of Professional and Managerial Workers: An International Comparison* (Tokyo, 1998), 171–90.

40. Motohiro Morishima, "Career Development of Japanese and U.S. Managers: Differences in Career Breadth," in JIL, *Human Resource Development*, 154–70.

41. Dore, *Stock Market Capitalism*, 25.

42. Boards also have time limits on how long a top executive may serve.

43. Aoki, *Information, Incentives, and Bargaining*. When the presidents of one hundred top Japanese companies were asked in 1990 to whom the firm should belong, they said shareholders (87 percent), employees (80 percent), and society (69 percent). Ulrike Schaede, "Understanding Corporate Governance in Japan: Do Classical Concepts Apply?" *Industrial and Corporate Change* 3 (1994), 285–323.

44. Tokyo Stock Exchange, *2001 Shareownership Survey* (Tokyo, 2002), table 2.

45. Okazaki, "The Japanese Firm under the Wartime Planned Economy."

46. Managing directors average nine times the starting annual salary for a new college graduate; the ratio for CEOs is only eleven times greater. Inagami Takeshi, "From Industrial Relations to Investor Relations? Persistence and Change in Japanese Corporate Governance, Employment Practices, and Industrial Relations," *Social Science Japan Journal* 4 (2001), 231. In the United States, by contrast, the ratio of the pay of CEOs to that of new college graduates was at least two hundred, if not higher. Kevin Phillips, *Wealth and Democracy* (New York, 2002), 153; U.S. Bureau of Labor Statis-

tics, *National Compensation Survey: Occupational Wages in the United States,* July 2002, table 1.

47. Katsuyuki Kubo, "The Determinants of Executive Compensation in Japan and the U.K," working paper, Hitotsubashi University, 2000; Toshiaki Tachibanaki, "Road to the Top," and Tomohiko Noda, "Determinants of Top Executives' Promotion and Remuneration," in Tachibanaki, ed. *Who Runs Japanese Business.* It would be wrong, however, to think that there is a divide between board members and employees. While board members call themselves *yakuin* (executives of the company), they also call themselves *shain jūgyōin* (employees, or members of the enterprise). Dore, *Stock Market Capitalism. Shain* is an interesting word because in a legal context it refers to shareholders, whereas in the corporate world it means core employees, thus suggesting some ambiguity as to who constitutes the Japanese corporation's residual claimant. See Ryuichi Yamakawa, "The Silence of Stockholders: Japanese Labor Law from the Viewpoint of Corporate Governance," *Japan Institute of Labor (JIL) Bulletin* 38 (November 1, 1999), 1.

48. Masahiro Abe, "Corporate Governance Structure and Employment Adjustment in Japan," *Industrial Relations* 41 (October 2002), 683–702. There is debate over the origins of the main bank system and its centrality to the Japanese economic system at different points in time. See Yoshiro Miwa and J. Mark Ramseyer, "The Myth of the Main Bank," working paper, Olin Center, Harvard Law School, 2001, and Juro Teranishi, *Nihon no Keizai Shisutemu (The Evolution of the Japanese Economic System)* (Tokyo, 2003).

49. It is difficult to say which came first, long-term employment relations—which, to reduce agency costs, led to managerial-promotion tournaments and bank bloc holding (this is Roe's interpretation)—or long-term creditor and supplier relations, which resulted in bloc holding and career employment as devices to secure relational investments. One thing to bear in mind is that career employment, a feature primarily of large companies, is less widespread than cross-holding and other distinctive goverance features. This would imply that the "fit" between the two is, to some extent, serendipitous rather than causal. Mark J. Roe, *Political Determinants of Corporate Governance: Political Context, Corporate Impact* (Oxford, 2003); Mari Sako, *Prices, Quality, and Trust: Interfirm Relations in Britain and Japan* (London, 1992).

50. Mitsuharu Miyamoto, "Decline of Employment Protection and Trust? The Case of Japan," working paper, Department of Economics, Senshu University, 2000.

51. Michio Nitta, "Business Diversification Strategy and Employee Relations: The Case of the Japanese Chemical Textile Industry," in Sako and Sato, ed., *Japanese Labour and Management in Transition,* 265–79.

52. Robert J. Gordon, "Why U.S. Wage and Employment Behavior Differs from That in Britain and Japan," *Economic Journal* 92 (March 1982), 13–44.

53. Michael Gerlach, *Alliance Capitalism: The Social Organization of Japanese Business* (Berkeley, 1993); Mark Gilson, "Reflections in a Distant Mirror: Japanese Governance through American Eyes," *Columbia Business Law Review* 1 (1998), 203; Masahiko Aoki, Hugh Patrick, and Paul Sheard, "The Japanese Main Bank System," in Aoki and Patrick, eds., *The Japanese Main Bank System* (Oxford, 1994), 3–50; Sako, *Prices, Quality, and Trust;* Ronald J. Gilson and Mark J. Roe, "Understanding the Japanese Keiretsu: Overlaps between Corporate Governance and Industrial Organization," *Yale Law Journal* 102 (1993), 871; Masaru Yoshitomi, "Whose Company is It?

The Concept of the Corporation in Japan and the West," *Long Range Planning* 28 (Aug. 1995), 33–44; Yishay Yafeh, "Corporate Governance in Japan: Past Performance and Future Prospects" *Oxford Review of Economic Policy* 16 (Summer 2000), 74–84. Some claim, however, that the bank role in corporate governance has been exaggerated. See Miwa and Ramseyer, "The Myth of the Main Bank."

54. Michio Nitta, "Corporate Governance, Japanese Style: Roles of Employees and Unions," *Social Science Japan* 20 (March 2001), 6–12. A recent Ministry of Finance study similarly finds that the greater the extent to which employees are involved in management, the more active are the firms in adopting corporate governance reforms. Hideaki Miyajima, "The Latest Report on Corporate Governance Reform, 'Progress in Corporate Governance Reforms and the Revitalization of Japanese Companies' by the Ministry of Finance's Policy Research Institute," Research Institute of Economy, Trade, and Industry (RIETI), Tokyo, September 2003.

55. Lucian Arye Bebchuk, Jesse Fried, and David Walker, "Executive Compensation in America: Optimal Contracting or Extraction of Rents?" NBER Working Paper No. 8661 (December 2001).

56. Steven Kaplan, "Top Executive Rewards and Firm Performance: A Comparison of Japan and the United States," *Journal of Political Economy* 102 (1994), 510; Kaplan, "Top Executives, Turnover, and Firm Performance in Germany," *Journal of Law, Economics, and Organization* 10 (1994), 142–59.

57. The lapses in corporate governance cited in the Japanese press—the paying of bribes to *sōkaiya* (professional extortionists) and the hiding of bad loans after the bubble's collapse—are examples of illegalities committed in the interests of the firm, not of personal gain at the expense of the company. Dore, *Stock Market Capitalism*. On U.S. corporate leaders, see Rakesh Khurana, *Searching for a Corporate Savior: The Irrational Quest for Charismatic CEOs* (Princeton, 2002).

58. Keisuke Nakamura and Michio Nitta, "Developments in Industrial Relations and Human Resource Practices in Japan," in Richard Locke, Thomas Kochan, and Michael Piore, eds., *Employment Relations in a Changing World Economy* (Cambridge, Mass.,1995), 325–58.

59. Ronald Dore, *Flexible Rigidities: Industrial Policy and Structural Adjustment in the Japanese Economy, 1970–80* (Stanford, 1986).

60. Edward J. Lincoln, *Arthritic Japan: The Slow Pace of Economic Reform* (Washington, D.C., 2001).

61. Robert J. Kramer, *Organizing for Global Competitiveness: The Corporate Headquarters Design*, Conference Board Research Report, 1233–99-RR (New York, 1999), 10–14.

62. Carla Koen, "The Japanese Main Bank Model: Evidence of the Pressure for Change," Wissenschaftszeutrum Berlin (WZB) Working paper, 2000; "Corporations Wince as Shares Unwind," *Nikkei Weekly* (24 December, 2001), 12; "Japanese Banks: Fiddling While Marunouchi Burns," *Economist* (27 January 2001), 67–69. The main bank system is hardly dead, however. Banks continue to play a role in helping distressed clients, as in the rescue package put together in April 2002 for Daikyo, a property developer.

63. Inagami, "From Industrial Relations to Investor Relations," 228; Nobuo Tateisi, "Corporate Governance in Tomorrow's Japan," *Glocom Global Communications Platform*, August 2001. On the economic illogic behind some of these reforms, see

Sanford M. Jacoby, "Corporate Governance in Comparative Perspective: Prospects for Convergence," *Comparative Labor Law and Policy Journal* 22 (Fall 2000), 5–32.

64. Paul Beamish, "Sony's Yoshide Nakamura on Structure and Decision Making," *Academy of Management Executive* (1999), 12–13. There is a resemblance here to the British practice of a two-board system (which, unlike the German system, leaves no role for employee representatives).

65. *Freeter* is a neologism coined from the English word *free* and the German word *arbeiter*.

66. Dore, *Stock Market Capitalism*, chap. 3.

67. "Japanese Workers Least Loyal to Firms, Survey Discovers," *Japan Times* (5 September 2002); James Lincoln and Arne Kalleberg, "Work Organization and Work-force Commitment: A Study of Plants and Employees in the U.S. and Japan," *American Sociological Review* 50 (December, 1985), 738–60.

68. Performance-based pay is not new; it's just that its weight in the pay system has increased. Endo Koshi, "Japanization of a Peformance Appraisal System: A Historical Comparison of the American and Japanese Systems," *Social Science Japan Journal* 1 (1998), 247–62; Hiromichi Shibata, "The Transformation of the Wage and Performance Appraisal System in a Japanese Firm," *International Journal of Human Resource Management* 11 (April 2000), 294–313.

69. In 2001 alone, membership in Rengo, the main labor-union federation, fell by 3 percent. Japan Institute of Labor, *Labor Flash* 11 (January 17, 2002).

70. Charles Weathers, "Japan's Fading Labor Movement," JPRI Working Paper no. 35 (July 1997); Yuji Genda and Marcus Rebick, "Japanese Labour Stagnation in the 1990s," *Oxford Review of Economic Policy* 16 (2000), 85–102; Tsuyoshi Tsuru and James Rebitzer, "The Limits of Enterprise Unionism: Prospects for Continuing Decline in Japan," *British Journal of Industrial Relations* 33 (September 1995), 459–92.

71. See the excellent discussions in D. Hugh Whittaker, "Labor Unions and Industrial Relations in Japan: Crumbling Pillar or Forging a Third Way?" *Industrial Relations Journal* 29 (1998), 280–94, and in Clair Brown, Yoshifumi Nakata, Michael Reich, and Lloyd Ulman, *Work and Pay in the United States and Japan* (New York, 1997).

72. Nikkeiren, *Creating a Society Rich in Choices* (Tokyo, 2001); Inagami, "From Industrial Relations to Investor Relations," 229; "Solution Sought to Employment Mismatch," *Japan Times* (16 March 2001); personal interview with Nikkeiren's Deputy Director General Yano Hironori, 2001; Koyama, "Flexibilization."

73. John C. Coffee Jr., "Shareholders versus Managers: The Strain in the Corporate Web," in John C. Coffee Jr, Louis Lowenstein, and Susan Rose-Ackerman, eds., *Knights, Raiders and Targets: The Impact of the Hostile Takeover* (New York, 1988), 77–134.

74. Christina L. Ahmadjian and Gregory Robbins, "A Clash of Capitalisms: Foreign Shareholders and Corporate Restructurings in 1990s Japan," working paper, Hitotsu-bashi University International School of Corporate Strategy, Tokyo, 2002.

75. Generally, see Cass Sunstein, "Social Norms and Social Roles," *Columbia Law Review*, (May 1996). 903–68; Curtis J. Milhaupt, "Creative Norm Destruction: The Evolution of Nonlegal Rules in Japanese Corporate Governance," *University of Pennsylvania Law Review* 149 (2001), 2083–2129; Geert Hofstede, *Cultures and Organizations: Softwares of the Mind* (New York, 1991).

76. Tokyo Stock Exchange, *2001 Shareownership Survey*, table 2; Christina Ahmadjian, "Changing Japanese Corporate Governance," Working Paper no. 188, Columbia University Graduate School of Business 2001; "Making Waves," *Nikkei Weekly* (5 November, 2001).

77. For a typical example of this reasoning, see "Limits Urged on Banks' Shareholding," *Nikkei Weekly* (11 June 2001). Evidence of how the media affects governance outcomes can be found in Alexander Dyck and Luigi Zingales, "The Corporate Governance Role of the Media," working paper, Harvard Business School, August 2002.

78. Takeshi Inagami and RIALS, *Gendai Nihon-no Kōporēto Gabanansu*, table 2–20.

79. Ronald Dore. "Time to Revive Incomes Policy," 3 September 2002, http://www.nation-online.com.

80. Dore, *Stock Market Capitalism*, chap. 4.

81. Randall Jones and Kotaro Tsuru, "Japan Corporate Governance: A System in Evolution," *OECD Observer* 204 (1997), 40–41; Hiroyuki Takahashi, "Corporate Governance in Japan: Reform of Top Corporate Management Structure," *JEI Reports*, 23 July 1999; Bao Gai, *Japan's Economic Dilemma: The Institutional Origins of Prosperity and Stagnation* (Cambridge, 2001); Sachiko Hirao, "Business Law Changes Just Scratch Surface," *Japan Times* (8 March 2001); "Commercial Code Revised to Allow U.S.-Style Corporate Governance," *Japan Labor Bulletin* 41 (August 2002).

82. Japan Institute of Labor, *The Labor Situation in Japan: 2001*, 92–93.

83. "Temp Work System in Change," *Japan Times* (14 March 2001); "Businesses Turn to Alternative Employment," *Nikkei Weekly* (7 January 2002); Japan Institute of Labor, "Rules Governing Employee Dismissals," *JIL Labor Flash* (3 December 2001); Takashi Araki, "A Comparative Analysis of Corporate Governance and Labor and Employment Relations in Japan," *Comparative Labor Law and Policy Journal* 22 (2000), 67–96; Mitsuharo Miyamoto, "Decline of Employment Protection and Trust? The Case of Japan," working paper, Senshu University, July 2000.

Chapter 3
Inside Japanese Companies Today

1. The interviews on which this chapter is based were conducted jointly with Professor Kazuro Saguchi.

2. Charles Ragin, *The Comparative Method: Moving Beyond Qualitative and Quantitative Strategies* (Berkeley, 1987).

3. Toyohiro Kono, "A Strong Head Office Makes a Strong Company," *Long Range Planning* 32 (1999), 225–36.

4. Jeffrey Pfeffer, *Power in Organizations* (Marshfield, 1981); Jeffrey Pfeffer and Gerald Salancik, *The External Control of Organizations* (New York, 1978); James G. March, "The Business Firm as a Political Coalition," *Journal of Politics* 24 (November 1962), 662–78.

5. Given the occupational homogeneity of finance and insurance companies, it comes as little surprise that firms in this sector have the highest proportion (46 percent) of senior executives who previously held leadership positions in the enterprise union. Takeshi Inagami and the Research Institute for the Advancement of Living Standards

(RIALS), *Gendai Nihon-no Kōporēto Gabanansu* (*Corporate Governance in Contemporary Japan*) (Tokyo, 2000), table 3–4.

6. One sign of the company's insularity and commitment to its "lifers" is the fact that it makes very few mid-career hires (*chūto saiyō*) and has no plans to change this.

7. Naoki Tsuchiya, "Diversification of Labor Patterns and Labor-Management Relations in the Trucking Industry," *Proceedings of the International Industrial Relations Research Association* (Tokyo, 2001).

8. Single-status policies do not discriminate between production, clerical, and managerial employees with respect to benefits or facilities (e.g., a single cafeteria for all).

9. A sign that training is taken seriously is the fact that the company's finance department keeps close track of training expenditures and considers these figures to be sensitive, confidential information.

10. Takeshi Inagami, "From Industrial Relations to Investor Relations? Persistence and Change in Japanese Corporate Governance, Employment Practices, and Industrial relations," *Social Science Japan Journal* 4 (2001), 231; Christina L. Ahmadjian, "Changing Japanese Corporate Governance," Working Paper no. 188, Graduate Business School, Columbia University April 2001.

11. In the past, shareholders viewed staff cuts, which were considered a signal of declines in product demand, as "bad news." This changed in the 1990s in the United States, which in turn led U.S. investors to pressure Japanese companies to restructure and downsize. The latest research on Japan shows positive share price reactions to announcements of labor shedding in 1999, as in the United States. Henry Farber and Kevin Hallock, "Have Employment Reductions Become Good News for Shareholders?" Working Paper, Princeton University, September 2000; Christina L. Ahmadjian and Gregory Robbins, "A Clash of Capitalisms: Foreign Shareholders and Corporate Restructurings in 1990s Japan," working paper, Hitotsubashi University, International School of Corporate Strategy, Tokyo, 2002; Noriko Tanisaka and Fumio Ohtake, "Impact of Labor Shedding on Stock Prices," *Japan Labor Bulletin* 42 (January 2003), 6–12.

12. Inagami and RIALS, *Kōporēto Gabanansu*, table 3–4.

13. These findings are consistent with more-aggregate data showing declining returns to tenure and rising return to market experience in the 1990s. See, for example, Ken Ariga, Giorgio Brunello, and Yasushi Ohkusa, *Internal Labour Markets in Japan* (Cambridge, 2000), or Motohiro Morishima, "Pay Practices in Japanese Organizations," *Japan Labor Bulletin* 41 (April 2002), 10, which finds that 41 percent of employers report that pay disparities have increased over the last five years. In addition, the pay ratio between between top and bottom deciles of male employees has widened from 2.6 to 2.8. However, this is still below the U.S. ratio of nearly 4.5. And when demographic changes are controlled for, the data show little or no widening of wage inequality. "Show Me the Money," *Economist* (16 January 2002), 56; Takehisa Shinozaki, "Wage Inequality and Its Determinants in the 1980s and 1990s," *Japan Labor Bulletin* 41 (August 2002), 6–12.

14. Paul DiMaggio and Walter Powell, "The Iron Cage Revisited: Institutional Isomorphism and Collective Rationality in Organizational Fields," *American Sociological Review* 48 (1983), 147–60.

15. A similar observation is made by Hiroyuki Fujimura, "Changes in the Spring Wage Offensive and the Future of the Wage Determination System in Japanese Firms," *JIL Labor Bulletin* (1 May 2003), 6–12.

16. Survey data show that performance-based pay is being integrated into, not replacing, the traditional pay system based on factors such as age, tenure, skill, and education. Only 6 percent of employers surveyed in 2001 used "market value" as the basis for pay raises for nonmanagerial employees. Morishima, "Pay Practices," 8–13.

17. Robert Ballon and Keikichi Honda, *Stakeholding: The Japanese Bottom Line* (Tokyo, 2000); Ronald Dore, William Lazonick, and Mary O'Sullivan, "Varieties of Capitalism in the Twentieth Century," *Oxford Review of Economic Policy* 15 (Winter 1999), 119.

18. Geert Hofstede, *Cultures and Organizations: Software of the Mind* (New York, 1997).

19. Christopher L. Erickson and Sanford M. Jacoby, "The Effect of Employer Networks on Workplace Innovation and Training," *Industrial & Labor Relations Review* 56 (January 2003), 203–43.

20. Robert E. Cole, *Small Group Activities in American, Japanese, and Swedish Industry* (Berkeley, 1989).

21. "Saying Sayonara," *Business Week* (7 September 2001), 109.

22. Yoshifumi Nakata and Ryoji Takehiro, "Joint Accounting System and Human Resource Management by Company Group," *Japan Labor Bulletin* 40 (October, 2001), 5–11. Consolidated accounting—which took effect in 1999—reduces the ability of companies to shift losses to subsidiaries, but these labor transfers are completely legal.

23. "Recent Trends in Transferring Employees," *Japan Labor Bulletin* 40 (1 December, 2001). Also see Hiroki Sato, ed., *Promotion and Allocation of White-Collar University Graduates* (Tokyo, 2001).

24. "Life Employment Ends Prematurely for Some," *Nikkei Weekly* (3 September 2001); Stephanie Strom, "A Shift in Japanese Culture Aids Some Workers Who Want to Go It Alone," *New York Times* (16 November 2000).

25. "Pay Hikes Not on Union Agenda," *Nikkei Weekly* (14 January 2002), 2; *Japan Labor Bulletin* 41 (January 2002), 3. In an opinion poll, 70 percent of Japanese executives said that they planned to cut salaries in 2002. James Brooke, "Bush to Encounter a Much Less Formidable Japan," *New York Times* (17 February 2002).

26. "Uncut," *Economist* (20 July 2002), 57; Takao Kato, "The End of Lifetime Employment in Japan? Evidence from National Surveys and Field Research," Colgate University, August 2001; Yuji Genda and Marcus Rebick, "Japanese Labour in the 1990s: Stability and Stagnation," *Oxford Review of Economic Policy* 16 (2000), 85–102; Noriko Tanisaka and Fumio Ohtake, "Impact of Labor Shedding on Stock Prices," *Japan Labor Bulletin* 42 (January 2003), 10; Michio Nitta, "Employment Relations after the Collapse of the Bubble Economy," in Banno Junji, ed., *The Political Economy of Japanese Society*, vol. 2 (Oxford, 1998), 267–84.

27. Takeshi Inagami and RIALS, *Kōporēto Gabanansu*, table 6–1; *JIL Labor Flash*, 1 November 2001, 15 March 2002; *JIL Labor Flash*, 1 August 2003.

28. Curtis J. Milhaupt, "On the (Fleeting) Existence of the Main Bank System and Other Japanese Economic Institutions," working paper, Columbia Law School, November 2001; Takashi Araki, "A Comparative Analysis of Corporate Governance

and Labor and Employment Relations in Japan," *Comparative Labor Law & Policy Journal* 22 (2000), 67–96; Nikkeiren, *Creating a Society Rich in Choices* (Tokyo, 2001); Hideaki Miyajima, "The Latest Report on Corporate Governance Reform, 'Progress in Corporate Governance Reforms and the Revitalization of Japanese Companies' by the Ministry of Finance's Policy Research Institute," RIETI, September 2003.

29. Christina L. Ahmadjian and Patricia Robinson, "Downsizing and the Deinstitutionalization of Permanent Employment in Japan," *Administrative Science Quarterly* 46 (2001), 622–54.

30. Strom, "Shift in Japanese Culture"; "Businesses Turn to Alternative Employment," *Nikkei Weekly* (7 January 2002); Hiroyuki Chuma, "Employment Adjustments of Japanese Firms during the Current Crisis," *Industrial Relations* (October 2002), 653–82.

31. Inagami and RIALS, *Kōporēto Gabanansu*, tables 6–2, 2–20.

32. Survey data support this finding. Most companies continue to have joint consultation committees (JCCs), which are composed of senior union officials and top executives and are a vehicle for two-way communication—upward, employee concerns are conveyed to headquarters, and, downward, confidential information about corporate plans and performance reaches employees. On the other hand, there is evidence that managements are sharing somewhat less information with unions, and fewer senior managers are participating in conferences with them. Motohiro Morishima, "Use of Joint Consultation Committees by Large Japanese Firms," *British Journal of Industrial Relations* 20 (1992), 405–23; Takao Kato, "The Recent Transformation of Participatory Employment Practices in Japan," working paper, Department of Economics, Colgate University, September 2000; Inagami and RIALS, *Kōporēto Gabanansu*, tables 6–5, 6–6.

33. Michio Nitta, "Corporate Governance, Japanese Style: Roles of Employees and Unions," *Social Science Japan* 20 (March 2001), 6–11; Tokyo Stock Exchange, *2001 Shareownership Survey*, table 2; Hideaki Miyajima, "The Latest Report on Corporate Governance Reform," 2003.

34. Hideaki Inoue, "The Accelerating Dissolution of Stock Cross-Holding," *NLI Research* (March 2000), 133; Fumiaki Kuroki, "Cross-Shareholdings Decline for the Eleventh Straight Year," *NLI Research* (October 2002), 4–8; Douglas Ostrom, "The Keiretsu System: Crackling or Crumbling?" *JEI Report* (7 April 2000); Hiroyuki Takahashi, "Corporate Governance in Japan: Reform of Top Corporate Management Structure," *JEI Report* (23 July 1999); Ryuichi Yamakawa, "The Silence of Stockholders: Japanese Labor Law from the Viewpoint of Corporate Governance," 38 *Japan Institute of Labor Bulletin* 1 (1 November, 1999); "Japan's Keiretsu: Undone," *Economist* (22 March 2003), 56. Note too that, in a recent survey, Inagami and RIALS found that stable shareholdings accounted for more than 50 percent of ownership in 719 out of 731 Tokyo Stock Exchange firms surveyed in 1999.

35. "Japan's Keiretsu Regrouping," *Economist* (25 November 2000), 74; "Japanese Companies Forge New Business Relationships: The Nissay Business Conditions Survey," NLI Research Institute no. 146 (2000).

36. Managers feel that this insulation is a good thing. They favor the system of stable shareholding because they think it facilitates a long-term perspective on business decisions. Inagami and RIALS, *Kōporēto Gabanansu*, table 2–10.

37. Inagami and RIALS, *Kōporēto Gabanansu*, table 2–19; *Sangyo Shimbun* (25 September 2000), courtesy of Suzuki Fujikazu; Ronald Dore, *Stock Market Capitalism, Welfare Capitalism: Japan and Germany versus the Anglo-Saxons* (Oxford, 2000), 119; "More Listed Companies Inviting Outside Directors on Board," *Nikkei Weekly* (13 October 2003), 3.

38. "Foreign Institutions Snap Up Greater Share of Japanese Firms," *Nikkei Weekly*, (16 July 2001); Brian Bremner, "How Merrill Lost Its Way in Japan," *Business Week* (12 November 2001), 104; "Toyota Board Gets Even Bigger," *Nikkei Weekly* (30 July 2001); "Toyota Steers Own Course by Picking Managing Officers," *Nikkei Weekly* (30 June 2003), 2.

39. Derek Jones and Takao Kato, "The Productivity Effects of Employee Stock Ownership Plans: Evidence from Japanese Panel Data," *American Economic Review* 85 (1995), 391–414.

40. Yoshiro Miwa and J. Mark Ramseyer, "The Myth of the Main Bank," working paper, Olin Center, Harvard Law School, 2001; Michael E. Porter, Hitotaka Takeuchi, and Mariko Sakakibara, *Can Japan Compete?* (London, 2000).

41. Ronald Dore, "Where We Are Now: Musings of an Evolutionist," *Work, Employment, & Society* 3 (December, 1989), 425–46; Hirokuni Tabata, "Community and Efficiency in the Japanese Firm," *Social Science Japan* 1 (1998), 199–215.

42. Inagami and RIALS, *Kōporēto Gabanansu*, table 2–3.

43. Often it is the most prosperous companies that are attuned to their public image and able to afford making faddish changes to pay systems and to corporate governance. Hence it is very difficult to estimate whether these reforms contribute to improved performance or whether causality runs in the opposite direction. See, for example, Hideaki Miyajima, "The Latest Report on Corporate Governance Reform," 2003. For an analysis of this issue with U.S. data, see Barry Staw and Lisa Epstein, "What Bandwagons Bring: Effects of Popular Management Techniques on Corporate Performance, Reputation, and CEO Pay," *Administrative Science Quarterly* 45 (2000), 523–56.

Chapter 4
The Evolution of Human Resource Management in the United States

1. This chapter is based on my essay "A Century of Human Resource Management," in Bruce E. Kaufman, Richard Beaumont, and Roy Helfgott, eds., *From Industrial Relations to Human Resources and Beyond* (Armonk, N.Y., 2003). Note that *personnel management* was the label used from the early years of the twentieth century through the 1980s, when it was replaced by *human resource management*.

2. Daniel Nelson, *Managers and Workers: Origins of the New Factory System in the U.S.* (Madison, 1975); Alfred D. Chandler Jr., *The Visible Hand: The Managerial Revolution in American Business* (Cambridge, Mass., 1977).

3. Joseph A. Litterer, "Systematic Management: Design for Organizational Recoupling in American Manufacturing Firms," *Business History Review* 37 (Winter 1963), 376–89.

4. Henry Eilbirt, "The Development of Personnel Management in the United States," *Business History Review* 33 (Autumn 1959), 345–64.

5. Daniel T. Rodgers, *Atlantic Crossings: Social Politics in a Progresssive Age* (Cambridge, Mass.,1998); Robert H. Wiebe, *The Search for Order: 1877–1920* (New York, 1967).

6. Stuart Brandes, *American Welfare Capitalism, 1880–1940* (Chicago, 1976); Edward Berkowitz and Kim McQuaid, "Businessman and Bureaucrat: The Evolution of the American Social Welfare System, 1900–1940," *Journal of Economic History* 38 (1978), 120–42.

7. Nikki Mandell, *The Corporation as Family: The Gendering of Corporate Welfare, 1890–1930* (Chapel Hill, 2002); Angel Kwolek-Folland, *Incorporating Women: A History of Women and Business in the United States* (New York, 1998); Frank B. Miller and Mary Coghill, "Sex and the Personnel Manager," *Industrial and Labor Relations Review* 18 (October 1964), 32–44.

8. Sanford M. Jacoby, *Employing Bureaucracy: Managers, Unions, and the Transformation of American Industry, 1900–1945* (New York, 1985), 137, 161.

9. Howard M. Gitelman, "Being of Two Minds: American Employers Confront the Labor Problem," 25 *Labor History* (1984), 189–216

10. Jacoby, *Employing Bureaucracy*, 181.

11. Sanford M. Jacoby, *Modern Manors: Welfare Capitalism since the New Deal* (Princeton, 1997).

12. Sanford M. Jacoby, "Unnatural Extinction: The Rise and Fall of the Independent Labor Union," *Industrial Relations* 40 (July 2001), 377–404.

13. Sanford M. Jacoby, "Employers and the Welfare State: The Role of Marion B. Folsom," *Journal of American History* 80 (1993), 525–56; Edward Berkowitz and Kim McQuaid, *Creating the Welfare State: The Political Economy of Twentieth-Century Reform* (Lawrence, Kans., 1992); Jennifer Klein, "The Business of Health Security: Employee Health Benefits, Commercial Insurers, and the Reconstruction of Welfare Capitalism, 1945–1960," *International Labor and Working Class History* 58 (Fall 2000), 293–313.

14. Jacoby, *Employing Bureaucracy*, 233, 242.

15. Ibid., 260–74. Also see James N. Baron, Frank Dobbin, and P. Devereaux Jennings, "War and Peace: The Evolution of Modern Personnel Administration in U. S. Industry," *American Journal of Sociology* 92 (September 1986), 350–83.

16. Sanford Jacoby and Sunil Sharma, "Employment Duration and Industrial Labor Mobility in the United States, 1880–1980," *Journal of Economic History* 52 (March 1992), 161–79.

17. Adolf A. Berle and Gardiner C. Means, *The Modern Corporation and Private Property* (New York, 1932).

18. Francis X. Sutton, Seymour Harris, Carl Kaysen, and James Tobin, *The American Business Creed* (Cambridge, Mass., 1956), 64–65.

19. Gordon Donaldson, *Corporate Restructuring: Managing the Change Process from Within* (Boston, 1994), 19. Donaldson's point about managerial careers is reminiscent of the traditional Japanese model.

20. Ibid.; Richard Tedlow, *Keeping the Corporate Image: Public Relations and Business* (Greenwich, Conn., 1979); Robert A. Hall, "The Importance of Lifetime Jobs in the U.S. Economy," *American Economic Review* 72 (September 1982), 716–24; Robert E. Cole, *Work, Mobility, and Participation: A Comparative Study of American and Japanese Industry* (Berkeley, 1979).

21. Sanford M. Jacoby, "Employee Attitude Surveys in Historical Perspective," *Industrial Relations* 27 (1988), 74–93; F. J. Roethlisberer and William Dickson, *Management and the Worker* (Cambridge, Mass., 1939); William J. Breen, "Social Science and State Policy in World War II: Human Relations, Pedagogy, and Industrial Training, 1940–1945," *Business History Review* 76 (Summer 2002), 233–66.

22. Louis E. Davis and Albert Cherns, *The Quality of Working Life* (New York, 1975); Robert Blake and Jane Mouton, *The Managerial Grid* (Houston, 1964); Harold M. F. Rush, *Behavioral Science: Concepts and Management Application* (New York, 1969).

23. Chester Evans and LaVerne Laseau, *My Job Contest* (Washington, D.C., 1950).

24. Stephen Habbe, "How Not to Have Grievances," *Management Record* 11 (June 1949), 247–49; Alan Zane, "The Grievance Procedure among Nonunion White-Collar Employees in Life Insurance Companies," M.S. thesis, UCLA, 1968; Ronald Berenbeim, *Nonunion Complaint Systems* (New York, 1980).

25. The Conference Board, *Personnel Administration: Changing Scope and Organization* (New York, 1966), 21, 28–29.

26. Alfred D. Chandler Jr., *Strategy and Structure* (Cambridge, Mass., 1962); Neil Fligstein, "The Spread of the Multidivisional Form," *American Sociological Review* 50 (June 1985), 377–91.

27. Conference Board, *Personnel Administration*, 13, 15, 31–37, 64–72.

28. See Peter Drucker's negative appraisal in *The Practice of Management* (New York, 1954), 273–88.

29. Neil Fligstein, "The Intraorganizational Power Struggle: Rise of Finance Presidents in Large Corporations, 1919–1979," *American Sociological Review* 52 (1987), 44–58; Dalton McFarland, *Cooperation and Conflict in Personnel Administration* (New York, 1962), 63; George Ritzer and Harrison Trice, *An Occupation in Conflict: A Study of the Personnel Manager* (Ithaca, 1969), 65.

30. Ivar Berg, Marcia Freedman, and Michael Freeman, *Managers and Work Reform: A Limited Engagement* (New York, 1978); *Work in America* (1973); George Strauss et al. eds., *Organizational Behavior: Research and Issues* (Madison, 1974).

31. Allen R. Janger, *The Personnel Function: Changing Objectives and Organization* (New York, 1977), 48–49.

32. Richard Freeman and James Medoff, *What Do Unions Do?* (New York, 1984); Thomas A. Kochan, Harry C. Katz, and Robert McKersie, *The Transformation of American Industrial Relations* (New York, 1986); Thomas A. Kochan and Peter Cappelli, "The Transformation of the Industrial Relations/Human Resources Function," in Paul Osterman, ed., *Internal Labor Markets* (Cambridge, Mass., 1984), 163–90.

33. Fred K. Foulkes, *Personnel Policies in Large Nonunion Companies* (Englewood Cliffs, N.J., 1980), 70–96; Audrey Freedman, *The New Look in Wage Policy and Employee Relations*, Conference Board Report no. 865 (New York, 1985), 29–33.

34. Frank Dobbin and John Sutton, "The Strength of a Weak State: The Rights Revolution and the Rise of Human Resources Management Divisions," *American Journal of Sociology* 104 (1998), 441–76.

35. Janger, *The Personnel Function*, 1, 4, 63.

36. The explanations for union decline in the United States include stiff employer resistance (partly for ideological reasons and partly to reduce impact of high union wages on profits); changing economic structures; and reduced employee interest in

unions as a result of rising education and provision of unionlike protection by progressive employers and by legislation. Assigning weights to these—and other—factors is a rather vexed task. See Richard B. Freeman and Joel Rogers, *What Workers Want* (New York, 1999); Freeman and Medoff, *What Do Unions Do?*; Sanford Jacoby, "American Exceptionalism Revisited: The Importance of Management" in Jacoby, ed., *Masters to Managers: Historical and Comparative Perspectives on American Employers* (New York, 1991); and Robert J. Flanagan, "Has Management Strangled U.S. Unions?" unpublished ms., Stanford University, 2003.

37. Steven Vogel, *More Rules: Regulatory Reform in Advanced Industrial Countries* (Ithaca, 1996); Barry Bluestone and Bennett Harrison, *The Deindustrialization of America* (New York, 1982); Lori Kletzer, "Job Displacement," *Journal of Economic Perspectives* 12 (Winter 1998); 115–36.

38. John C. Coffee Jr., "Shareholders versus Managers: The Strain in the Corporate Web," in John C. Coffee Jr., Louis Lowenstein, and Susan Rose-Ackerman, eds., *Knights, Raiders, and Targets: The Impact of the Hostile Takeover* (New York, 1988), 77–134; Rakesh Khurana, *Searching for a Corporate Savior: The Irrational Quest for Charismatic CEOs* (Princeton, 2002); Kevin J. Murphy and Jan Zabojnik, "Managerial Control and the Market for CEOs," unpublished paper, 2003.

39. R. Comment and G. Jarrell, "Corporate Focus, Stock Returns, and the Market for Corporate Control," *Journal of Financial Economics* 37 (1995), 67–88; Neil Fligstein, *The Architecture of Markets* (Princeton, 2001); Sanford M. Jacoby, "Risk and the Labor Market: Societal Past as Economic Prologue," in Ivar Berg and Arne Kalleberg, eds., *Sourcebook of Labor Markets* (New York, 2001), 31–60.

40. Michael Hammer and James Champy, *Reengineering the Corporation: A Manifesto for Business Revolution* (New York, 1993); Sanford M. Jacoby, "Are Career Jobs Headed for Extinction?" *California Management Review* 42 (Fall 1999), 123–45. However, the brunt of downsizing continued to fall on nonmanagerial employees, even though the rate of managerial downsizing rose in the 1980s and 1990s. See William J. Baumol, Alan S. Blinder, and Edward N. Wolff, *Downsizing in America: Reality, Causes, and Consequences* (New York, 2003), 213.

41. Robert J. Kramer, *Organizing for Global Competitiveness: The Corporate Headquarters Design* (New York, 1999).

42. Robert J. Shiller, *Irrational Exuberance* (Princeton, 2001); Terrance Odean, "Do Investors Trade Too Much?" *American Economic Review* 89 (1999), 1270. The argument sometimes is made that there is no such thing as myopia, that share prices reflect all information presently available about a company and that maximizing long-run value is equivalent to maximizing today's share price. This is the efficient-markets hypothesis. In fact, however, the evidence for efficient markets is less compelling than one might think. After all, if prices were at their appropriate level yesterday, why did the NASDAQ market come crashing down today? Warren Buffett, Bill Nygren, and other investors have repeatedly observed that quarterly earnings forecasts are a distraction to long-term corporate planning and, now that the stock market is in a post-bubble phase, a growing number of companies are moving away from them. Purely statistical evidence on myopia is ambiguous, as much of it is based on R&D figures that are not a reliable measure of "long term," and one can find empirical support on both sides of the issue. For a balanced overview, see Kevin J. Laverty, "Economic Short-Termism: The Debate, the Unresolved Issues, and the Implications for Management," *Academy*

of Management Review 21 (July 1996), 825–60. See also "Coca Cola to Stop Giving Forecasts," *Los Angeles Times* (15 December 2002).

43. Peter Cappelli, *The New Deal at Work* (Boston 1999). However, it is crucially important to recognize that, although there was a shift to market-oriented criteria and a transfer of risk from employers to employees, this was a not a slide all the way down to the pure-market end of the pole. That is, there continue to be significant organization-oriented elements of the employment relationship. While the percentage of adults in jobs lasting ten years or more fell from 1979 to 1996, the drop was modest: from 40 to 35 percent. Pay and benefits continue to reward tenure, although not as much as before. And many of the companies that reported downsizing actually ended up *increasing* their total employment later on. For a more detailed look at these issues, see Jacoby, "Are Career Jobs Headed for Extinction?" (passim); Baumol, Blinder, and Wolff, *Downsizing in America*.

44. John Cassidy, "The Greed Cycle," *New Yorker* (23 September 2002); *Economist* (6 April 2002), 12; Lucian Arye Bebchuk, Jesse Fried, and David I. Walker, "Managerial Power and Rent Extraction the Design of Executive Compensation," *University of Chicago Law Review* 69 (2002), 751–846; Forrest Briscoe, James Maxwell, and Peter Temin, "HR versus Finance: Who Controls Corporate Health Care Decisions and Does It Matter?" working paper, MIT, 2002.

45. Rosabeth Moss Kanter, *When Giants Learn to Dance* (New York, 1990).

46. Vincent Caimano, Pat Canavan, and Linda Hill, "Trends and Issues Affecting Human Resources and Global Business" and Arthur Yeung and Wayne Brockbank, "Reengineering HR through Information Technology," in Karl Price and James W. Walker, eds., *The New HR: Strategic Positioning of the HR Function* (New York, 1999), 23–38, 161–81; Robert E. Cole, *Managing Quality Fads: How American Business Learned to Play the Quality Game* (New York, 1999).

47. Scott Lever, "An Analysis of Managerial Motivations behind Outsourcing Practices," *Human Resource Planning* 20 (1997), 37–48.

48. Louis Csoka, *Rethinking Human Resources*, Conference Board Report, no. 1124-95-RR (1995), 11.

49. Ibid., 31.

50. See the case studies on strategic HRM in *Human Resource Management* 38 (Winter 1999).

51. John Purcell and Bruce Ahlstrand, *Human Resource Management in the Multidivisional Company* (Oxford, 1994); Paul Marginson, Peter Armstrong, Paul Edwards, John Purcell, and Nancy Hubbard, "The Control of Industrial Relations in Large Companies: An Initial Analysis of the Second Company-Level Industrial Relations Survey," Warwick Papers in Industrial Relations no. 45, Industrial Relations Research Unit, University of Warwick, Coventry, U.K., 1993; Anthony Buono and James L. Bowditch, *The Human Side of Mergers and Acquisitions* (San Francisco, 1989); Elaine McShulskis, "A Bigger Role in Mergers and Acquisitions," *HR Magazine* 43 (January 1998), 22–24; Conference Board, *Post-merger Integration: A Human Resources Perspective* (New York, 2000); "Mergers: Why Most Big Deals Don't Pay Off," *Business Week* (14 October 2002), 60ff.; L. Gratton, V. Hope-Hailey, P. Stiles, and C. Truss, "Linking Individual Performance to Business Strategy: The People Process Model," in Randall Schuler and Susan Jackson, eds., *Strategic Human Resource Management* (Malden, Mass., 1999).

52. Michael Lombardo and Robert Eichinger, "Human Resources' Role in Building Competitive Edge Leaders" in Dave Ulrich, Michael Losey, and Gerry Lake, eds., *Tomorrow's HR Management* (New York, 1997), 57–66; Csoka, "Rethinking," 9.

53. Jeffrey Pfeffer, "Pitfalls on the Road to Measurement: The Dangerous Liaison of Human Resources with the Ideas of Accounting and Finance," *Human Resource Management* 36 (1997), 357; Csoka, "Rethinking," 22; Karen Legge, "HRM: Rhetoric, Reality, and Hidden Agendas," in John Storey, ed., *Human Resource Management: A Critical Text* (London, 1995), 33–59.

54. Elizabeth Chambers, Mark Foulon, Helen Handfield Jones, Steve Hankin, and Edward Michaels, "The War for Talent," *McKinsey Quarterly* 3 (1998), 44–57.

55. Lucian Bebchuk and Allen Ferrell, "A New Approach to Takeover Law and Regulatory Competition," *Virginia Law Review* 87 (2001), 111–66; Bengt Holmstrom and Steven N. Kaplan, "Corporate Governance and Merger Activity in the United Sates: Making Sense of the 1980s and 1990s," *Journal of Economic Perspectives* 15 (Spring 2001), 121–44.

56. Marianne Bertrand and Sendhil Mullainathan, "Is There Discretion in Wage Setting? A Test Using Takeover Legislation," *Rand Journal of Economics* 30 (Autumn 1999), 535–54.

57. Shiller, *Irrational Exuberance*; Bebchuk, Fried, and Walker, "Executive Compensation"; Financial Markets Center, "Employee Stock Options," Background Report, April 2000.

58. "The Downsizing of America," series, *New York Times* (1996); Frederick F. Reichheld, *The Loyalty Effect: The Hidden Force behind Growth, Profits, and Lasting Value* (Boston, 1996), 151.

59. Jay Barney, "Firm Resources and Sustained Competitive Advantage," *Journal of Management* 17 (1991), 99–120; Nicolai Foss, ed., *Resources, Firms, and Strategies* (Oxford, 1997); John Purcell, "Corporate Strategy and its Link with HRM Strategy," in Storey, *Human Resource Management*, 63–86; Gary Hamel and C. K. Prahalad, *Competing for the Future* (Boston, 1994).

60. As recently as 1978, the book value of property, plant, and equipment of publicly traded corporations accounted for 83 percent of the market value of financial claims on the firm. By the end of 1997, it accounted for less than one-third of the market value of those claims. Margaret M. Blair and Lynn A. Stout, "Team Production in Business Organizations: An Introduction," *Journal of Corporation Law* 24 (1999), 744.

61. Martha Groves, "In Tight Job Market, Software Firm Develops Programs to Keep Employees," *Los Angeles Times* (14 June, 1998), D5; David J. Teece, "Capturing Value from Knowledge Assets," *California Management Review* 40 (1998), 77; Jacoby, "Are Career Jobs Headed for Extinction?"

62. Brian Becker and Mark Huselid, "Strategic HRM in Five Leading Firms," *Human Resource Management* 38 (Winter 1999), 287–301; Charles A. O'Reilly and Jeffrey Pfeffer, *Hidden Value: How Great Companies Achieve Extraordinary Results with Ordinary People* (Boston, 2000). For the Japanese version, see Hiroyuki Itami, *Mobilizing Invisible Assets* (Cambridge, Mass., 1987).

63. Jeffrey Pfeffer, *Competitive Advantage through People: Unleashing the Power of the Workforce* (Boston, 1994); John Kotter and James Heskett, *Corporate Culture and Performance* (New York, 1992); David I. Levine, *Working in the Twenty-first Century: Policies for Economic Growth through Training, Opportunity, and Education* (Armonk,

N.Y., 1998); Blinder, Baumol, and Wolff, *Downsizing in America*; Wayne Cascio, "Corporate Restructuring and the No-Layoff Payoff," *Perspectives on Work* 7 (2003), 4–6.

64. Currently around 13 percent of private workers own stock in firms where employee ownership exceeds 4 percent of total market value. Joseph Blasi and Douglas Kruse, *The New Owners: The Mass Emergence of Employee Ownership* (New York, 1991), 14.

65. One very rough gauge of the prevalence of the resource-based model is the percentage of employees who agree that their company thinks of them as its most important asset, which stood at 34 percent in a 2003 survey of around two thousand U.S. employees. Walker Information, *Loyalty in the Workplace* (Indianapolis, 2003). In theory, the resource-based approach could coexist with shareholder primacy, although in practice the combination is rare and difficult to sustain. See Simon Deakin, Richard Hobbs, Suzanne Konzelmann, and Frank Wilkinson, "Partnership, Ownership, and Control: The Impact of Corporate Governance on Employment Relations," Center for Business Research, Cambridge University, June 2001.

66. In 1999, women made up 49 percent of all managers but 60 percent of all personnel and labor-relations managers; for blacks, the figures are 8 percent of managers but 11 percent of personnel managers (U.S. Bureau of Labor Statistics, ftp://ftp.bls.gov/pub/special.requests/lf/aat11.txt). Among those in ten primary management occupations, HR managers ranked eighth in average annual earnings, slightly above those in purchasing and transportation but well below information systems, marketing, finance, and operations (Bureau of Labor Statistics, Occupational Employment Statistics, http://stats.bls.gov/news.release/ocwage.t01.htm).

Chapter 5
Inside U.S. Companies Today

1. Note that families wield influence at 35 percent to 45 percent of America's largest listed companies, depending on how influence is defined. "Under the Influence," *Economist* (17 November 2001), 57.

2. Terrence Deal and Allan Kennedy, *Corporate Cultures: The Rites and Rituals of Corporate Life* (Reading, Mass., 1982).

3. There is limited outsourcing of HR responsibilities. The only major outsourcing is for health and other nonfinancial benefits. For financial benefits—like 401(k)s—the company serves as its own third party.

4. In many respects this is like the supplemental unemployment benefit offered to blue-collar auto- and steel-workers in the 1960s and 1970s, which were intended to maintain the employment relation over the course of a temporary layoff.

5. Fred Foulkes, *Personnel Policies in Large Nonunion Companies* (Englewood Cliffs, N.J., 1980).

6. Michael Tushman and Charles O'Reilly, "Ambidextrous Organizations: Managing Evolutionary and Revolutionary Change," *California Management Review* 38 (Summer 1996), 8–30.

7. Sanford M. Jacoby, "Pacific Ties: Industrial Relations and Employment Systems in Japan and the United States since 1900" in Howell J. Harris and Nelson Lichtenstein, eds., *Industrial Democracy in America* (Cambridge, 1993), 206–48.

Chapter 6
Comparative Survey Data

1. The actual sample size was 1,007 in Japan and 977 in the United States. HR questionnaires from 103 U.S. firms were returned as undeliverable, usually because the company had merged with another or because it did not participate in surveys. One Japanese survey was discarded because of incomplete data.

2. Allen R. Janger, *The Personnel Function: Changing Objectives and Organization* (New York, 1977), 37.

3. Raghuram G. Rajan and Julie Wulf, "The Flattening Firm: Evidence from Panel Data on the Changing Nature of Corporate Hierarchies," NBER Working Paper no. 9633 (April 2003).

4. The correlation between being a CEO report and being concerned with employee job security was $-.18$ ($p < .05$).

5. Rajan and Wulf, "The Flattening Firm."

6. As described below, we created an index to measure centralization of operating decisions. For CEO reports, it was 25.8; for others, it was 28.2. The ratio of HR staff to employees for CEO reports was 1:211; for nonreports, it was 1:145.

7. This figure is virtually unchanged from more than twenty years ago, when it was 80 percent. See Audrey Freedman, *Managing Labor Relations* (New York, 1979), 29. The corresponding Japanese figure is 39 percent.

8. Despite the many changes that have buffeted the HR profession in the United States, this figure is not much lower than it was in the late 1960s, when it stood at 34 percent. George Ritzer and Harrison Trice, *An Occupation in Conflict: A Study of the Personnel Manager* (Ithaca, N.Y., 1969), 35. However, the Ritzer and Trice data are based on a survey of personnel managers at all levels, not just senior executives.

9. While the average sample unionization rate is 16 percent, the unionization rate for those companies spending "a lot more" time on labor relations is 25 percent.

10. This reverses a trend from earlier years. According to one study, headquarters HR staff fell 13 percent between 1990 and 1995. Susan Mohrman, Edward E. Lawler III, and Gary McMahan, "New Directions for the Human Resources Organization," Center for Effective Organizations, University of Southern California, 1996.

11. Spin-offs are akin to the U.S. practice of an internal chargeback system for use of central HR services by divisional and business-unit "customers" as is done with information technology.

12. Outsourcing is significantly associated with use of stock options in Japan ($r = .15$, $p < .05$). Both are examples of market-oriented practices being brought in from abroad.

13. Julekha Dash, "Outsourcing Wave Hits Japanese Market," *Computerworld* 35 (6 August 2001), 13. The U.S. outsourcing data are consistent with those reported earlier in Louis Csoka, "Rethinking Human Resources," Conference Board Report no. 1124–95-HR (New York, 1995), 20.

14. Four of the five chi-square tests in table 6.2 are significant.

15. We create indices of the first and of the last column in table 6.3 and refer to them as "index of line operating authority" and "index of headquarter operating authority." They are shown in the last row of table 6.3.

16. We ran two-sample t-tests with unequal variances and found five of the six differences in the Japan-U.S. means for headquarters operating authority (including the overall means) to be significant at the .0001 level.

A Japan Productivity Center survey in 1986 asked respondents to assess the power of the headquarters HR department. The greatest levels of influence ("very strong") were found in recruitment and hiring; pay structure, including negotiations with the union; and promotion and transfer of managers. Hideo Inohara, *Human Resource Development in Japanese Companies* (Tokyo, 1990), 4. Keep in mind that a respondent's rank affects his or her sense of how centralized decisions are; managing directors perceive greater centralization than do those further down the hierarchy.

17. Robert E. Cole, "Learning from the Quality Movement: What Did Happen and Didn't Happen and Why?" *California Management Review* 41 (Fall 1998), 43–73. When TQM and the like were first introduced into U.S. companies there was substantially more headquarters involvement than one sees today. In 1985, the primary responsibility for introducing employee participation plans was the HR executive (58 percent) rather than the line manager (28 percent); compare these figures to those in table 6.4. However, even in 1985 it was reported that responsibility for participation was being decentralized along with training and development. Audrey Freedman, *The New Look in Wage Policy and Employee Relations* (New York, 1985), 30.

18. For Japan, the correlation between operating authority and staff per employee is .20 ($p < .01$). In the United States the correlation is .09 but not significant.

19. These stages originally were identified in Paul Marginson et al., "The Control of Industrial Relations in Large Companies," Warwick Papers in Industrial Relations no. 45, Coventry, December 1993.

20. The findings mesh with another study, which found that only a third of U.S. HR executives said that HR had a major influence in the planning and/or negotiation of M&As but that 80 percent said they became involved once the deal had been made. Elaine McShulskis, "A Bigger Role in Mergers and Acquisitions," *HR Magazine* (January 1998), 22–24.

21. On investing in new sites, 35 percent of HR executives said they were involved in final decisions, whereas only 10 percent of the CFOs said that their HR executives were involved in these final decisions.

22. National Industrial Conference Board, *Personnel Administration: Changing Scope and Organization* (New York, 1966), 17. We calculated these figures in the same manner as was done in 1966, when the survey did not distinguish between "not involved" and "did not occur."

23. For the matched companies, 77 percent of HR executives said that they took part in final decisions on executive pay and selection, whereas CFOs reported an HR involvement figure of only 45 percent. On payroll budgets, 50 percent of HR executives said they were involved in final decisions; only 23 percent of CFOs said that HR was involved.

24. For education, the correlation with full-time employment in Japan is .14; for the U.S., it is .19. Both are significant at the .05 level. For union membership, the correlation with full-time employment is .14 and significant at the .05 level. For the United States the correlation is .12 but not significant.

25. See the tests of national difference shown in table 6.6, all four of which are significant at the .001 level.

26. See Sanford M. Jacoby, "Reply: Premature Reports of Demise," *California Management Review* 42 (Fall 1999), 168–79; William Baumol, Alan Blinder, and Edward Wolff, *Downsizing in American: Reality, Causes, and Consequences* (New York, 2003), 47–48. We ran two-sample t-tests with unequal variances and found the difference in the Japanese-U.S. means for internal labor markets to be significant at the .001 level.

27. The correlation between managerial internal labor markets and operating centralization in Japan is .17 ($p < .01$).

28. The correlation between internal labor market strength (the combined supervisory-plus-nonsupervisory measure) and the change in headquarters HR staff is $-.17$ ($p < .05$).

29. The correlation between the combined measure of internal labor market strength and the number of board members with an HR background is .20 ($p < .05$).

30. The correlation between pay for performance and line-manager involvement is .23 ($p < .01$).

31. Rajan and Wulf, "The Flattening Firm."

32. Lucian Arye Bebchuk and Jesse M. Fried, "Executive Compensation as an Agency Problem," Harvard Law School, Working Paper 421 (April 2003).

33. Christina Ahmadjian, "Changing Japanese Corporate Governance," Working Paper no. 188, Columbia University Graduate School of Business, 2001; Hideaki Miyajima, "The Latest Report on Corporate Governance Reform, 'Progress in Corporate Governance Reforms and the Revitalization of Japanese Companies' by the Ministry of Finance's Policy Research Institute," RIETI, September 2003. The symbolic motivation for organizational reform provides one explanation why the MOF study reported on by Miyajima fails to find a significant relationship between adoption of the corporate officer system and corporate financial performance. In our own data, too, we found no evidence that use of this system is associated with employment change over the last five years; the correlation was negative and insignificant, $-.03$ ($p = .67$).

34. Ulrike Schaede, "Understanding Corporate Governance in Japan: Do Classical Concepts Apply?" *Industrial and Corporate Change* 3 (1994), 285–323.

35. We refer to "influence over strategic decisions" as defined in table 6.5. However, strategic influence was slightly higher in firms with the corporate-officer system when using the strategy categories shown in table 6.4.

36. James Westphal and Edward Zajac, "The Symbolic Management of Stockholders: Corporate Governance Reforms and Shareholder Reactions," *Administrative Science Quarterly* 43 (1998), 127–53. More generally, see W. W. Powell and P. J. DiMaggio, "The Iron Cage Revisited: Institututional Isomorphism and Collective Rationality in Organizational Fields," *American Sociological Review* 48 (April 1983), 147–60.

37. Korn/Ferry data as of February 2002, courtesy of Caroline Nahas and Jeremy Lawrence. If we assume that all of the non-*shikkō yakuin* companies have their senior HR manager on the board, the contrast is sharp: 72 percent of Japanese firms versus 0.7 percent of U.S. firms have their top HR executive on the board of directors.

38. See Charles Perrow, "Departmental Power and Perspectives in Industrial Firms," in Mayer N. Zald, ed., *Power in Organizations* (Nashville, 1970).

39. In the matched-pair companies, finance rated itself 8.5 and rated HR 4.1, while HR rated finance 8.7 and rated itself 6.7.

40. $r = -.29$ ($p < .01$.)

41. As shown in table 6.7, Spearman's rank correlation was insignificant, indicating that the national rankings are dissimilar.

42. We found the greatest accretion of power by planning departments occurring in companies that were unrelated diversifiers—i.e., companies having no single business contributing more than 70 percent of sales and whose businesses were mostly unrelated. These are the companies feeling the greatest pressure to divest or restructure to achieve greater synergy.

43. See also Ahmadjian, "Corporate Governance."

44. A recent study found a split among U.S. companies between those who reserved options for their top officers and those—predominantly in high tech—who shared them more widely. Joseph Blasi, Douglas Kruse, and Aaron Bernstein, *In the Company of Owners: The Truth about Stock Options (and Why Every Employee Should Have Them)* (New York, 2003).

45. In both countries, power has a significant negative association with changes in employment levels during the past five years. That is, employment cuts are associated with higher HR power levels. This could be a reflection of the prominence of HR when layoffs must be made. However, employment cuts were most prevalent in large firms, so the relationship could also be a proxy for the size-power relationship discussed below.

46. Lawrence J. White, "What's Been Happening to Aggregate Concentration in the U.S.?" working paper, New York University, December 2001, 44; James L. Medoff and Michael Calabrese, *The Impact of Labor Market Trends on Health and Pension Benefit Coverage and Inequality*, Final Report to the U.S. Pension and Welfare Agency, 28 February 2001.

47. Data from Japanese Bureau of Statistics, courtesy of Professor Michio Nitta, Tokyo University. In our sample, the Japanese companies are smaller than the U.S. companies: Mean (median) employment was 5,083 (2,215) in Japan versus 18,260 (5,200) in the United States.

48. The classic (British) studies on firm size found an opposite result—that centralization was positively related to size—perhaps because the studies were done before the M-form approach had diffused widely in the United Kingdom See S. Pugh, D. J. Hickson, and C.R. Hinings, "An Empirical Taxonomy of Structures of Work Organisations," *Administrative Science Quarterly* 14 (1969), 115–26.

49. We also looked at some three-way relationships, which are not shown. In the United States, size is important and tends to trump business strategy when predicting operating authority and staffing levels. But in Japan, regardless of firm size, it is the unrelated diversifiers who have had the largest cuts in HR staff and whose HR executives report the least amount of power. This supports what was found in the case studies and fits with the received wisdom about divestment and its effects in Japan.

50. Michael Porter, Hirotaka Takeuchi, and Mariko Sakakibara, *Can Japan Compete?* (London, 2000).

51. Masayuki Morikawa, "Business Diversification of Japanese Companies," MITI Discussion Paper no. 99, Tokyo, November 1999. Thanks to Professor Yoshiji Suzuki for bringing this paper to my attention.

52. Cynthia Montgomery, "Corporate Diversification," *Journal of Economic Perspectives* 8 (Summer 1994), 163–78. Contrast this study to R. Comment and G. Jarrell,

"Corporate Focus, Stock Returns, and the Market for Corporate Control," *Journal of Financial Economics* 37 (1995), 67–88.

53. White, "What's Been Happening to Aggregate Concentration."

54. Personal communication from Professor Tadao Kagono, Kobe University.

55. Jay Barney, "Firm Resources and Sustained Competitive Advantage," *Journal of Management* 17 (1991), 91–120.

56. That is, Japan relies on employee voice to judge HR performance, whereas the United States tends to rely more on retention patterns. Sanford M. Jacoby, *Employing Bureaucracy: Managers, Unions, and the Transformation of Work in American Industry, 1900–1945* (New York, 1985); Richard Freeman and James Medoff, *What Do Unions Do?* (New York, 1984).

57. We created a "cost factor" comprised of labor costs and revenue per employee and a "human capital" factor comprised of employee morale and union relations. In Japan, the factors are positively associated ($r = .22$, $p < .001$) but in the United States, the association is negative, although not significant.

58. Harry C. Triandis, *Individualism and Collectivism* (Boulder, 1995); Geert H. Hofstede, *Culture's Consequences: Comparing Values, Behaviors, Institutions, and Organizations Across Nations*, 2d ed. (Thousand Oaks, Calif., 2001).

59. Observe, however, that on two key values—maximizing share price and safeguarding employee jobs—U.S. CFOs look more like U.S. HR executives than the latter look like Japanese HR executives. We also asked U.S. CFOs to tell us what measures were reported to headquarters for gauging business-unit performance. Employee-based measures such as sales per employee and labor costs were cited much less frequently than purely financial measures such as return on investment, profit/sales, and total sales. It would appear that, from the CFO perspective, employment costs—and employees—are relatively unimportant, and that finance is influencing the perspective of HR managers more than the other way around, a point we return to in the final chapter.

60. Sometimes it is alleged that in Japan a kind of "groupthink" ensues from strong societal norms and that in the United States shared norms are weaker. We find evidence for this claim: There is less overall variance of values in the Japanese than in the U.S. HR sample. Mean Japanese and U.S. variances are .59 and .65, respectively. Also note that the samples are significantly different (at the .0001 level) in what they reveal about the importance attached to shareholder values (stronger in the United States) and stakeholder values (stronger in Japan).

61. In Japan, variations in the percentage of an executive's career spent in HR do not have the same meaning, given the generalist career pattern that exists in many companies.

62. On these issues see Rakesh Khurana, *Searching for a Corporate Savior* (Princeton, 2002), 115.

Chapter 7
Taking Stock and Looking Ahead

1. Kazuhiko Murata, "Personnel Management in Japanese Business Enterprises," *Hitotsubashi Journal of Commerce and Management* 25 (1990), 35–46.

2. On this point, we replicated a survey question recently asked of Japanese corporate directors and put it to CFOs in the United States: "Do you agree that corporations are the property of shareholders, and employees are merely one of the factors of production?" In Japan, 9 percent of directors agreed with this question; in the United States, 67 percent of CFOs agreed. The split is striking. For Japan, see International Industrial Relations Association (IIRA) twelfth World Congress, Special Seminar, *Corporate Governance and Industrial Democracy* (Tokyo, June 2000), 105.

3. The survey data show that standard deviations for operating authority, HR power, and executive values are larger in the United States than in Japan.

4. Thus, the contemporary U.S. distribution shown in figure 7.2 actually is bimodal, with one small, and one much larger, hump. For further evidence on this point, based on structural equation modeling of the survey data, see Sanford M. Jacoby, Emily Lau, and Kazuro Saguchi, "Corporate Governance, Business Strategy, and Employment Relations in Japanese and U.S. Corporations: A Structural Analysis," working paper, UCLA, 2004.

5. Christopher L. Erickson and Sanford M. Jacoby, "The Effect of Employer Networks on Workplace Innovation and Training," *Industrial and Labor Relations Review* 56 (January 2003), 203–43.

6. For a theoretical elaboration on the point that motivating employees to invest in firm-specific human capital may require ceding a role to them in corporate governance, see John Roberts and Eric Van den Steen, "Shareholder Interests, Human Capital Investment, and Corporate Governance," working paper, Stanford Graduate School of Business, April 2000.

7. Charles O'Reilly and Jeffrey Pfeffer, *Hidden Value: How Great Companies Achieve Extraordinary Results with Ordinary People* (Boston, 2000).

8. David Barstow and Lowell Bergman, "At a Texas Foundry, an Indifference to Life," *New York Times* (8 January 2003).

9. Forrest Briscoe, J. Maxwell, J. and Peter Temin,, "HR versus Finance: Who Controls Corporate Health Care Decisions?" working paper, Sloan School of Management, MIT, 2002.

10. See, for example, Sandra Waddock and Samuel B. Graves, "Performance Characteristics of Social and Traditional Investments," *Journal of Investing* 9 (Summer 2000), 27; Mark Huselid, "The Impact of Human Resource Management Practices on Turnover, Productivity, and Corporate Financial Performance," *Academy of Management Journal* 38 (June 1995), 635–73.

11. Golin/Harris International, "American Business Faces a Crisis of Trust," February 2002.

12. Lucian Arye Bebchuk, Jesse Fried, and David I. Walker, "Managerial Power and Rent Extraction the Design of Executive Compensation," *University of Chicago Law Review* 69 (2002), 751–846.

13. A group of corporate directors from major U.S. companies attended an accounting workshop at the University of Chicago. Only 32 percent were able to supply correct answers to a basic accounting test. One of the questions asked for a definition of "retained earnings." Fewer than 20 percent answered it correctly. Andrew Ross Sorkin, "Back to School, But This One Is for Top Corporate Officials," *New York Times* (3 September 2002).

14. A recent study by the Federal Reserve Bank of New York reported that "there is presently no theoretical or empirical consensus on how stock options affect . . . firm performance." John Core, Wayne Guay, and David Larcker, "Executive Equity Compensation and Incentives: A Survey," Federal Reserve Bank of New York, *Economic Policy Review* (April 2003), 27–50.

15. Eugene F. Fama, "Agency Problems and the Theory of the Firm," *Journal of Political Economy* 88 (1980), 288–307.

16. Micheline Maynard, *The End of Detroit: How the Big Three Lost Their Grip on the American Car Market* (New York, 2003).

17. Jeff Madrick, "Welch's Juice," *New York Review of Books* (14 February 2002), 16–18.

18. Mike McNamee, "Pitt's Accounting Fix Leaves a Lot Broke," *Business Week* (4 February 2002).

19. Sheila McNulty, "Unions Urge Groups to Act on Enron Directors," *Financial Times* (26 January 2002); Kathy M. Kristof, "Shareholders Join Others in Calling for Reductions in CEO Packages," *Los Angeles Times* (2 June 2002), C1; P. Plitch, "Investors Seek Proxy Election Reform," *Los Angeles Times* (17 February 2003), C3.

20. "Board, Interrupted," *Business Week* (13 October 2003), 114–15.

21. Sheila McNulty, "Unions Urge Groups to Act on Enron Directors," *Financial Times* (26 January 2002); Kathy M. Kristof, "Shareholders Join Others in Calling for Reductions in CEO Packages," *Los Angeles Times* (2 June 2002), C1; P. Plitch, "Investors Seek Proxy Election Reform," *Los Angeles Times* (17 February 2003), C3; Richard C. Breeden, "Restoring Trust: Report to the Honorable Jed Rakoff, U.S. District Court for the Southern District of New York, on Corporate Governance for the Future of MCI Inc.," August 2003; Brendan Barber, "Unions Must Have a Voice on the Board," *Guardian* (21 December 2002).

22. Peter Coy, "High Turnover, High Risk," *Business Week* 50 (Spring 2002), 24.

23. "Out of the Back Room," *Economist* (1 December 2001), 55–56.

24. Michael Goold and Andrew Campbell, *Designing Effective Organizations: How to Create Structured Networks* (San Francisco, 2002); "Cisco's Comeback," *Business Week* (24 November 2003), 116–24.

25. "Human Resource Positions Get Cut," *Wall Street Journal* (August 28, 2001), 1.

26. Charles Kupchan, *The End of the American Era: U.S. Foreign Policy and the Geopolitics of the Twenty-first Century* (New York, 2002).

27. Yoshi Nakamura, "Corporate Governance in Japan," *Japan Economic Currents* 11 (August 2001), 1–4.

28. "Revised Commercial Code Introduces U.S.-Style Corporate Governance," *JIL Labor Bulletin* (1 May 2003), 2–4; "More Listed Companies Inviting Outside Directors on Board," *Nikkei Weekly* (13 October 2003), 3.

29. Tokyo Stock Exchange, *2001 Shareownership Survey* (Tokyo, 2002), table 2.

30. Japan offers less generous unemployment benefits than can be found in Europe, although the benefits are on par with those of the United States. Hence it is not unemployment insurance that is the main explanation of U.S.-Japanese differences in layoff activity by employers but instead the factors mentioned in the text. "U.S. Unemployment Insurance: A Safety Net with Holes," Clearinghouse on International Developments in Child, Youth, and Family Policies, Columbia University, issue brief, December 2001.

31. "Culture Is Our Core Competency," *Nikkei Weekly* (18 March 2002), 1. Canon derives 70 percent of its sales outside Japan. Despite its profitability, Canon's traditional approach to corporate governance has earned it the enmity of foreign investment analysts like Goldman Sachs. See Richard Katz, *Japanese Phoenix: The Long Road to Economic Revival* (Armonk, N.Y., 2003), 323.

32. Byron K. Marshall, *Capitalism and Nationalism in Prewar Japan: The Ideology of the Business Elite, 1868–1941* (Stanford, 1967).

33. "Canon President Defends Current Japanese Structure," *Nikkei Weekly* (30 June 2003), 9.

34. Michael Porter, Hirotaka Takeuchi, and Mariko Sakakibara, *Can Japan Compete?* (London, 2000).

35. Andrew Campbell, Michael Goold, and Marcus Alexander, "The Value of the Parent Company," *California Management Review* 38 (Fall 1995), 75–97.

36. A year after the deal, the losers' average return was 25 percentage points below their industry peers. "Mergers: Why Most Big Deals Don't Pay Off," *Business Week* (14 October 2002), 63. Despite these facts, foreign financial analysts in Japan continue to be infatuated with M&As as the solution to what ails Japan. See the remarks by Jesper Koll of Merrill Lynch in Katz, *Japanese Phoenix*, 230.

37. Ronald Lipsey and Kelvin Lancaster, "The General Theory of Second Best," *Review of Economic Studies* 24 (1956), 11.

38. Charles E. Lindblom, *The Market System: What It Is, How it Works, What to Make of It* (New Haven, 2001).

39. Ronald J. Gilson, "Globalizing Corporate Governance: Convergence of Form or Function," *American Journal of Comparative Law* 49 (Spring 2001), 329–58. On the link between human capital and business strategy in the world economy, see Margarita Estevez-Abe, Peter Hall, and David Soskice, "Social Protection and the Formation of Skills: A Reinterpretation of the Welfare State," in Peter A. Hall and David Soskice, eds., *Varieties of Capitalism: The Institutional Foundations of Comparative Advantage* (Oxford, 2001), 145–83. An example of functional convergence are the different methods by which Japanese and U.S. companies get rid of incompetent presidents. Another example is the methods that U.S. and Japanese manufacturers have adopted to reduce labor costs without cutting wage rates: layoffs and outsourcing in the United States, bonus reductions, early retirement, and *kogaisha* spin-offs in Japan. Steven N. Kaplan, "Top Executive Rewards and Firm Performance: A Comparison of Japan and the U.S.," *Journal of Political Economy* 102 (1994), 510–46; Truman F. Bewley, *Why Wages Don't Fall during a Recession* (Cambridge, Mass., 2000).

40. For a more optimistic appraisal of the possibilities for discontinuous change, see Christopher L. Erickson and Sarosh Kuruvilla, "Industrial Relations System Transformation," *Industrial and Labor Relations Review* 52 (October 1998), 3–21.

41. Paul Krugman, "Mind the Gap," *New York Times* (16 August 2002); "Greenspan Says Fed Ready to Fight Deflation," *International Herald Tribune* (21 May 2003).

42. Richard B. Freeman and Lawrence F. Katz, "Introduction and Summary," in Freeman and Katz, eds., *Differences and Changes in Wage Structure* (Chicago, 1995), 1–21; Larry Mishell, Jared Bernstein, and John Schmitt, *The State of Working America 2001* (Ithaca, N.Y., 2001).

43. Philippe Aghion et al., "Inequality and Economic Growth: The Perspective of the New Growth Theories," *Journal of Economic Literature* 37 (1999), 1615–60; Al-

berto Alesina and Dani Rodrik, "Distributive Politics and Economic Growth," *Quarterly Journal of Economics* 109 (1994), 465–90.

44. Geoffrey Garrett, *Partisan Politics in the Global Economy* (Cambridge, 1998); Clair Brown, Yoshifumi Nakata, Michael Reich and Lloyd Ulman, *Work and Pay in the United States and Japan* (New York, 1997).

45. Mark J. Roe calls this "social democracy," but the broader designation of egalitarianism makes the theory fit both Europe and Japan. Roe, *Political Determinants of Corporate Governance* (Oxford, 2003). Also see Emmanuel Saez and Thomas Piketty, "Income Inequality in the United States, 1913–1918," NBER Working Paper no. 8467 (September 2001), on social norms and fluctuations in the distribution of income.

46. For a spirited statement of this view, but one that ignores distributional issues, see Raghuram Rajan and Luigi Zingales, *Saving Capitalism from the Capitalists: Unleashing the Power of Financial Markets to Create Wealth and Spread Opportunity* (New York, 2003). For evidence that downsizing is associated with a shift of income from workers to owners but *not* with improved productivity, see William J. Baumol, Alan S. Blinder, and Edward N. Wolff, *Downsizing in America: Reality, Causes, and Consequences* (New York, 2003).

47. Sanford M. Jacoby, "Risk and the Labor Market: Societal Past as Economic Prologue," in Ivar Berg and Arne Kalleberg, eds., *Sourcebook of Labor Markets: Structures and Processes* (New York, 2001), 31–60.

48. The richest fifth in the United States earn 11 times more than the poorest fifth, whereas the ratio in Japan is 4.3. In 1998, the very rich—the top 0.01 percent of U.S. taxpayers—received more than 3 percent of all income in America; this group includes the prime beneficiaries of the institutional changes of the 1990s. Kevin Phillips, *Wealth and Democracy: A Political History of the American Rich* (New York, 2002), 124; "Radical Birthday Thoughts," *Economist* (28 June 2003), 8; Paul Krugman, "For Richer," *New York Times* (20 October 2002).

49. These factors are not independent, however. Were unions stronger, they would undoubtedly restrain corporate governance and public policy from favoring shareholders over all others. For proof, consider the recent negotiations at American Airlines. American's unions gave the nearly bankrupt company over $1 billion in labor concessions, while top management secretly arranged for executive-retention bonuses and pension protections. When the arrangements were revealed, the unions angrily forced the CEO to rescind them. The CEO subsequently tendered his resignation. "Carty Resigns as AMR Chief over Pension Gaffe," *Wall Street Journal* (25 April 2003). On the standard factors, see Lawrence Katz and David Autor, "Changes in the Wage Structure and Earnings Inequality," in Orley Ashenfelter and David Cards, eds., *Handbook of Labor Economics* (Amsterdam, 1999), 1463–1555.

Acknowledgments

1. Sanford M. Jacoby, "The Origins of Internal Labor Markets in Japan," *Industrial Relations* 18 (Spring 1979), 184–96.

Index

A. G. Edwards, 99
accounting rules and practices, 14, 23, 192n.22
acquisitions. *See* mergers and acquisitions
AFL-CIO, 164–65
Albert, Michel, 13
Alexander, Magnus W., 82
American Institute for Social Service, 80
American Management Association, 81
AT & T, 86

banks, 30–32, 34–35, 73
Barnevik, Percy, 54
behavioral sciences, 86–87, 89, 104, 112
Berkshire Hathaway, 184n.18
Berle, Adolf A., 85
"best practices" innovations, 12–14, 16, 19, 68, 111
boards of directors, ix, 91; accountability of, 31–32, 162–65; finance membership on, 29, 56–57, 146, 159; HR membership on, 2, 7, 60–61, 74, 160; pay systems for, 30; resource-based models and, 160; size of, 7, 15, 30, 35, 74–75, 105–6, 144; union membership and, 28, 145
bonus pay, 24, 30–31, 67
Breeden, Richard C., 165
Britain. *See* United Kingdom
business-government relations, x, 1, 9, 38–40, 82–85, 89–91. *See also* legal and regulatory environments
business-partner models, 9–10, 94–96, 99–100, 159–61, 163–65
business-university linkages, 14–15, 89

California Public Employee Retirement System (CalPERS), 38
Canada, 15–16
Canon, 158, 168
Cappelli, Peter, 9
career planning: in construction companies, 52–53, 69, 123–24, 126, 128; in delivery companies, 46–47, 110–12; in electrical/electronics companies, 51, 55–56, 63–64, 69–70, 120–21; in energy companies, 123–24, 126, 128; executives, identification/pro-

motion of, and, 2, 7, 22, 26–27, 32, 63, 88, 92, 95, 136, 141, 163–64; information systems and, 22, 26–27, 32, 82, 90; job rotation and, 2, 7, 25–26, 32, 136; mid-career movers and, 64, 69–70; in parts manufacturing companies, 48–49, 58, 64, 69–70, 116–17; performance evaluations and, 7, 26, 82, 136; recruitment and, 22, 62, 70, 82, 93–94, 135, 143–44; in securities companies, 43–45, 53, 63, 67, 70, 102, 106–7; training and, 7, 11, 18, 21–22, 25, 58–60, 82, 86–87, 94, 135
CEOs (chief executive officers). *See* executives
CFOs (chief finance officers). *See* finance departments and financialization
Chandler, Alfred D., 79
China, 6, 171
Cisco Systems, 166
collective bargaining. *See* unions
complaints and grievances, employee, 71, 82, 87, 103, 109–11, 121–22, 127
Confederation of British Industry, 37
construction companies: in Japan, 42, 52–54, 58, 61, 66–67, 69–70, 72, 74–75, 77; in United States, 101–2, 123–28, 130, 161
consultants 67–69, 86, 96, 111, 116–17
contingent employees. *See* part-time employees
convergence theories, x, 3–4, 10–20, 77, 98; converging divergences and, 17, 19, 129; directional, 12; dominant-model, 16–17; incrementalism and, 18, 35, 166; institutional complementarities and, 14–15, 18, 65; path dependence and, 17–20, 170–72
corporate governance, 15–16, 60–61, 73–75, 91–93, 144–45; boards of directors and, ix, 2, 7, 15, 28–32, 35, 56–57, 60–61, 74–75, 91, 105–6, 144–46, 159–60, 162–65; in construction companies, 61, 75; corporate-officer system and, 35, 56, 60, 74–75, 144–45, 157; in delivery companies, 47, 61, 75, 101, 111; in electrical/electronics companies, 56–57, 60–61, 65, 101, 119; executives and, ix, 2, 4, 6–8, 17–18, 22, 25–29, 31–32, 37, 186n.46; HR departments and, 2, 7, 32–33, 60–62, 74, 132–33, 144–45;

corporate governance (*cont.*)
mergers/acquisitions and, ix, 6, 64, 88, 96, 137, 139, 141, 168–69; in parts manufacturing companies, 49–50, 101, 115; in securities companies, 44–45, 61, 101, 103, 105–6, 108; shareholders and, ix, 1–2, 9, 12, 15–16, 19, 31, 61, 75, 85, 91–92, 96–97, 129, 152, 156, 157, 165; shocks/scandals and, ix, 8, 31–32, 162, 164, 188n.57; stakeholders and, ix, 1–2, 5, 7, 11, 29–33, 35, 58, 71–72, 75, 86, 98–99
corporate officer system. *See* corporate governance
Corporate Governance Forum (Japan), 35
cross-shareholding, 73, 170
culture, corporate, 2, 9–10, 25, 68, 152, 154–56; in delivery companies, 47, 129; in electrical/electronics companies, 57, 118–19; individualism and, 7, 11, 35–36, 63–64, 68; in parts manufacturing companies, 48, 116; in securities companies, 104–5, 107, 129. *See also* market-oriented companies; organization-oriented companies

Daei, 73
Darbishire, Owen, 17
delivery companies: in Japan, 41, 45–47, 61, 65, 67, 74–77, 110, 114, 129; in United States, 101–2, 108–14, 129, 160
deregulation, 6, 18, 39, 91
Digital Equipment Company, 92
directors. *See* boards of directors
diversification, 22, 24–25, 31, 41, 88, 148–52. *See also* spin-offs
Donaldson, Gordon, 85–86
downsizing, 92, 97, 143
Dunlap, Al, 164

electrical/electronics companies: in Japan, 41, 50–51, 54–65, 67, 69–72, 74–77, 120, 129; in United States, 101–2, 118–23, 128–29, 160
employees: career-type, ix–x, 5, 11, 21–22, 25, 61, 70–71, 133, 167–68; mobility/turnover of, ix–x, 2, 9, 11–12, 15, 21, 80–81, 84, 133; part-time/temporary/contingent, 6, 39, 45–47, 65, 71, 141
employee-stock-ownership plans (ESOPs), 30, 75, 108
employer organizations, 28, 36–37
energy companies, 101–2, 123–28, 130, 161
England. *See* United Kingdom

Enron, ix, 32, 162, 164
enterprise unions, 5, 11, 21–22, 27–29, 33, 36–37, 72–73, 76, 129, 133, 145
Europe, 1, 6, 13–14, 17, 171–72
evaluations. *See* performance evaluations
executives, ix, 4, 8, 101–2; accountability of, 31–32; identification/promotion of, 2, 7, 22, 26–27, 32, 63, 88, 92, 95, 136, 141, 163–64; pay systems for, 34, 37, 57, 93, 97, 141, 162, 165, 186n.46; previous experience of, 25, 29, 88, 91–92; replacement of, 6, 17–18, 31–32; union membership and, 28, 145

finance departments and financialization, ix, 22; board membership and, 29, 56–57, 146, 159; business-partner role of, 163–64; in construction companies, 74; in delivery companies, 74; in electrical/electronics companies, 56–57, 60–61, 74; pay systems and, 93, 97, 141; performance evaluations and, 141; power/status of, x, 2–3, 25, 33, 88, 93, 139, 141, 145–47, 159–61; recruitment by, 93; survey participation by, 131–32; welfare/benefits issues and, 93
first-mover advantages, 14–15
Folsom, Marion, 84
Ford Motor Company, 80
foreign investments, 6, 35, 38, 54, 56, 69, 75, 167
France, 13
Freeman, Richard, 16
"freeters," 35–36

General Electric, 23–24, 115, 184n.18
General Foods, 90
General Motors Corporation, 3, 87, 89
Germany, 1, 12, 15, 17–18, 25
Gerschenkron, Alexander, 12, 14
Gerstner, Lou, 54
Ghosn, Carlos, 35, 69
Global Crossing, ix, 162
globalization, x, 3–4, 11, 16–17, 57, 76, 93, 170
Goodyear, 80
Greenspan, Alan, 171

headhunters, 64, 106, 116
Hicks, Clarence J., 82
hiring. *See* recruitment practices
hiring freezes, 58
Hitachi, 184n.18

hostile takeovers, 91–92, 96
human resources departments (HR), ix, 19–20, 41–42, 131–56; advocacy role of, 2, 9, 27–29, 33, 87, 94; behavioral sciences and, 87, 89; business-partner role of, 9–10, 94–96, 99–100, 159–61; as career choice, 29, 133, 161; career planning by, 2, 7, 21–22, 25–27, 32, 36, 69–71, 88, 92, 94, 136; corporate governance and, 2, 7, 32–33, 60–62, 74, 132–33, 144–45; disciplinary/dismissal process and, 82, 84; executives, identification/promotion of, and, 2, 7, 22, 26–27, 32, 88, 92, 95, 136, 141, 163–64; information functions of, 22, 26–27, 32, 82, 90; job rotation control by, 2, 7, 25–26, 32, 136; organization orientation of, 21–22, 25–26, 33; outside consultants and, 67–69, 96, 111; pay systems and, 21, 27–28, 64, 70, 82, 93–94, 141; performance evaluations and, 7, 26, 82, 136; power/status of, x, 1–3, 7–8, 11–12, 21, 25–27, 33, 42, 57–58, 65–66, 76, 78–79, 83, 88–89, 91, 94, 99–100, 137–41, 145–47; pressures for change and, 7, 9–10, 33–40; professionalization of, 78, 96, 99, 161–62; recruitment by, 22, 62, 70, 82, 93–94, 143–44; training and, 7, 11, 21–22, 25, 58–60, 82, 94, 135; union relations and, 21, 27–29, 33, 61–62, 72–73, 83–84, 87–88, 90, 133–34; welfare/benefits issues and, 21–22, 58–60, 62, 80–81. *See also specific types of companies*

IBM, 9, 92, 121
incrementalism, 18, 35, 166
individualism, 7, 11, 35–36, 63–64, 68
institutional complementarities models, 14–15, 18, 65
intellectual property laws, 15
Investor Responsibility Research Center, 38

Japanese Business Federation, 37
Japanese companies, 5–8, 157–59, 166–73; business-government relations in, 1, 23, 38–40; centralization/decentralization in, 8, 22–24, 33, 62, 67, 75, 136–37, 148–52; consultants and, 67–69, 86; convergence theories and, 10–20, 77; distributional issues in, 3, 34–35, 37–38, 171–72; incrementalism and, 35, 166; individualism in, 11, 35–36, 63–64, 68; life employees in, ix–x, 5, 11, 21–22, 25, 61, 70–71, 133, 167–68; mergers/acquisitions in, 6, 64, 139,

168; organization/market-orientation in, 2, 10–11, 19, 21–22, 33, 39, 143, 157–58, 167; pay systems in, 5, 11, 17, 21–22, 24, 27–28, 34, 36, 38, 63–64, 67, 70; pressures for change in, 2, 6–7, 33–40; resource allocation in, 134–36; resource-based business strategies in, 10, 24, 33, 98, 151–52, 158; scandals and, 31–32, 188n.57; stakeholders/shareholders in, ix, 1–2, 5–7, 11, 19, 29–33, 35, 58, 61, 71–72, 75, 152, 154, 156, 157; structure of, 22–26, 34–35, 39, 41–42, 57–60, 67, 168–69; unions in, 5, 11, 21–22, 27–29, 33, 36–37, 72–73, 76, 129, 133, 145. *See also specific types of companies*
Japan Productivity Council, 68
job cuts: attrition and, 71; downsizing and, 92, 97, 143; hiring freezes and, 58; layoffs and, 6, 27, 31, 40, 63, 65, 70–72, 122, 183n.3; resource allocation and, 134–36; retirements and, 59, 65, 71; small companies and, 72; transfer/absorption of surplus employees and, 23, 58–59, 65, 69, 71, 122, 168
job duration. *See* turnover, employee
job rotation, 2, 7, 25–26, 32, 136; in construction companies, 52–53; in delivery companies, 47; in electrical/electronics companies, 51, 55–56, 70; in parts manufacturing companies, 49; in securities companies, 43–45, 53
junk bonds, 91, 96
just-in-time production methods, 14

Kanter, Rosabeth Moss, 93
Katz, Harry C., 17
Keidanren, 36–37, 68
keiretsu (business-groups), 7, 28, 32, 68, 73, 167
Keizai Doyukai, 35
Kodak, 92
kogaisha (spin-offs), 22–23, 44, 52, 67, 68–69, 168
Koizumi, Junichiro, 39
Korea, 6
Krugman, Paul, 171

labor organizations. *See* unions
late-developing countries model, 12–14
layoffs, 6, 27, 31, 40, 63, 65, 70–72, 183n.3; in construction companies, 70; in

layoffs (*cont.*)
  electrical/electronics companies, 122; in
    securities companies, 108
Lazarsfeld, Paul, 87
legal and regulatory environments, x; deregu-
    lation and, 6, 18, 39, 91; intellectual prop-
    erty laws and, 15; in Japan, 23, 38–40; in
    United States, 2, 6, 9, 96. *See also individ-
    ual laws*
Liberal Democratic Party (Japan), 38–39
life employees/lifetime employment, ix–x, 5,
    11, 21–22, 25, 61, 70–71, 133, 167–68
Lincoln Electric, 99
Lordstown Syndrome, 89

Maine, Henry, 180n.26
market globalization. *See* globalization
marketing departments, 2–3, 29, 146–47
market-oriented companies, 2, 9, 11, 19, 39,
    92–93, 129–30, 143, 157–59, 167
Matsushita Electric, 23–24
Mayo, Elton, 86
Means, Gardiner C., 85
Men's Wearhouse, 10, 160
mergers and acquisitions, ix, 6, 64, 88, 96,
    137, 139, 141, 168–69
Merrill Lynch, 75
M-form type organizations, 3–4, 22–25, 39,
    50, 88
mid-career movers (*chūto saiyō*), 64, 69–70
Mitarai, Fujio, 168, 170
Mitsui, 184n.18
Mitsukoshi, 31
Mizuho Securities, 38
mobility. *See* turnover, employee
mochikabukai (employee-stock-ownership
    funds), 30, 75

National Association of Employment Manag-
    ers (U.S.), 81
National Association of Manufacturers (U.S.),
    85
National Civic Federation (U.S.), 80
National Industrial Conference Board (U.S.),
    82
National Industrial Recovery Act (U.S.), 83
National Labor Relations Act (U.S.), 109
New York Stock Exchange, 162, 164
Nikkeiren, 28, 36–37, 68, 72, 157
Nissan, 68–69
norm entrepreneurs, 37–38, 66, 166, 172

oil-shocks (1970s), 28, 31, 33
organization-oriented companies, 2, 10–11,
    21–22, 32–33, 84, 157
outsourcing, 9, 59, 94, 96, 135–36, 165,
    200n.3
overnight-package-delivery companies. *See* de-
    livery companies
ownership, company, 15, 33, 85, 160

package delivery. *See* delivery companies
parts manufacturing companies: in Japan, 41,
    48–50, 58–59, 61–62, 64–66, 69–70, 75; in
    United States, 101–2, 114–18, 130, 132,
    169
part-time employees, 6, 39, 45–47, 65, 71, 141
path dependence theories, 17–20, 170–72
pay systems, 11; bonuses in, 24, 30–31, 67; in
    construction companies, 75, 123–24; in de-
    livery companies, 46, 61, 75; in electrical/
    electronics companies, 50, 55, 57, 63–64,
    67, 120, 122; in energy companies, 123–
    24; for executives, 34, 37–38, 57, 93, 97,
    141, 162, 165, 186n.46; incentives and, 79;
    outsourcing and, 94, 135; in parts manufac-
    turing companies, 49, 64; performance-
    based, 36, 63–64, 67–68, 124, 143–44, 157;
    in securities companies, 43–44, 63–64,
    106–7; seniority-based, 5, 21–22, 27, 36;
    stock option plans and, 30, 38–39, 55, 57,
    74–75, 91, 93, 97, 107–8, 122, 124, 147,
    157, 164; union negotiations and, 17, 28
performance evaluations, 7, 82; in construc-
    tion/energy companies, 124–27; in delivery
    companies, 47; in electrical/electronics
    companies, 67, 120; of executives and
    boards, 26, 31–32, 136; finance depart-
    ments and, 141; in parts manufacturing
    companies, 49; pay bonuses and, 24, 30–
    31, 67; in securities companies, 43, 104,
    106–7
personnel management. *See* human re-
    sources departments
production departments, x, 2, 146
psychology. *See* behavioral sciences
punctuated equilibrium models, 77, 183n.49

quality circles, 14, 68

Railway Labor Act (U.S.), 109–10, 113
recruitment practices, 22, 62, 70, 82, 93–94,
    143–44; in construction companies, 53,

126; in electrical/electronics companies, 55; in energy companies, 126; outsourcing and, 94, 135; in parts manufacturing companies, 48–49; in securities companies, 43
Reichheld, Frederick, 97
Rengo, 37, 39, 71, 189n.69
resource-based business strategies, 2, 10, 24, 33, 97–100, 129–30, 151–52, 158, 160
Rockefeller, John D., Jr., 82
Rockefeller Foundation, 38
Russia, 12, 183n.49

SAS Institute, 10, 99
scandals, corporate, ix, 8, 31–32, 162, 164, 188n.57
scientific management, 13, 79
securities companies: in Japan, 41–45, 50, 53, 61, 63–65, 67, 70, 75–76, 102–3, 107–8, 158, 169; in United States, 101–8, 129–30, 160
Securities Exchange Commission (U.S.), 162, 164
seishain (core employees), 2, 27, 30–31, 45, 50, 61–62, 167–68
shareholders, ix, 1–2, 9, 12, 15–16, 19, 31, 61, 75, 85, 91–92, 96–97, 129, 152, 156–57, 165
shikkō yakuin (corporate-officer system), 35, 56, 60, 74–75, 144–45, 157
shukkō (employee transfer practices), 23, 58–59, 65, 69, 71, 168
Silicon Valley companies, 7, 9, 14–15, 166
Snow Brand Dairy Company, 31–32
social norms and values, x, 4, 8, 11, 35–38. See also culture, corporate
Social Security Act (U.S.), 83
Softbank, 17
Sogo, 73
Son, Masayoshi, 17
Sony, 35, 56, 60, 68, 144
Soskice, David, 17
Southwest Airlines, 10, 160
Soviet Union, former. See Russia
Special Conference Committee (U.S.), 82–83
spin-offs, 31; in electrical/electronics companies, 59–60, 62, 65; kogaisha as, 17, 22–24, 44, 52, 67, 68–69, 168; in parts manufacturing companies, 58–59, 62. See also diversification

stakeholders, ix, 1–2, 5, 7, 11, 29–33, 58, 71–72, 75, 86, 98–99
stock option plans: ESOPs and, 30, 75, 108; in Japan, 38–39, 55, 57, 74–75, 147, 157; in United States, 91, 93, 97, 107–8, 122, 124, 164
strikes, 27, 36, 48, 80–81, 89
subsidiaries. See spin-offs
Sweden, 17, 89

Tateisi, Nobuo, 35
Taylor, Frederick, 79, 96
temporary employees. See part-time employees
Thurow, Lester, 13
TIAA-CREF, 38
Toshiba, 23, 24, 68
Toyota, 66, 68, 73, 75, 158
training, 7, 11, 18, 21–22, 25, 82, 129; behavioral sciences and, 86–87; in delivery companies, 46, 47; in electrical/electronics companies, 59–60, 120; outsourcing of, 94, 135; in parts manufacturing companies, 48–49, 58–59, 62; in securities companies, 43–44, 107; spin-offs of, 58–60, 62, 135
Training Within Industry program, 86
trucking companies, 113
turnover, employee, ix–x, 2, 9, 11–12, 15, 21, 80–81, 84, 133
Tyco, 32, 162

U-form type organizations, 22–23, 109
unemployment trends, 14, 71–72, 81, 91
unions, 2, 9, 14, 61–62, 82–83, 85, 87–91; in construction companies, 72; in delivery companies, 47, 61, 102, 109–10; in electrical/electronics companies, 50, 55, 58, 61–62, 72, 102, 118; enterprise, 5, 11, 21–22, 27–29, 33, 36–37, 72–73, 76, 145; executive/management membership in, 28, 145; industrial and craft, 12, 80, 82; legal/regulatory environments and, 39; in parts manufacturing companies, 48–50, 61–62; in securities companies, 43, 103; strikes and, 27, 36, 48, 80–81, 89; unfair dismissal complaints and, 71; wage negotiations and, 17, 28
United Kingdom, 1, 13, 14, 15–16
United States companies, 8–10, 159–66, 172; business-government relations in, 2, 6, 9, 82–85, 89–91, 96; consultants and, 86, 96, 111; convergence theories and, 10–20, 98; decentralization/centralization in, 8–9, 22,

United States companies (*cont.*) 88, 90–91, 93, 95, 136–37, 148–52, 165–66, 169; distributional issues in, 3, 85, 96–97, 172; employee mobility/turnover in, 2, 9, 11–12, 80–81, 84, 86, 102, 133; individualism in, 11; market/organization-orientation of, 2, 9, 11, 84, 86, 92–93, 98, 129–30, 143, 159; mergers/acquisitions in, 169; pay systems in, 11, 17, 28, 34, 37, 79, 82, 93–94, 106–7, 124, 191n.13; pressures on, 93–96; resource allocation in, 134–36; resource-based business strategies in, 2, 10, 97–99, 129–30, 151–52, 160; scandals and, ix, 8, 162, 164; shareholders/stakeholders in, ix, 1–2, 9, 12, 15–16, 85–86, 91–92, 96–99, 129, 154, 165; structure of, 3–4, 6, 22–23, 34, 93, 128, 169, 191n.11; unions and, 2, 9, 12, 14, 28, 36, 82–83, 85, 87–91, 129, 133. *See also specific types of companies*

venture-capital funds, 14–15, 17
Vogel, Steven, 18

wages. *See* pay systems
War Labor Board (U.S.), 82, 84
Welch, Jack, 54, 164
welfare benefits, employee, 21–22, 82; in delivery companies, 47; in electrical/electronics companies, 59–60, 62, 118–19; in parts manufacturing companies, 48, 58–59, 62; in securities companies, 43; spin-offs of, 58–60, 62, 135
welfare capitalism, 9, 13, 80–84, 129
Western Electric, 86
Worker Dispatch Law (Japan), 39
WorldCom, ix, 32, 162, 165

Yamaha Motor, 73
Yashiro, Naohiro, 7, 36, 66